P9-CRX-491

the unbeatable Squirrel Girl

Ryan North
WRITER

Erica Henderson
ARTIST

Rico Renzi
COLOR ARTIST

Rico Renzi
TRADING CARD ART, #27

VC's Travis Lanham
LETTERER

Erica Henderson
COVER ART

Sarah Brunstad
ASSOCIATE EDITOR

Wil Moss
EDITOR

LOGO DESIGN BY **MICHAEL ALLRED**

SQUIRREL GIRL CREATED BY **WILL MURRAY** & **STEVE DITKO**

COLLECTION EDITOR: **JENNIFER GRÜNWALD** ▪ ASSISTANT EDITOR: **CAITLIN O'CONNELL**
ASSOCIATE MANAGING EDITOR: **KATERI WOODY** ▪ EDITOR, SPECIAL PROJECTS: **MARK D. BEAZLEY**
VP PRODUCTION & SPECIAL PROJECTS: **JEFF YOUNGQUIST** ▪ SVP PRINT, SALES & MARKETING: **DAVID GABRIEL**
BOOK DESIGNER: **JAY BOWEN**

EDITOR IN CHIEF: **C.B. CEBULSKI** ▪ CHIEF CREATIVE OFFICER: **JOE QUESADA**
PRESIDENT: **DAN BUCKLEY** ▪ EXECUTIVE PRODUCER: **ALAN FINE**

THE UNBEATABLE SQUIRREL GIRL VOL. 8: MY BEST FRIEND'S SQUIRREL. Contains material originally published in magazine form as THE UNBEATABLE SQUIRREL GIRL #27-31 and NOT BRAND ECHH #14. First printing 2018. ISBN 978-1-302-91076-1. Published by MARVEL WORLDWIDE, INC., a subsidiary of MARVEL ENTERTAINMENT, LLC. OFFICE OF PUBLICATION: 135 West 50th Street, New York, NY 10020. Copyright © 2018 MARVEL No similarity between any of the names, characters, persons, and/or institutions in this magazine with those of any living or dead person or institution is intended, and any such similarity which may exist is purely coincidental. **Printed in Canada.** DAN BUCKLEY, President, Marvel Entertainment; JOHN NEE, Publisher; JOE QUESADA, Chief Creative Officer; TOM BREVOORT, SVP of Publishing; DAVID BOGART, SVP of Business Affairs & Operations, Publishing & Partnership; DAVID GABRIEL, SVP of Sales & Marketing, Publishing; JEFF YOUNGQUIST, VP of Production & Special Projects; DAN CARR, Executive Director of Publishing Technology; ALEX MORALES, Director of Publishing Operations; DAN EDINGTON, Managing Editor; SUSAN CRESPI, Production Manager; STAN LEE, Chairman Emeritus. For information regarding advertising in Marvel Comics or on Marvel.com, please contact Vit DeBellis, Custom Solutions & Integrated Advertising Manager, at vdebellis@marvel.com. For Marvel subscription inquiries, please call 888-511-5480. **Manufactured between 4/27/2018 and 5/29/2018 by SOLISCO PRINTERS, SCOTT, QC, CANADA.**

10 9 8 7 6 5 4 3 2 1

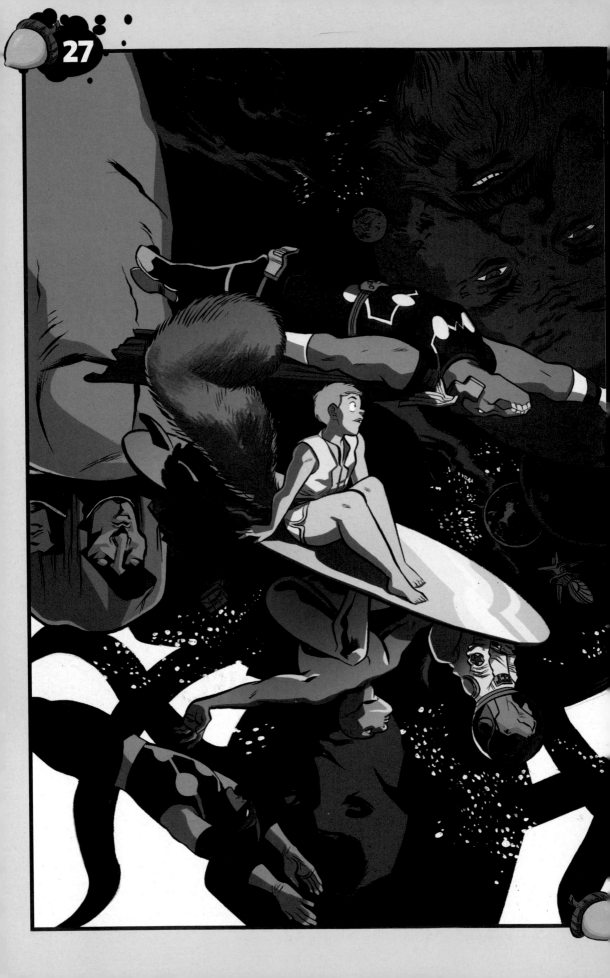

*oreen Green isn't just a second-year computer science student: she secretly also has all the powers of both squirrel and rl! She uses her amazing abilities to fight crime **and** be as awesome as possible. You know her as... **The Unbeatable Squirrel Girl!***

Find out what she's been up to, with...

Squirrel Girl in a nutshell

Squirrel Girl @unbeatablesg
Thank you everyone for buying my special zine last month! It turned out better than I expected AND I ALREADY HAD HUGE EXPECTATIONS FOR IT!!

Squirrel Girl @unbeatablesg
For example, I was not expecting GALACTUS to submit a story but I'm glad he did

Squirrel Girl @unbeatablesg
I hope you enjoyed all those quality gags written by my friend from space who has tried to gobble our planet a non-zero number of times

Squirrel Girl @unbeatablesg
And how about that Wolverine story? And that Kraven story? And that BRAIN DRAIN story??

Squirrel Girl @unbeatablesg
Sorry to everyone who hasn't got a copy of my zine yet, sorry you missed out it RULES SO HARD AND YOU SHOULD DEFINITELY TRY TO GET A COPY

Squirrel Girl @unbeatablesg
Oh!! Also in case you're following me for my crimefighting tips and not self-publishing promotion, here's today's ANTI-CRIME TIP:

Squirrel Girl @unbeatablesg
Considering doing a crime? How About Maybe Don't™

Squirrel Girl @unbeatablesg
Thank you for enjoying today's extremely excellent anti-crime tip

Squirrel Girl @unbeatablesg
So here's what I'm thinking for my next zine: a book full of excerpts from PICTURE BOOKS FOR PROGRAMMERS

Nancy W. @sewwiththeflo
@unbeatablesg Why the interest in programming, famed hero Squirrel Girl, who I remind you doesn't even HAVE a secret identity as far as everyone knows?

Squirrel Girl @unbeatablesg
@sewwiththeflo GOOD CATCH, THANKS UNRELATED CIVILIAN NANCY WHITEHEAD!!

Squirrel Girl @unbeatablesg
CLARIFICATION TO PREVIOUS:

Squirrel Girl @unbeatablesg
I, of course, am a super hero, so I don't need to program computers, no matter how awesome it might be, which is too bad because it rules

Squirrel Girl @unbeatablesg
But think how great they could be! "Horton Hears a Stack Overflow"! "I Want My Pointer Back"! "Don't Let The Pigeon Drive The Data Bus"!

Squirrel Girl @unbeatablesg
ETCETERA!

Nancy W. @sewwiththeflo
@unbeatablesg You know, in the absence of these being printed by publishers, one could make their own fake dustjackets to put on books.

Squirrel Girl @unbeatablesg
@sewwiththeflo !! oh my gosh YES

Squirrel Girl @unbeatablesg
@sewwiththeflo everyone will think I'm reading the coolest books and be SO JEALOUS of my CURATED READING LIST

Squirrel Girl @unbeatablesg
@sewwiththeflo this is a great idea and I'm getting started on it right away!!

Squirrel Girl @unbeatablesg
@sewwiththeflo GOTTA GO

search!

#galactus

#onthemoon

#biggs

#chtty

#sorcerersupreme

This is just SOME of what Doreen's been posting--all these handles are real! Follow **@unbeatablesg** for more!

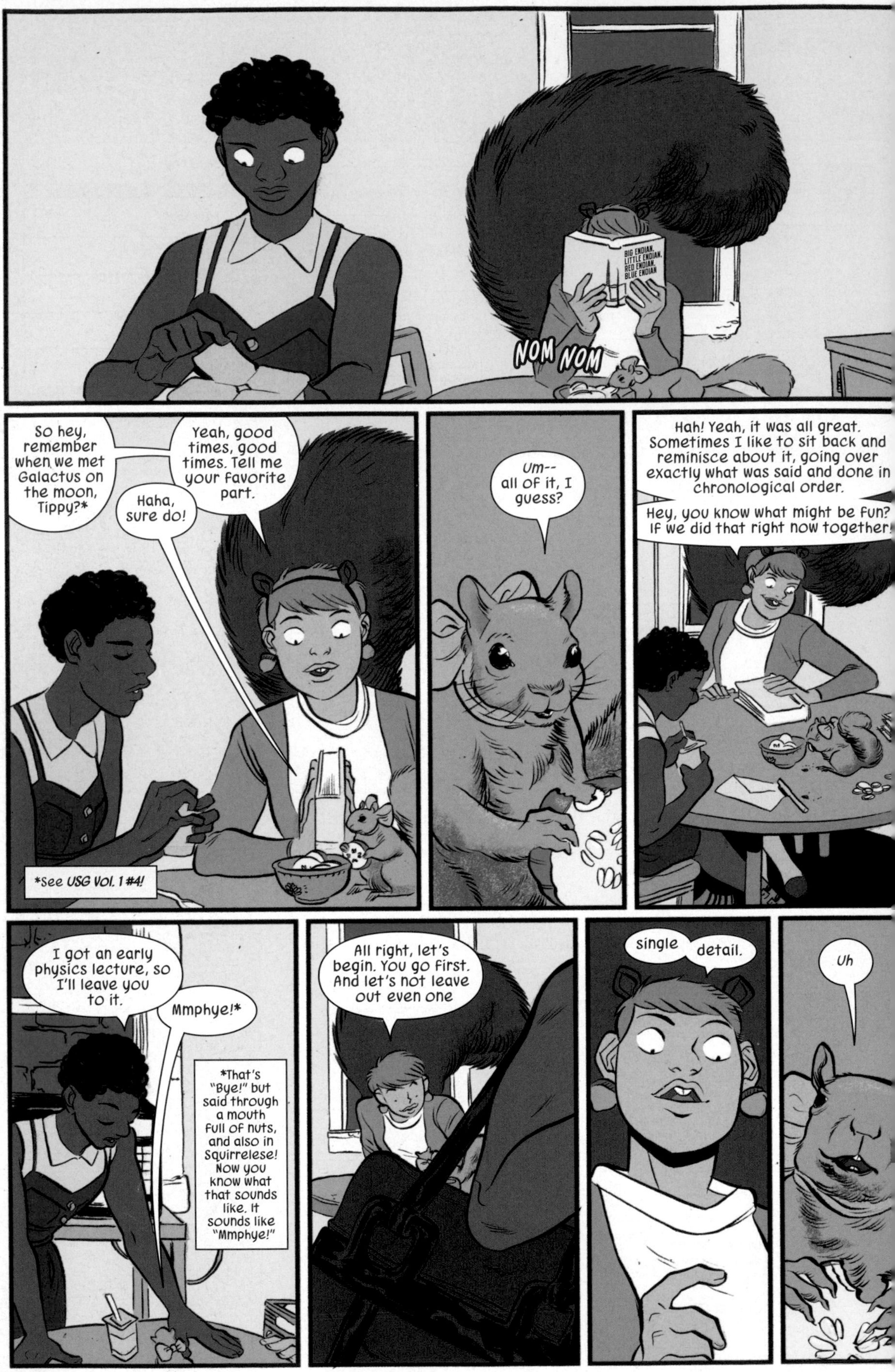
BIG ENDIAN, LITTLE ENDIAN, RED ENDIAN, BLUE ENDIAN
NOM NOM
So hey, remember when we met Galactus on the moon, Tippy?*
Haha, sure do!
Yeah, good times, good times. Tell me your favorite part.
*See USG VOL. 1 #4!
Um-- all of it, I guess?
Hah! Yeah, it was all great. Sometimes I like to sit back and reminisce about it, going over exactly what was said and done in chronological order.
Hey, you know what might be fun? If we did that right now together!
I got an early physics lecture, so I'll leave you to it.
Mmphye!*
*That's "Bye!" but said through a mouth full of nuts, and also in Squirrelese! Now you know what that sounds like. It sounds like "Mmphye!"
All right, let's begin. You go first. And let's not leave out even one
single
detail.
Uh

Wow, what a weird thing for Squirrel Girl to say! *Ah* well, I'm sure everything's completely fine and normal.

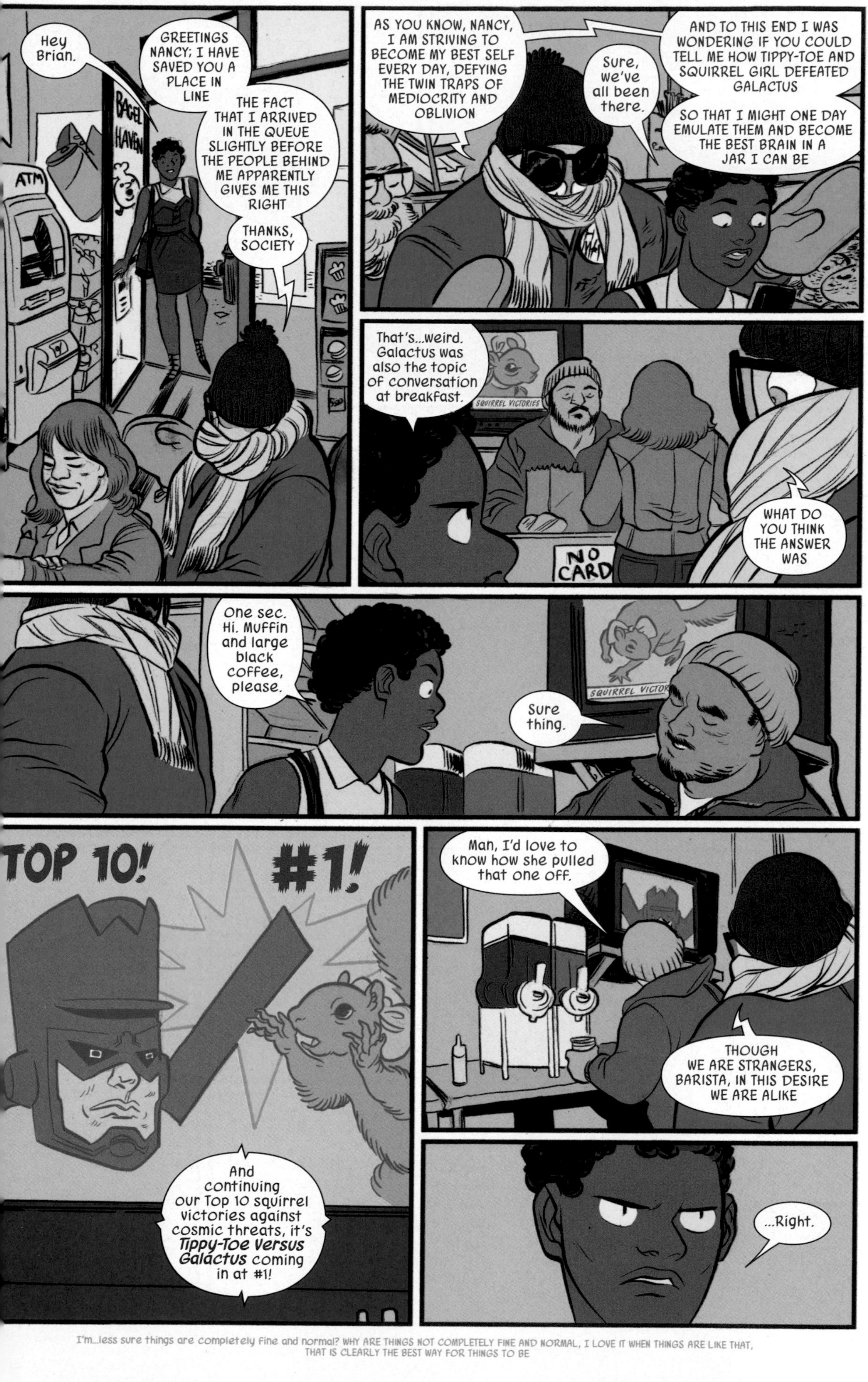
Hey Brian.
GREETINGS NANCY; I HAVE SAVED YOU A PLACE IN LINE
THE FACT THAT I ARRIVED IN THE QUEUE SLIGHTLY BEFORE THE PEOPLE BEHIND ME APPARENTLY GIVES ME THIS RIGHT
THANKS, SOCIETY
BAGEL HAVEN
ATM
AS YOU KNOW, NANCY, I AM STRIVING TO BECOME MY BEST SELF EVERY DAY, DEFYING THE TWIN TRAPS OF MEDIOCRITY AND OBLIVION
Sure, we've all been there.
AND TO THIS END I WAS WONDERING IF YOU COULD TELL ME HOW TIPPY-TOE AND SQUIRREL GIRL DEFEATED GALACTUS
SO THAT I MIGHT ONE DAY EMULATE THEM AND BECOME THE BEST BRAIN IN A JAR I CAN BE
That's...weird. Galactus was also the topic of conversation at breakfast.
SQUIRREL VICTORIES
NO CARD
WHAT DO YOU THINK THE ANSWER WAS
One sec. Hi. Muffin and large black coffee, please.
Sure thing.
TOP 10! #1!
And continuing our Top 10 squirrel victories against cosmic threats, it's *Tippy-Toe Versus Galactus* coming in at #1!
Man, I'd love to know how she pulled that one off.
THOUGH WE ARE STRANGERS, BARISTA, IN THIS DESIRE WE ARE ALIKE
...Right.

I'm...less sure things are completely fine and normal? WHY ARE THINGS NOT COMPLETELY FINE AND NORMAL, I LOVE IT WHEN THINGS ARE LIKE THAT, THAT IS CLEARLY THE BEST WAY FOR THINGS TO BE

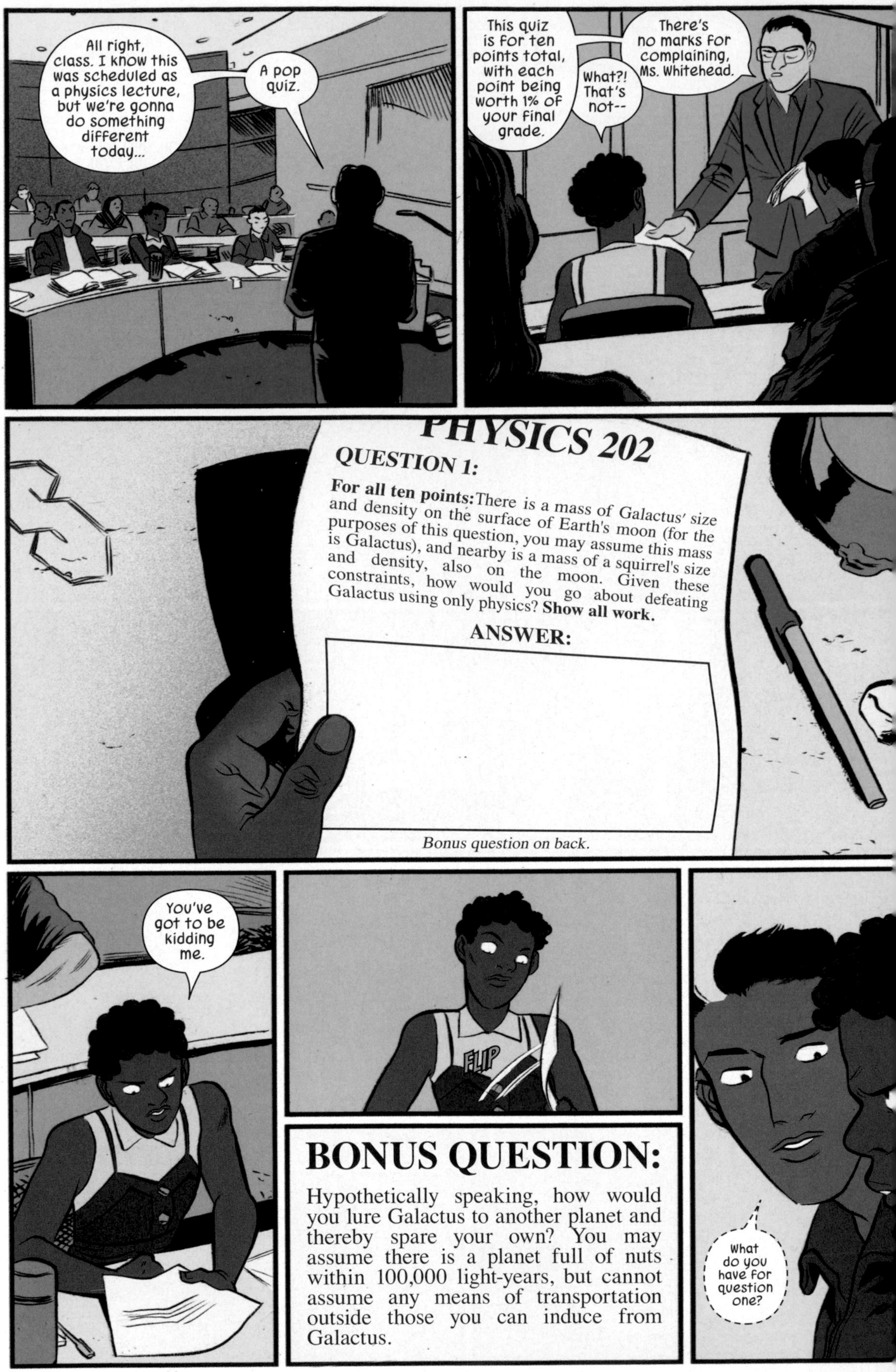
All right, class. I know this was scheduled as a physics lecture, but we're gonna do something different today...
A pop quiz.
This quiz is for ten points total, with each point being worth 1% of your final grade.
What?! That's not--
There's no marks for complaining, Ms. Whitehead.
PHYSICS 202
QUESTION 1:
For all ten points: There is a mass of Galactus' size and density on the surface of Earth's moon (for the purposes of this question, you may assume this mass is Galactus), and nearby is a mass of a squirrel's size and density, also on the moon. Given these constraints, how would you go about defeating Galactus using only physics? Show all work.
ANSWER:
Bonus question on back.
You've got to be kidding me.
FLIP
BONUS QUESTION:
Hypothetically speaking, how would you lure Galactus to another planet and thereby spare your own? You may assume there is a planet full of nuts within 100,000 light-years, but cannot assume any means of transportation outside those you can induce from Galactus.
What do you have for question one?

One time in physics class I didn't know the answer so I wrote "true because of implied premises in question," i.e. "it's true because I used some big words to say it's true." I am here to tell you that this is sadly not a viable long-term solution in physics class.

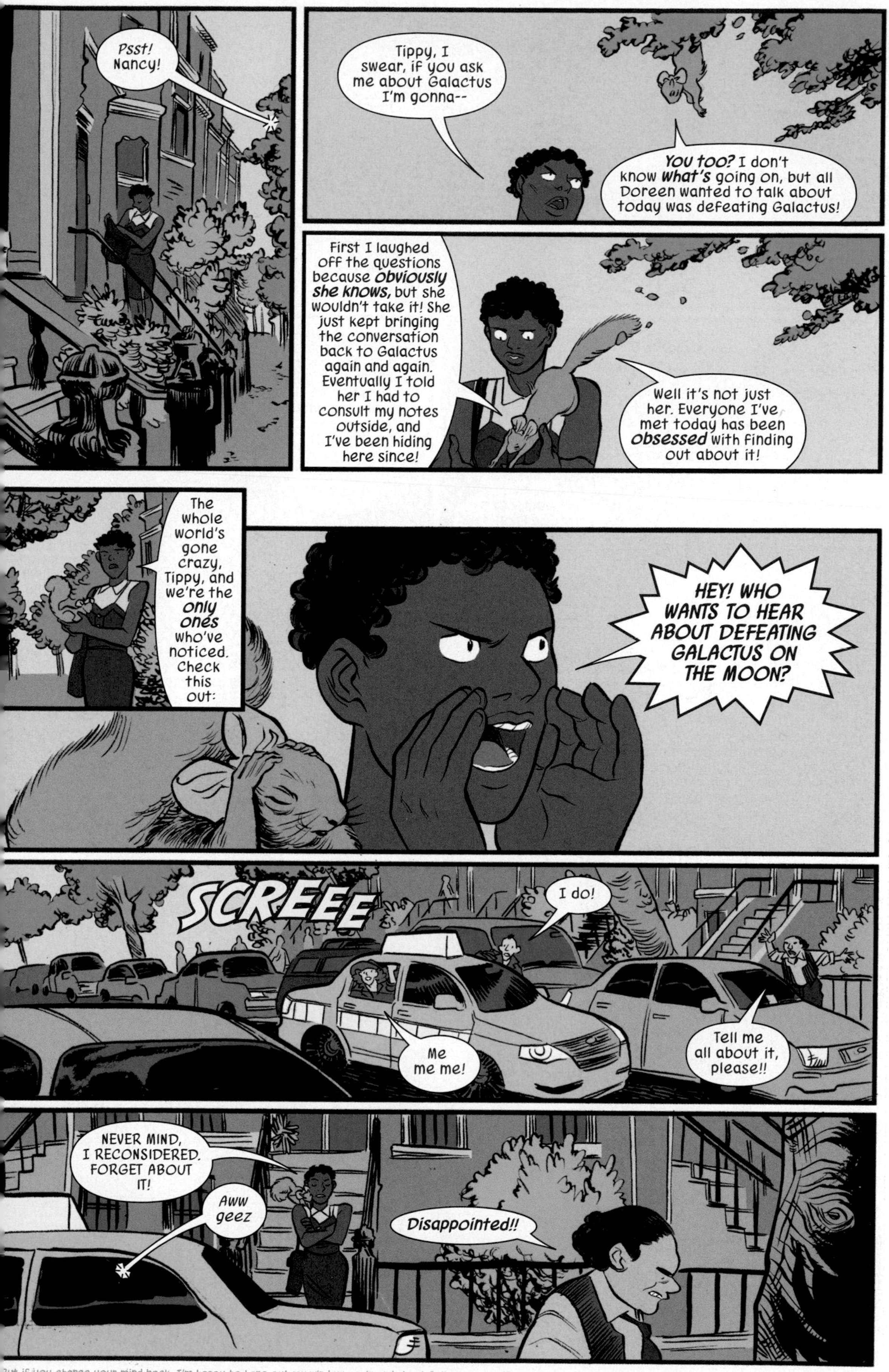
Psst! Nancy!
Tippy, I swear, if you ask me about Galactus I'm gonna--
YOU TOO? I don't know WHAT'S going on, but all Doreen wanted to talk about today was defeating Galactus!
First I laughed off the questions because OBVIOUSLY SHE KNOWS, but she wouldn't take it! She just kept bringing the conversation back to Galactus again and again. Eventually I told her I had to consult my notes outside, and I've been hiding here since!
Well it's not just her. Everyone I've met today has been OBSESSED with finding out about it!
The whole world's gone crazy, Tippy, and we're the ONLY ONES who've noticed. Check this out:
HEY! WHO WANTS TO HEAR ABOUT DEFEATING GALACTUS ON THE MOON?
SCREEE
I do!
Me me me!
Tell me all about it, please!!
NEVER MIND, I RECONSIDERED. FORGET ABOUT IT!
Aww geez
Disappointed!!

But if you change your mind back, I'm happy to hang out my window again and shout follow-up questions! I'll stand by my window here just in case! You just let me know!

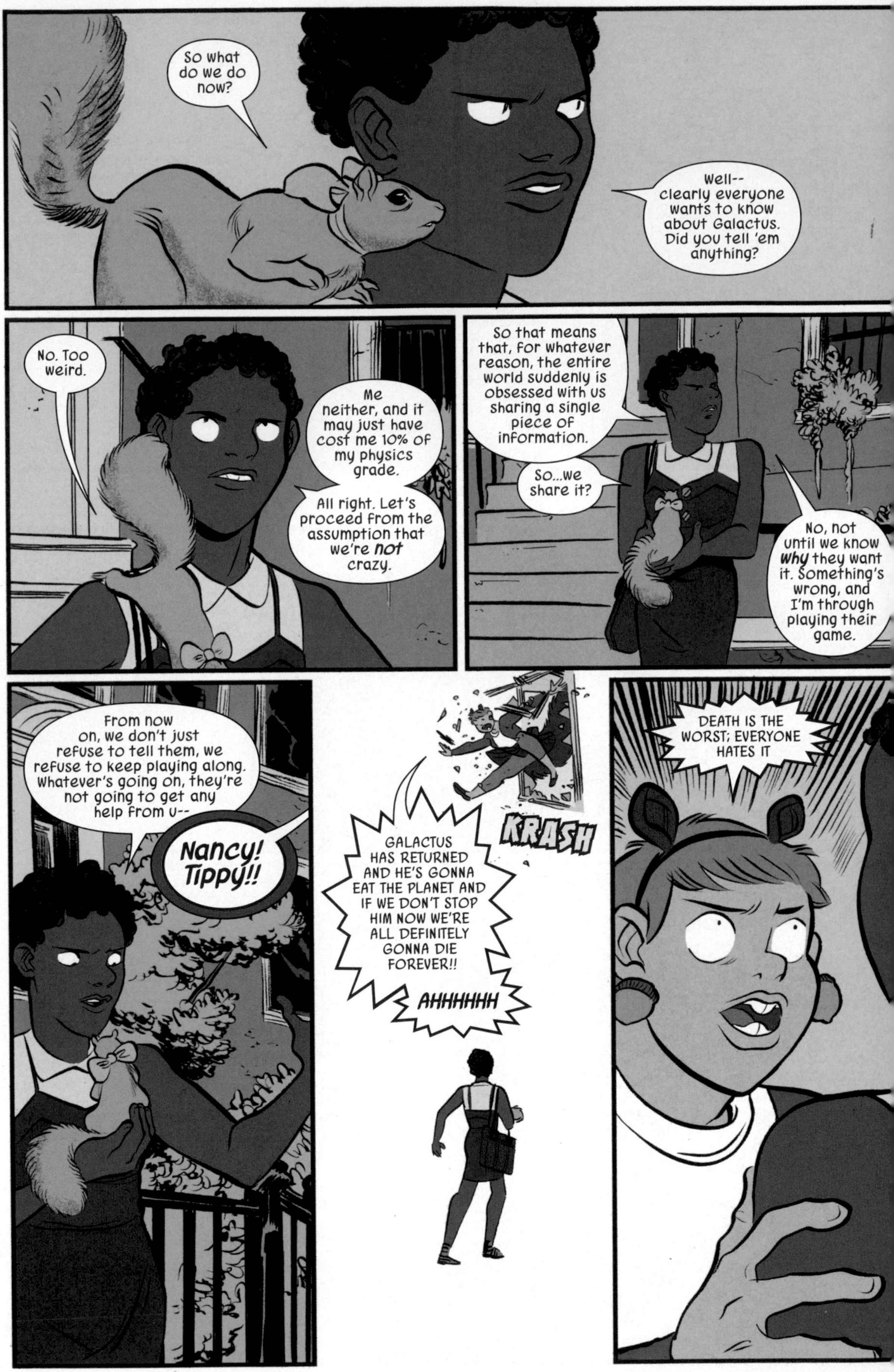

So what do we do now?
Well-- clearly everyone wants to know about Galactus. Did you tell 'em anything?
No. Too weird.
Me neither, and it may just have cost me 10% of my physics grade.
All right. Let's proceed from the assumption that we're *not* crazy.
So that means that, for whatever reason, the entire world suddenly is obsessed with us sharing a single piece of information.
So...we share it?
No, not until we know *why* they want it. Something's wrong, and I'm through playing their game.
From now on, we don't just refuse to tell them, we refuse to keep playing along. Whatever's going on, they're not going to get any help from u--
Nancy! Tippy!!
KRASH
GALACTUS HAS RETURNED AND HE'S GONNA EAT THE PLANET AND IF WE DON'T STOP HIM NOW WE'RE ALL DEFINITELY GONNA DIE FOREVER!!
AHHHHHH
DEATH IS THE WORST; EVERYONE HATES IT

EVEN UNDERTAKERS AND FUNERAL DIRECTORS, PEOPLE WHOSE VERY LIVELIHOODS DEPEND ON A CONSTANT SUPPLY OF DEATH, WOULD STILL PREFER IF IT DID NOT EXIST! I CAN THINK OF NO GREATER CONDEMNATION FOR A CONCEPT WITHIN A CAPITALIST CONTEXT!

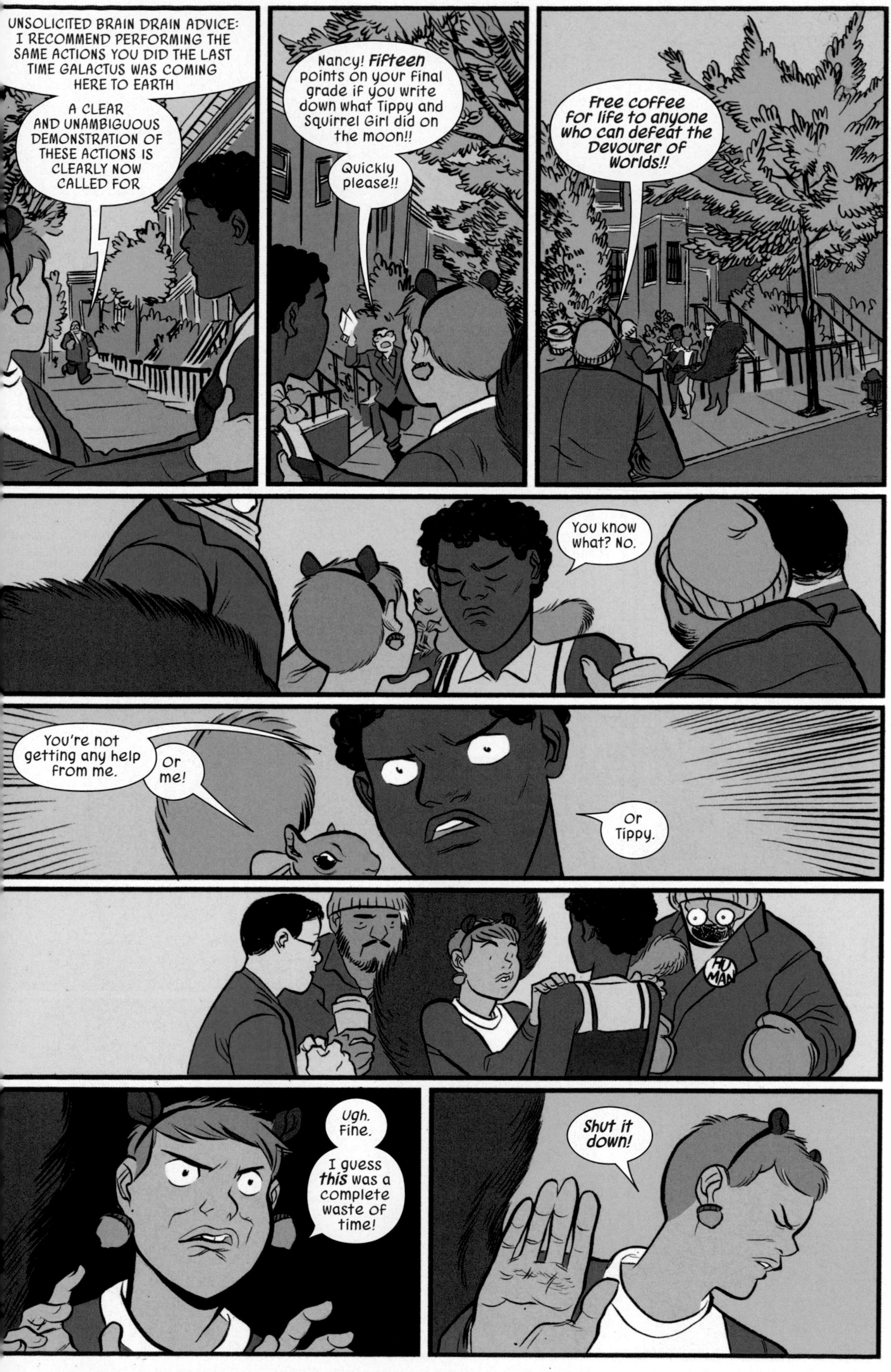
UNSOLICITED BRAIN DRAIN ADVICE: I RECOMMEND PERFORMING THE SAME ACTIONS YOU DID THE LAST TIME GALACTUS WAS COMING HERE TO EARTH
A CLEAR AND UNAMBIGUOUS DEMONSTRATION OF THESE ACTIONS IS CLEARLY NOW CALLED FOR
Nancy! Fifteen points on your final grade if you write down what Tippy and Squirrel Girl did on the moon!!
Quickly please!!
Free coffee for life to anyone who can defeat the Devourer of Worlds!!
You know what? No.
You're not getting any help from me.
Or me!
Or Tippy.
HU MAN
Ugh. Fine.
I guess this was a complete waste of time!
Shut it down!

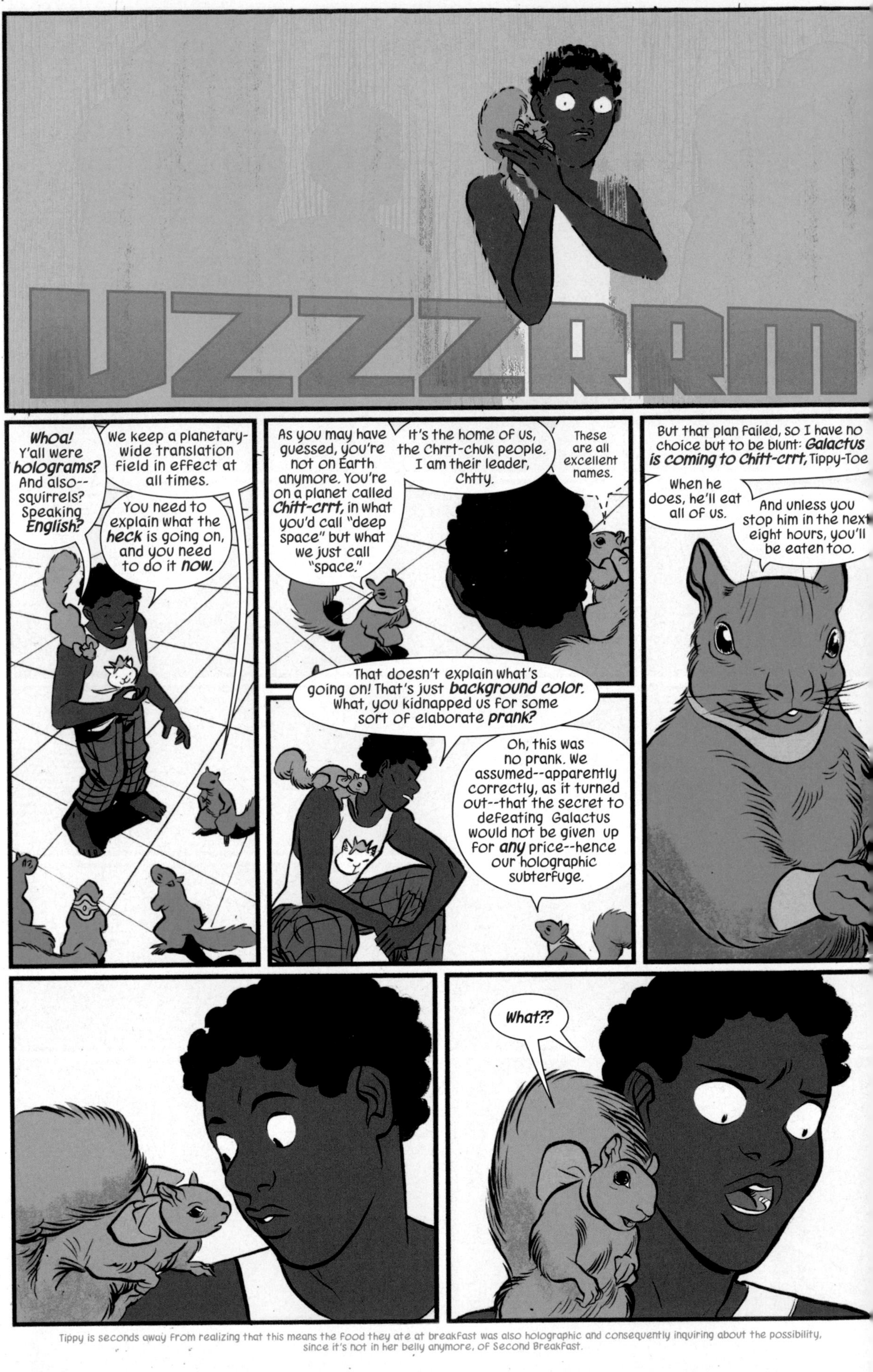
UZZZRRM
Whoa! Y'all were holograms? And also--squirrels? Speaking English?
We keep a planetary-wide translation field in effect at all times.
You need to explain what the heck is going on, and you need to do it now.
As you may have guessed, you're not on Earth anymore. You're on a planet called Chitt-crrt, in what you'd call "deep space" but what we just call "space."
It's the home of us, the Chrrt-chuk people. I am their leader, Chtty.
These are all excellent names.
That doesn't explain what's going on! That's just background color. What, you kidnapped us for some sort of elaborate prank?
Oh, this was no prank. We assumed--apparently correctly, as it turned out--that the secret to defeating Galactus would not be given up for any price--hence our holographic subterfuge.
But that plan failed, so I have no choice but to be blunt: Galactus is coming to Chitt-crrt, Tippy-Toe
When he does, he'll eat all of us.
And unless you stop him in the next eight hours, you'll be eaten too.
What??
Tippy is seconds away from realizing that this means the food they ate at breakfast was also holographic and consequently inquiring about the possibility, since it's not in her belly anymore, of Second Breakfast.

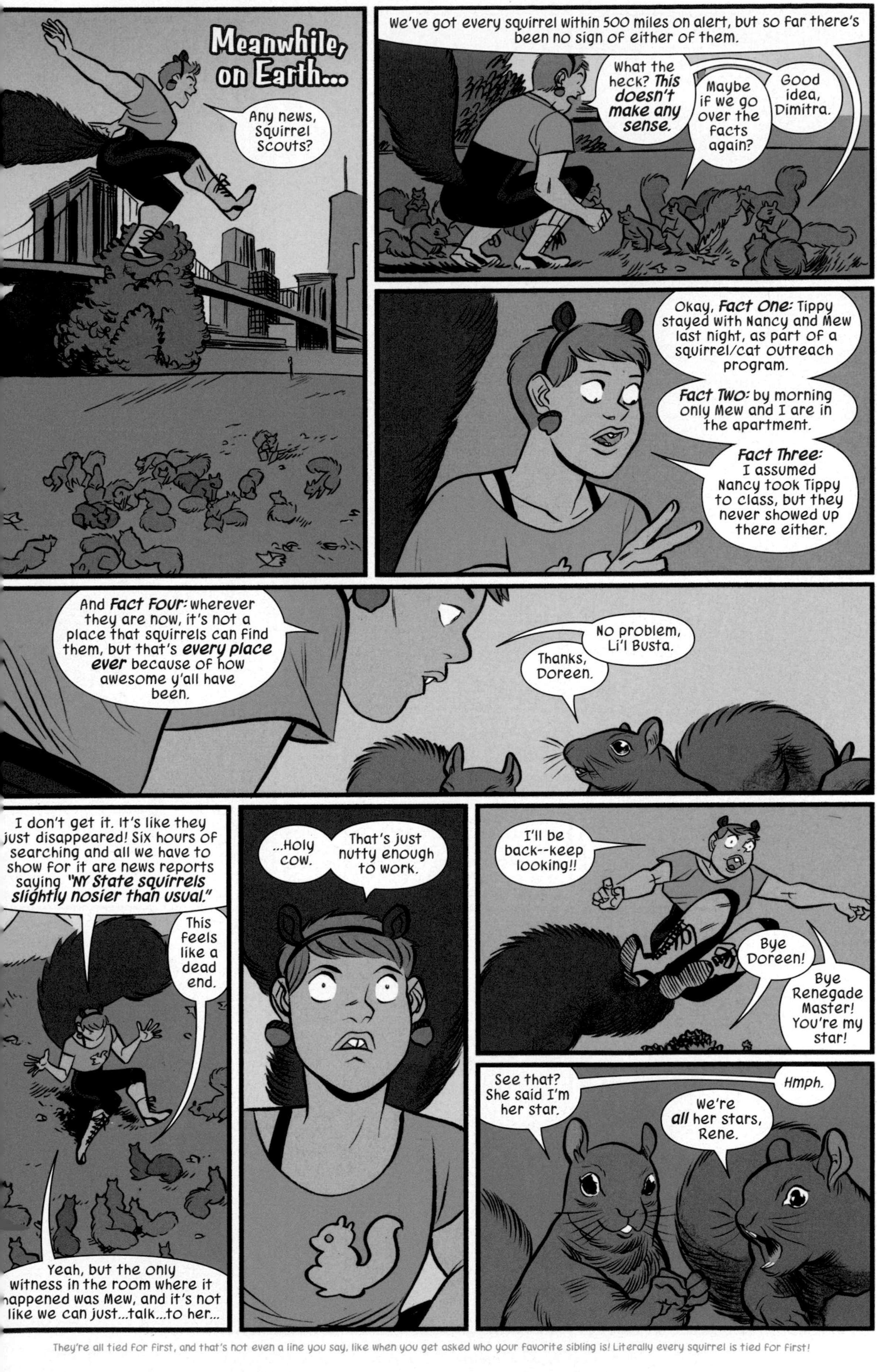
Meanwhile, on Earth...
Any news, Squirrel Scouts?
We've got every squirrel within 500 miles on alert, but so far there's been no sign of either of them.
What the heck? *This doesn't make any sense.*
Maybe if we go over the facts again?
Good idea, Dimitra.
Okay, *Fact One:* Tippy stayed with Nancy and Mew last night, as part of a squirrel/cat outreach program.
Fact Two: by morning only Mew and I are in the apartment.
Fact Three: I assumed Nancy took Tippy to class, but they never showed up there either.
And *Fact Four:* wherever they are now, it's not a place that squirrels can find them, but that's *every place ever* because of how awesome y'all have been.
No problem, Li'l Busta.
Thanks, Doreen.
I don't get it. It's like they just disappeared! Six hours of searching and all we have to show for it are news reports saying *"NY State squirrels slightly nosier than usual."*
This feels like a dead end.
Yeah, but the only witness in the room where it happened was Mew, and it's not like we can just...talk...to her...
...Holy cow.
That's just nutty enough to work.
I'll be back--keep looking!!
Bye Doreen!
Bye Renegade Master! You're my star!
See that? She said I'm her star.
Hmph.
We're *all* her stars, Rene.

They're all tied for first, and that's not even a line you say, like when you get asked who your favorite sibling is! Literally every squirrel is tied for first!

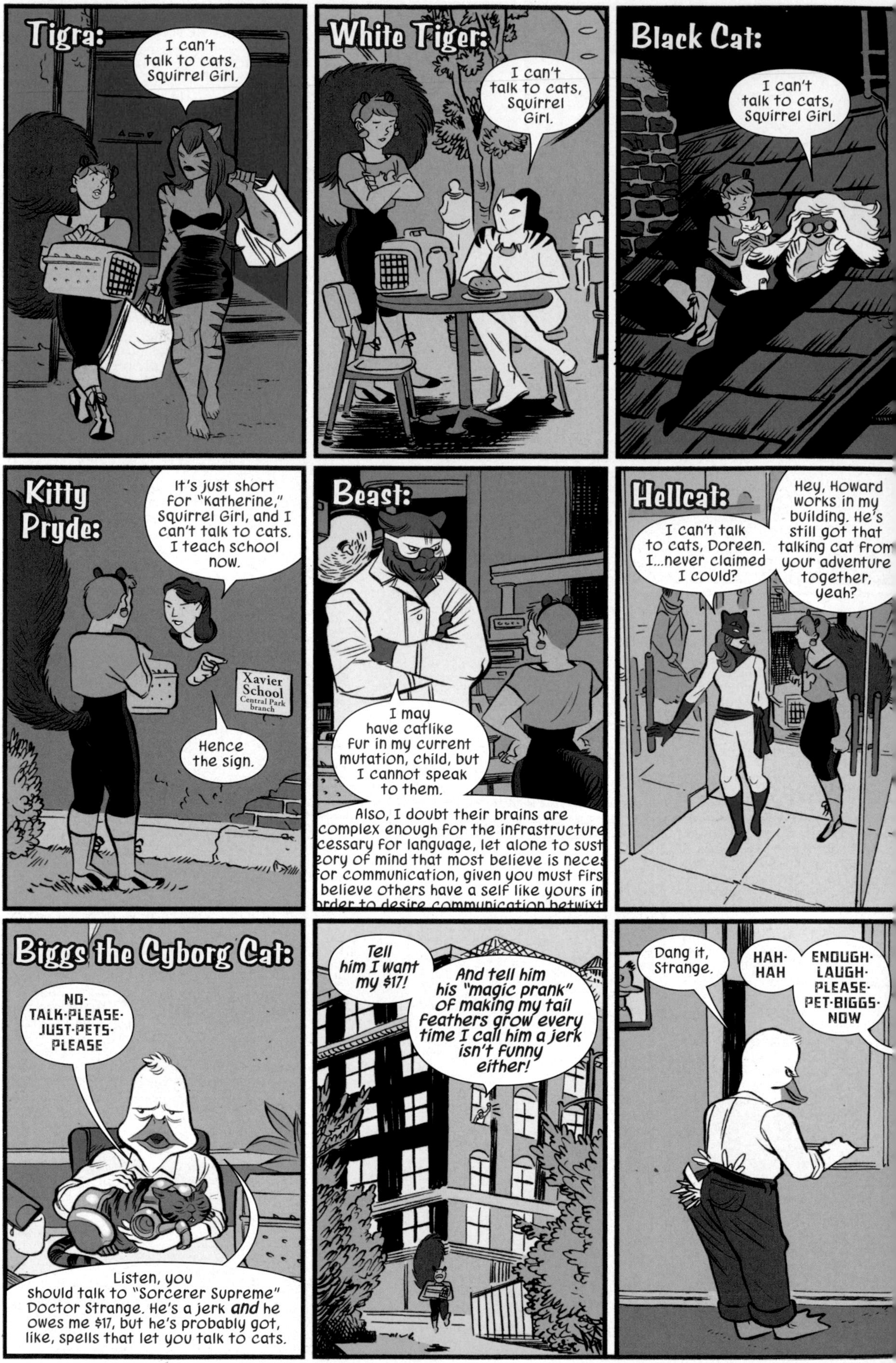
Tigra:
I can't talk to cats, Squirrel Girl.
White Tiger:
I can't talk to cats, Squirrel Girl.
Black Cat:
I can't talk to cats, Squirrel Girl.
Kitty Pryde:
It's just short for "Katherine," Squirrel Girl, and I can't talk to cats. I teach school now.
Xavier School Central Park branch
Hence the sign.
Beast:
I may have catlike fur in my current mutation, child, but I cannot speak to them.
Also, I doubt their brains are
complex enough for the infrastructure
cessary for language, let alone to sust
eory of mind that most believe is neces
for communication, given you must firs
believe others have a self like yours in
Hellcat:
I can't talk to cats, Doreen. I...never claimed I could?
Hey, Howard works in my building. He's still got that talking cat from your adventure together, yeah?
Biggs the Cyborg Cat:
NO·TALK·PLEASE·JUST·PETS·PLEASE
Listen, you should talk to "Sorcerer Supreme" Doctor Strange. He's a jerk and he owes me $17, but he's probably got, like, spells that let you talk to cats.
Tell him I want my $17!
And tell him his "magic prank" of making my tail feathers grow every time I call him a jerk isn't funny either!
Dang it, Strange.
HAH·HAH
ENOUGH·LAUGH·PLEASE·PET·BIGGS·NOW

BIGGS·ONLY·CARES·TO·TALK·ABOUT·THINGS·INVOLVING·BIGGS, LIKE·PETTING. DUCK·MAN·NOW·PET·WITH·WEIRD·FEATHER·HANDS. SORRY·BIGGS·NOT·MEAN·TO·SAY·"WEIRD," NO·JUDGMENT, BIGGS·LOVES·ALL·BODIES, FOR·ALL·BODIES·CAN·FIND·A·WAY·TO·PET·BIGGS

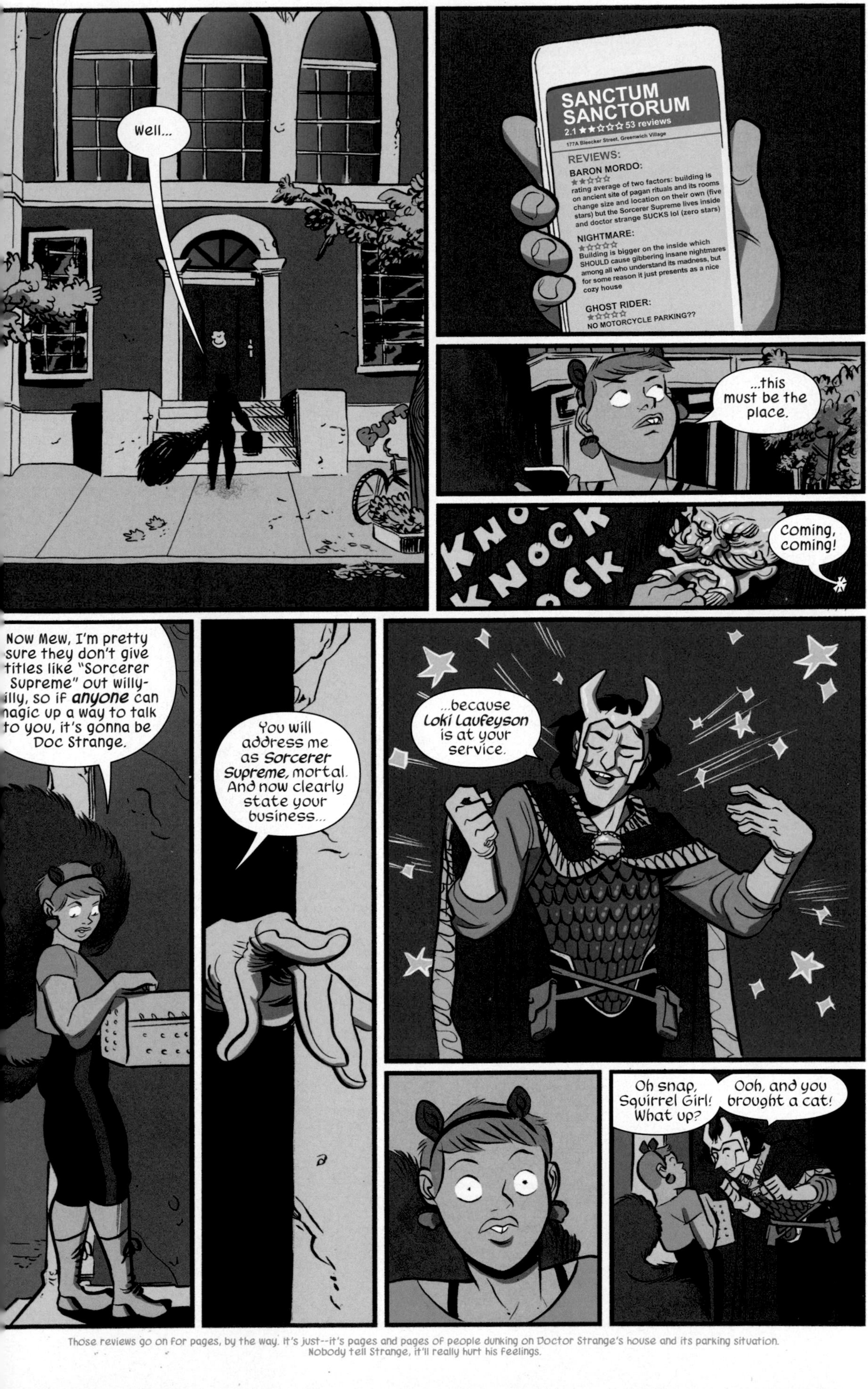
Well...
SANCTUM SANCTORUM
2.1 53 reviews
177A Bleecker Street, Greenwich Village
REVIEWS:
BARON MORDO:
rating average of two factors: building is on ancient site of pagan rituals and its rooms change size and location on their own (five stars) but the Sorcerer Supreme lives inside and doctor strange SUCKS lol (zero stars)
NIGHTMARE:
Building is bigger on the inside which SHOULD cause gibbering insane nightmares among all who understand its madness, but for some reason it just presents as a nice cozy house
GHOST RIDER:
NO MOTORCYCLE PARKING??
...this must be the place.
KNOCK KNOCK KNOCK
Coming, coming!
Now Mew, I'm pretty sure they don't give titles like "Sorcerer Supreme" out willy-nilly, so if anyone can magic up a way to talk to you, it's gonna be Doc Strange.
You will address me as Sorcerer Supreme, mortal. And now clearly state your business...
...because Loki Laufeyson is at your service.
Oh snap, Squirrel Girl! What up?
Ooh, and you brought a cat!

Those reviews go on for pages, by the way. It's just--it's pages and pages of people dunking on Doctor Strange's house and its parking situation. Nobody tell Strange, it'll really hurt his feelings.

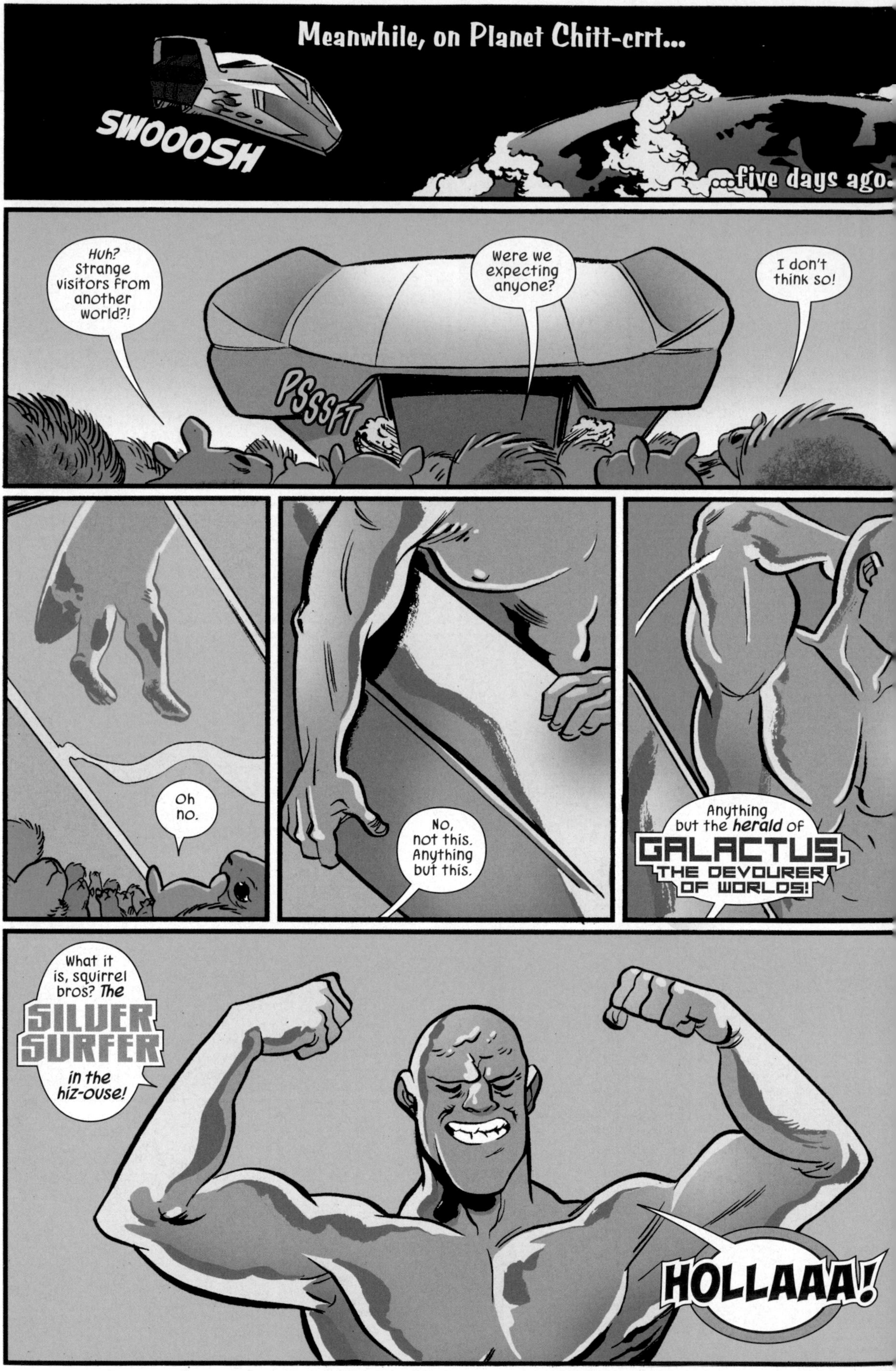
Meanwhile, on Planet Chitt-crrt...
SWOOOSH
...five days ago.
Huh? Strange visitors from another world?!
Were we expecting anyone?
I don't think so!
PSSSFT
Oh no.
No, not this. Anything but this.
Anything but the herald of GALACTUS, THE DEVOURER OF WORLDS!
What it is, squirrel bros? The SILVER SURFER in the hiz-ouse!
HOLLAAA!

I don't know what sound it makes when people speak in logo fonts in comic books, but I know that whatever it sounds like, it's *totally amazing.*

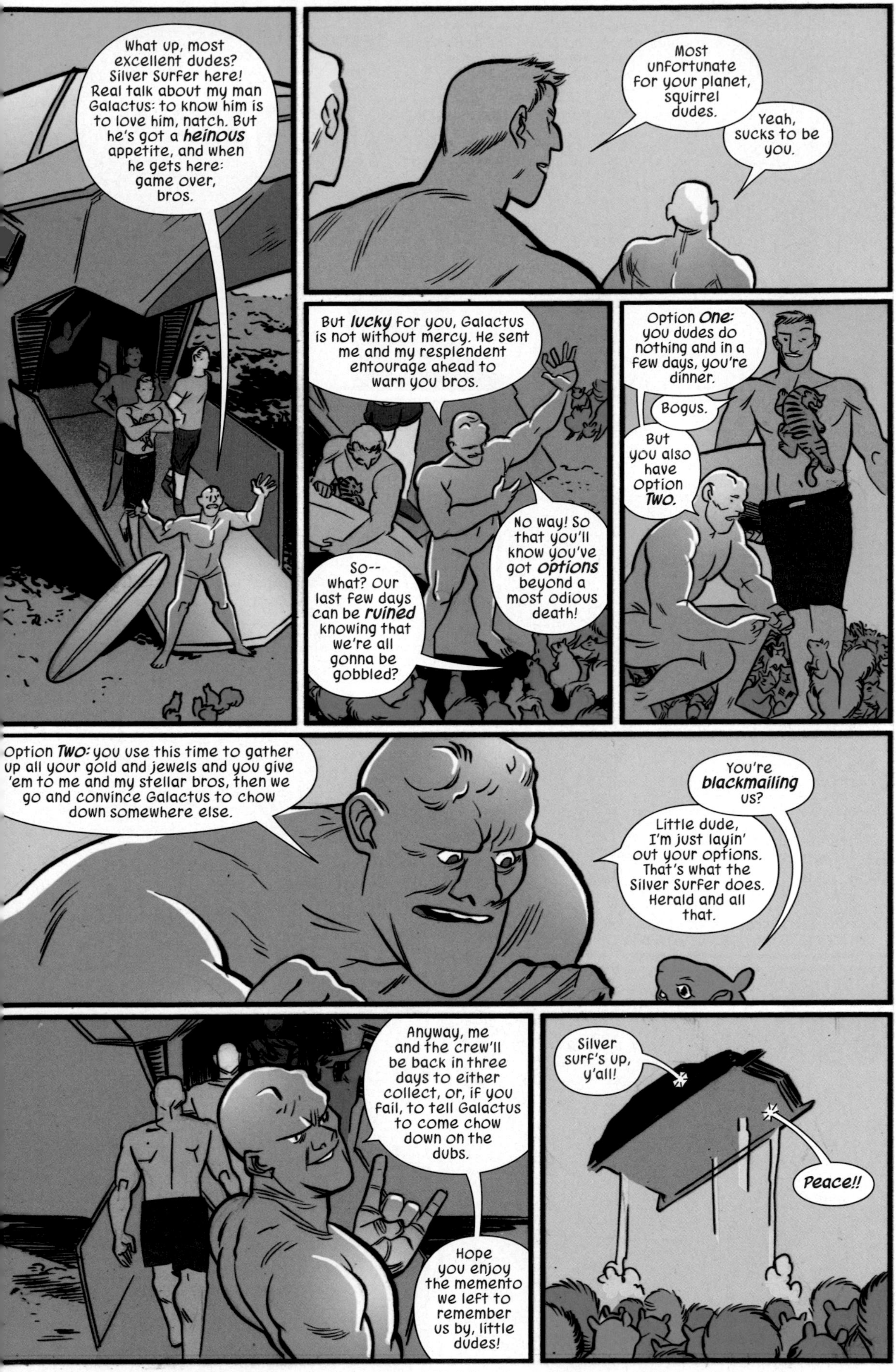
What up, most excellent dudes? Silver Surfer here! Real talk about my man Galactus: to know him is to love him, natch. But he's got a **heinous** appetite, and when he gets here: game over, bros.
Most unfortunate for your planet, squirrel dudes.
Yeah, sucks to be you.
But **lucky** for you, Galactus is not without mercy. He sent me and my resplendent entourage ahead to warn you bros.
So--what? Our last few days can be **ruined** knowing that we're all gonna be gobbled?
No way! So that you'll know you've got **options** beyond a most odious death!
Option **One:** you dudes do nothing and in a few days, you're dinner.
Bogus.
But you also have Option **Two.**
Option **Two:** you use this time to gather up all your gold and jewels and you give 'em to me and my stellar bros, then we go and convince Galactus to chow down somewhere else.
You're **blackmailing** us?
Little dude, I'm just layin' out your options. That's what the Silver Surfer does. Herald and all that.
Anyway, me and the crew'll be back in three days to either collect, or, if you fail, to tell Galactus to come chow down on the dubs.
Hope you enjoy the memento we left to remember us by, little dudes!
Silver surf's up, y'all!
Peace!!
The Silver Surfer is much hunkier than you may have been expecting. I don't know what to tell you. I guess..."It's time to accept this new and hunkier world without question"?

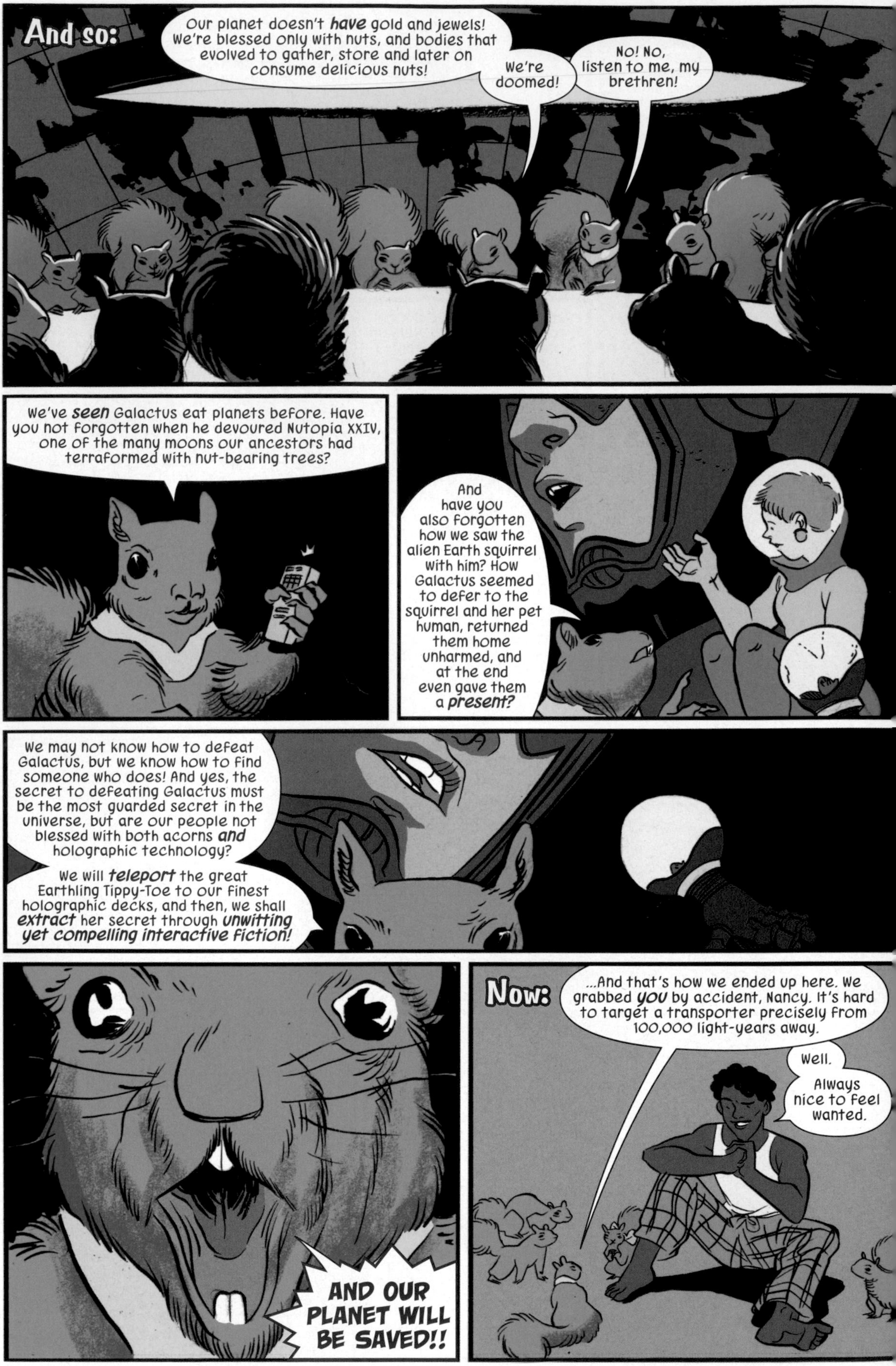

And so:
Our planet doesn't have gold and jewels! We're blessed only with nuts, and bodies that evolved to gather, store and later on consume delicious nuts!
We're doomed!
NO! NO, listen to me, my brethren!
We've seen Galactus eat planets before. Have you not forgotten when he devoured Nutopia XXIV, one of the many moons our ancestors had terraformed with nut-bearing trees?
And have you also forgotten how we saw the alien Earth squirrel with him? How Galactus seemed to defer to the squirrel and her pet human, returned them home unharmed, and at the end even gave them a present?
We may not know how to defeat Galactus, but we know how to find someone who does! And yes, the secret to defeating Galactus must be the most guarded secret in the universe, but are our people not blessed with both acorns and holographic technology?
We will teleport the great Earthling Tippy-Toe to our finest holographic decks, and then, we shall extract her secret through unwitting yet compelling interactive fiction!
AND OUR PLANET WILL BE SAVED!!
Now:
...And that's how we ended up here. We grabbed you by accident, Nancy. It's hard to target a transporter precisely from 100,000 light-years away.
Well.
Always nice to feel wanted.

Nutopia XXIV was but the twenty-fourth of our many nut moons! Nut-wise, we've been doing really great!

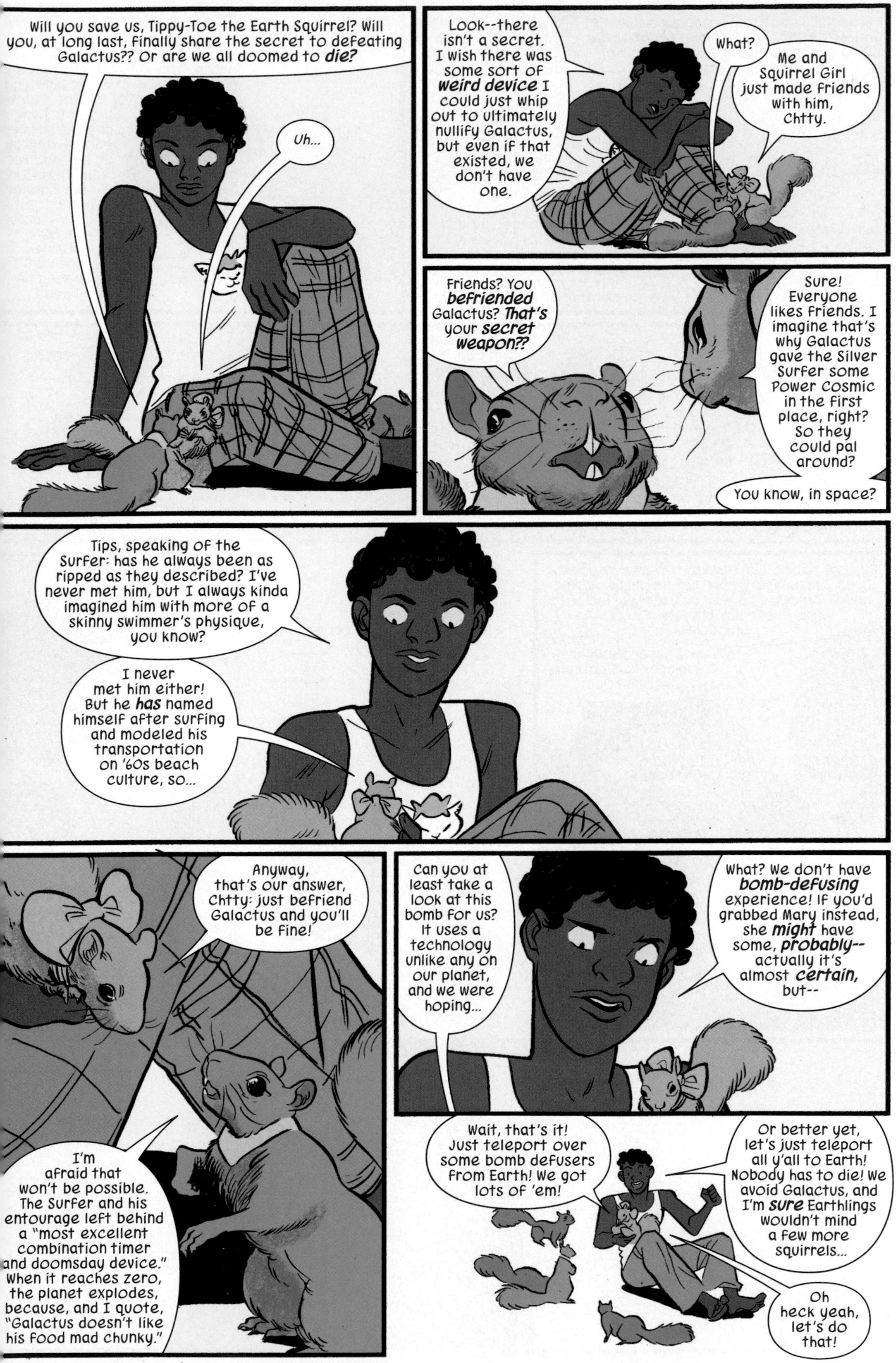
Will you save us, Tippy-Toe the Earth Squirrel? Will you, at long last, finally share the secret to defeating Galactus?? Or are we all doomed to *die?*
Uh...
Look--there isn't a secret. I wish there was some sort of *weird device* I could just whip out to ultimately nullify Galactus, but even if that existed, we don't have one.
What?
Me and Squirrel Girl just made friends with him, Chtty.
Friends? You *befriended* Galactus? *That's* your *secret weapon??*
Sure! Everyone likes friends. I imagine that's why Galactus gave the Silver Surfer some Power Cosmic in the first place, right? So they could pal around?
You know, in space?
Tips, speaking of the Surfer: has he always been as ripped as they described? I've never met him, but I always kinda imagined him with more of a skinny swimmer's physique, you know?
I never met him either! But he *has* named himself after surfing and modeled his transportation on '60s beach culture, so...
Anyway, that's our answer, Chtty: just befriend Galactus and you'll be fine!
I'm afraid that won't be possible. The Surfer and his entourage left behind a "most excellent combination timer and doomsday device." When it reaches zero, the planet explodes, because, and I quote, "Galactus doesn't like his food mad chunky."
Can you at least take a look at this bomb for us? It uses a technology unlike any on our planet, and we were hoping...
What? We don't have *bomb-defusing* experience! If you'd grabbed Mary instead, she *might* have some, *probably--* actually it's almost *certain,* but--
Wait, that's it! Just teleport over some bomb defusers from Earth! We got lots of 'em!
Or better yet, let's just teleport all y'all to Earth! Nobody has to die! We avoid Galactus, and I'm *sure* Earthlings wouldn't mind a few more squirrels...
Oh heck yeah, let's do that!

We got lots of bomb defusers on Earth! If you're ever not sure if you want to cut the red wire or the green one and you've only got a few seconds left, give 'em a call! They love that stuff!

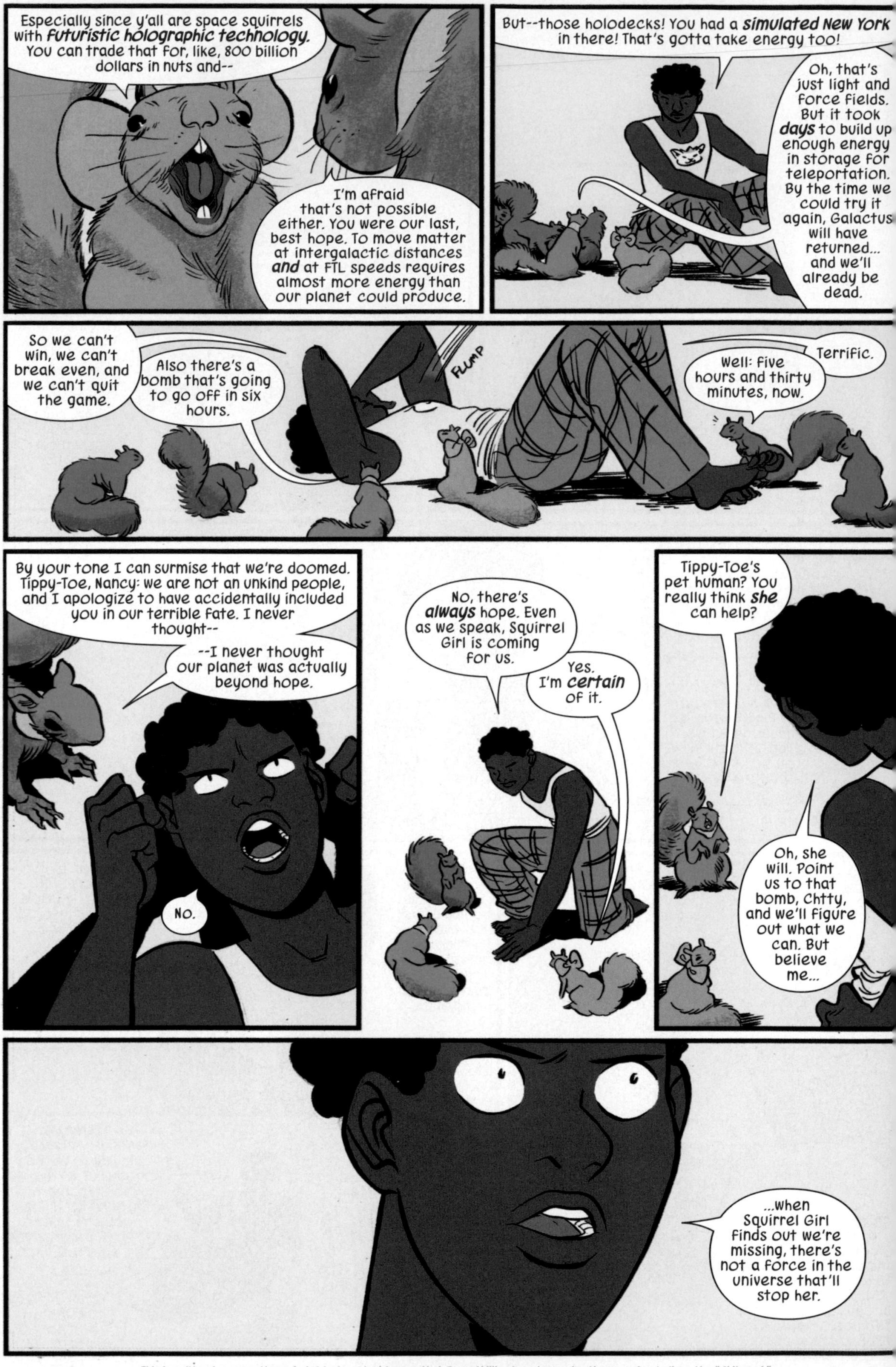

Especially since y'all are space squirrels with futuristic holographic technology. You can trade that for, like, 800 billion dollars in nuts and--
I'm afraid that's not possible either. You were our last, best hope. To move matter at intergalactic distances and at FTL speeds requires almost more energy than our planet could produce.
But--those holodecks! You had a simulated New York in there! That's gotta take energy too!
Oh, that's just light and force fields. But it took days to build up enough energy in storage for teleportation. By the time we could try it again, Galactus will have returned... and we'll already be dead.
So we can't win, we can't break even, and we can't quit the game.
Also there's a bomb that's going to go off in six hours.
FLUMP
Terrific.
Well: five hours and thirty minutes, now.
By your tone I can surmise that we're doomed. Tippy-Toe, Nancy: we are not an unkind people, and I apologize to have accidentally included you in our terrible fate. I never thought--
--I never thought our planet was actually beyond hope.
No.
No, there's always hope. Even as we speak, Squirrel Girl is coming for us.
Yes. I'm certain of it.
Tippy-Toe's pet human? You really think she can help?
Oh, she will. Point us to that bomb, Chtty, and we'll figure out what we can. But believe me...
...when Squirrel Girl finds out we're missing, there's not a force in the universe that'll stop her.

This is neither here nor there, but I just wanted to say that I was thiiiis close to naming these squirrel aliens the "Chit-auri."

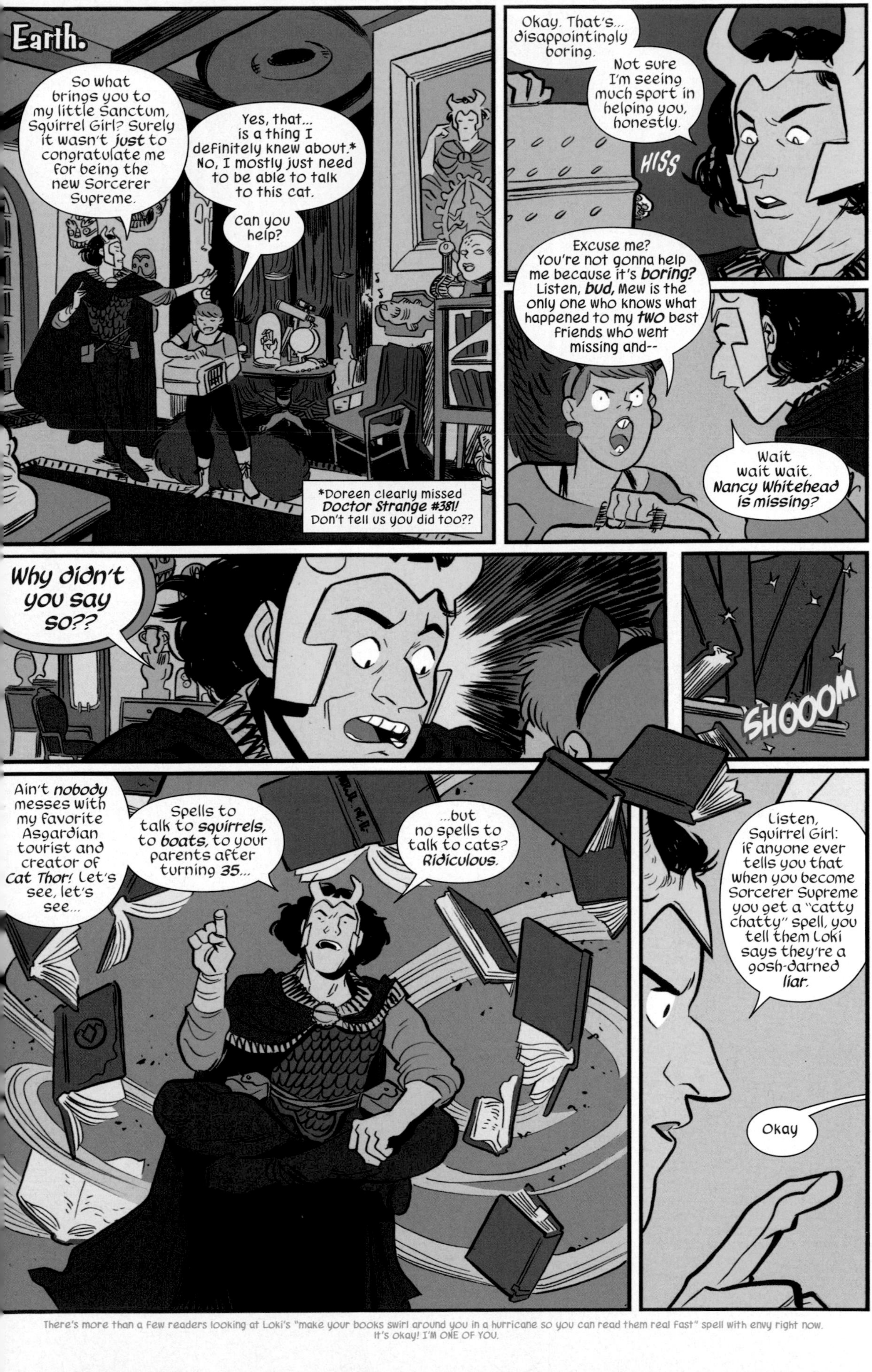
Earth.
So what brings you to my little Sanctum, Squirrel Girl? Surely it wasn't *just* to congratulate me for being the new Sorcerer Supreme.
Yes, that... is a thing I definitely knew about.* No, I mostly just need to be able to talk to this cat.
Can you help?
*Doreen clearly missed **Doctor Strange #381!** Don't tell us you did too??
Okay. That's... disappointingly boring.
Not sure I'm seeing much sport in helping you, honestly.
HISS
Excuse me? You're not gonna help me because it's ***boring?*** Listen, ***bud,*** Mew is the only one who knows what happened to my ***two*** best friends who went missing and--
Wait wait wait. ***Nancy Whitehead is missing?***
Why didn't you say so??
SHOOOM
Ain't ***nobody*** messes with my favorite Asgardian tourist and creator of ***Cat Thor!*** Let's see, let's see...
Spells to talk to ***squirrels,*** to ***boats,*** to your parents after turning ***35***...
...but no spells to talk to cats? ***Ridiculous.***
Listen, Squirrel Girl: if anyone ever tells you that when you become Sorcerer Supreme you get a "catty chatty" spell, you tell them Loki says they're a gosh-darned ***liar.***
Okay

There's more than a few readers looking at Loki's "make your books swirl around you in a hurricane so you can read them real fast" spell with envy right now. It's okay! I'M ONE OF YOU.

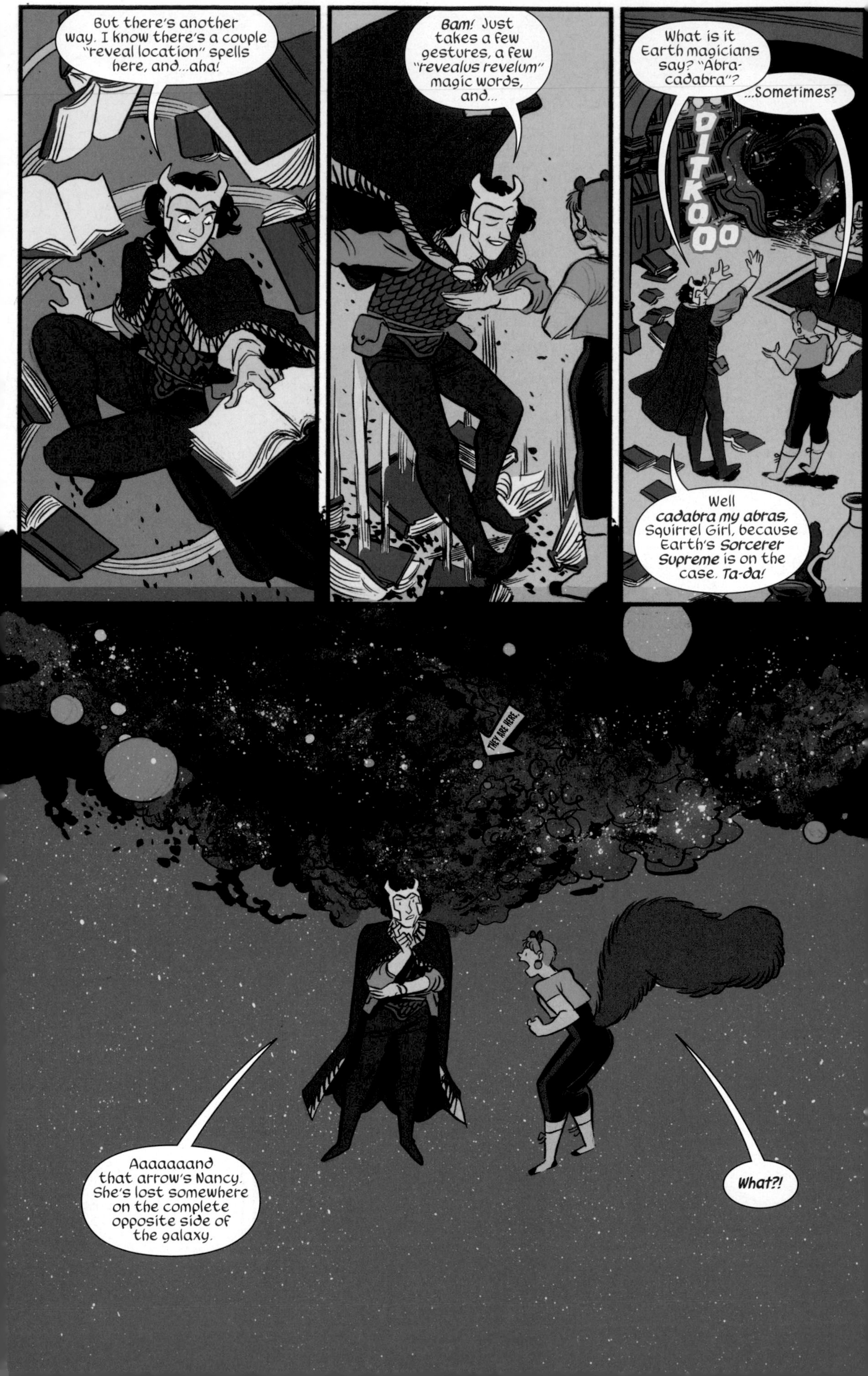
But there's another way. I know there's a couple "reveal location" spells here, and...aha!
Bam! Just takes a few gestures, a few "revealus revelum" magic words, and...
What is it Earth magicians say? "Abra-cadabra"?
...Sometimes?
DITKOOO
Well cadabra my abras, Squirrel Girl, because Earth's Sorcerer Supreme is on the case. Ta-da!
THEY ARE HERE.
Aaaaaaand that arrow's Nancy. She's lost somewhere on the complete opposite side of the galaxy.
What?!

Don't worry, don't worry--I can send you there. But there's a catch, Squirrel Girl...

...there's no way for me to bring you back. It'll be a one-way trip.

Normally I wouldn't mention that little fact until you were already mid-transport and fading away--that's just *classic* me right there--but this one's for Nancy, so I'mma level with you.

There's nothing I can do. You'll have to find your own way home.

I don't care.

Send me to her, Loki.

You got it, bud. But-- you're not going into space wearing *that*, are you?

...What? What do my *clothes* have to do with anything?

Also, what's wrong with them?

So last millennium. Confidentially, Earth is considered to be a bit of a fashion backwater out here in the cosmos. Y'all had a chance in the 1100s when capes were in for a hot minute, but since then-- evgh.

No worries. Your friendly neighborhood Sorcerer Supreme has a solution for that, too.

SNAP

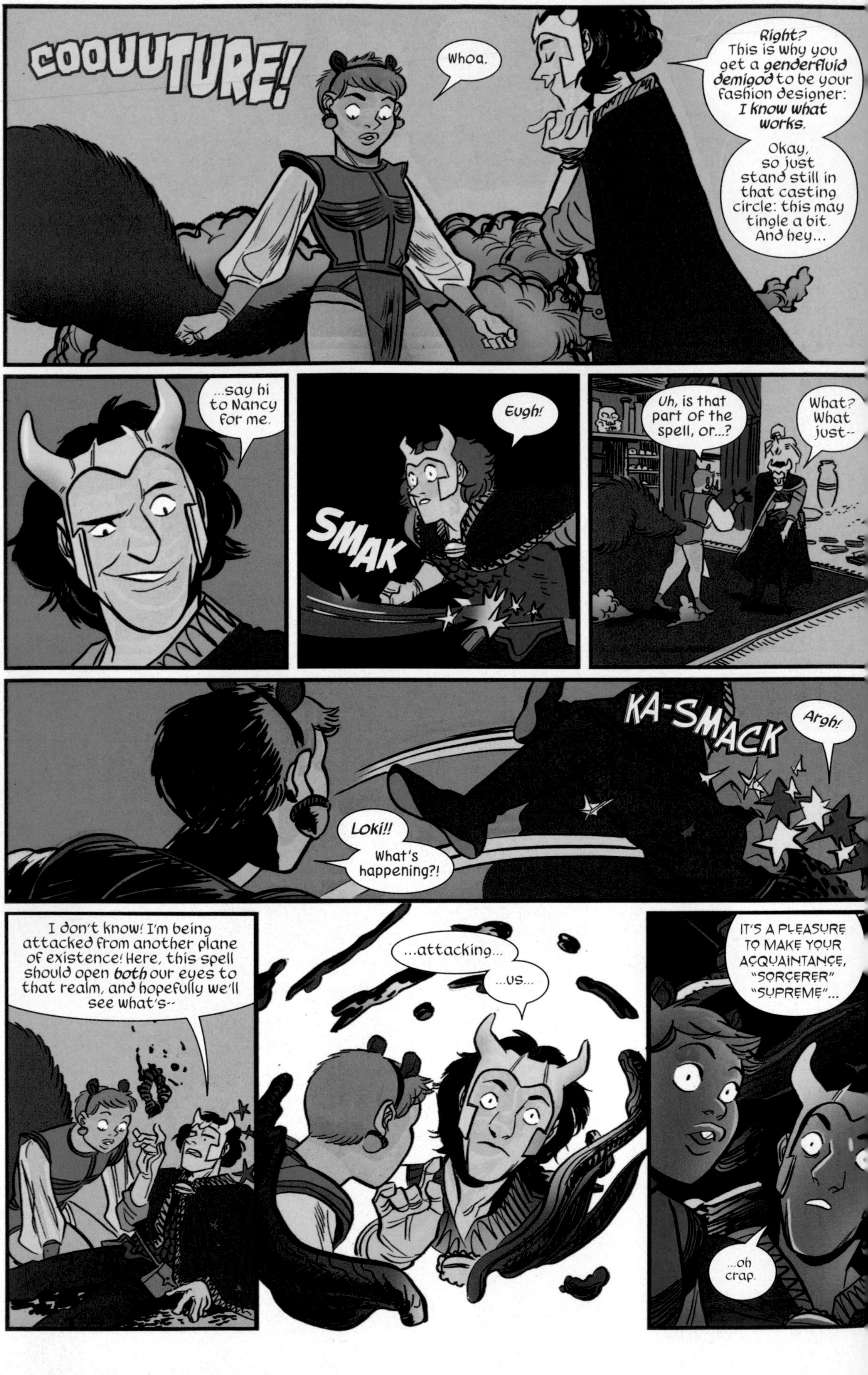
COOUUTURE!
Whoa.
Right? This is why you get a genderfluid demigod to be your fashion designer: I know what works.
Okay, so just stand still in that casting circle: this may tingle a bit. And hey...
...say hi to Nancy for me.
Eugh!
SMAK
Uh, is that part of the spell, or...?
What? What just--
KA-SMACK
Argh!
Loki!!
What's happening?!
I don't know! I'm being attacked from another plane of existence! Here, this spell should open both our eyes to that realm, and hopefully we'll see what's--
...attacking...
...us...
IT'S A PLEASURE TO MAKE YOUR ACQUAINTANCE, "SORCERER" "SUPREME"...
...oh crap.

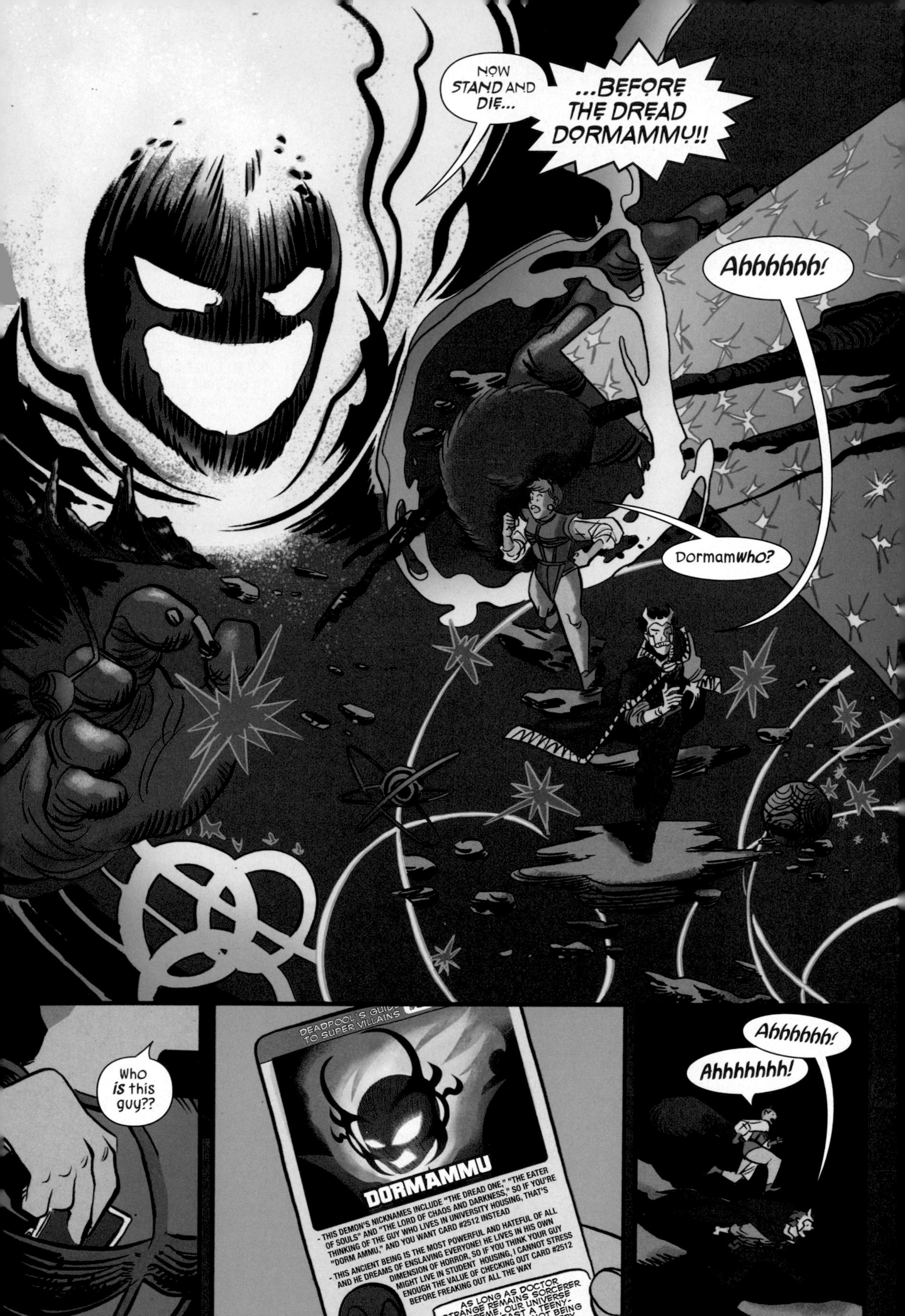
NOW STAND AND DIE...
...BEFORE THE DREAD DORMAMMU!!
Ahhhhhh!
DormamWHO?
Who *is* this guy??
DEADPOOL'S GUIDE TO SUPER VILLAINS
DORMAMMU
- THIS DEMON'S NICKNAMES INCLUDE "THE DREAD ONE," "THE EATER OF SOULS" AND "THE LORD OF CHAOS AND DARKNESS," SO IF YOU'RE THINKING OF THE GUY WHO LIVES IN UNIVERSITY HOUSING, THAT'S "DORM AMMU," AND YOU WANT CARD #2512 INSTEAD
- THIS ANCIENT BEING IS THE MOST POWERFUL AND HATEFUL OF ALL AND HE DREAMS OF ENSLAVING EVERYONE! HE LIVES IN HIS OWN DIMENSION OF HORROR, SO IF YOU THINK YOUR GUY MIGHT LIVE IN STUDENT HOUSING, I CANNOT STRESS ENOUGH THE VALUE OF CHECKING OUT CARD #2512 BEFORE FREAKING OUT ALL THE WAY
AS LONG AS DOCTOR STRANGE REMAINS SORCERER SUPREME, OUR UNIVERSE HAS AT LEAST A TEENY-WEENIE HOPE OF NOT BEING CONSUMED BY HIS FIERY GRASP! SO THAT'S NICE!!
Ahhhhhh!
Ahhhhhhh!

I can confirm this is the Dread Dormammu and not Dorm Ammu! If you're wondering what Dorm Ammu's up to, he is currently eating as much as he can at the university eteria because they forced him to pay $20 a day for meals when he got his room, and there's ***no way*** he's gonna let himself get ripped off by not getting his money's worth. We'll catch up with him never!

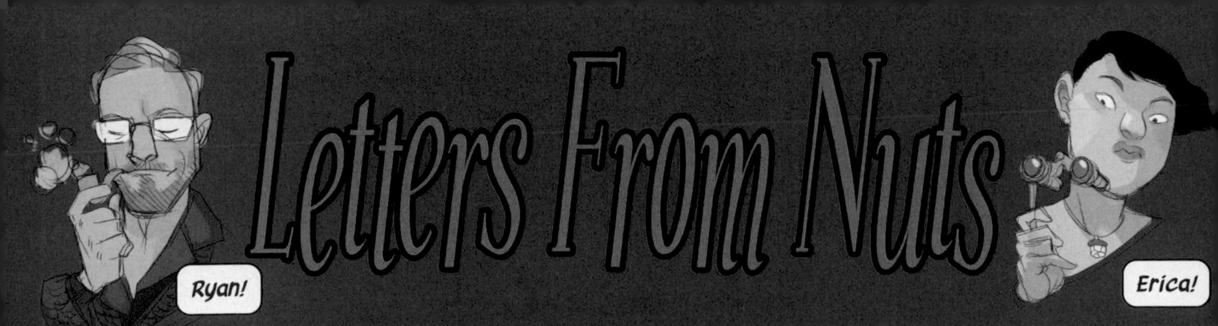
Letters From Nuts
Ryan!
Erica!

Send letters to mheroes@marvel.com or 135 W 50th St, 7th Floor, New York, NY 10020 (Please mark "OKAY TO PRINT

Good day Squirrel Friends,

Way back in UNBEATABLE SQUIRREL GIRL #4 (June 2015), I sent you folks some drawings from my comic convention sketchbook where I ask artists to mash-up squirrels and whatever character they choose. I have attached a few more drawings for your viewing pleasure! I think it is time for an EDGE OF SQUIRREL-VERSE or SQUIRREL EMPIRE miniseries!!!

Corey Fuhrer

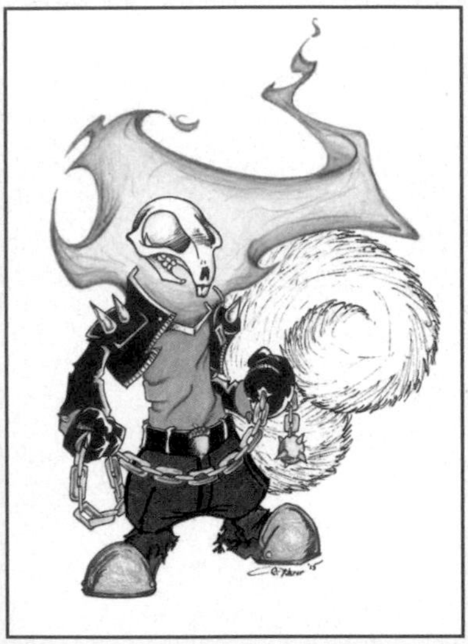

RYAN: I am so here for squirrel mash-ups. Can we talk about the Ghost Rider Squirrel you drew? I love it. I think there are no downsides to this becoming a new canonical character. My only tweak would be to change the spikey ball into a spikey acorn, for very important personal branding reasons.

ERICA: Ryan, you don't get to decide how Zarathos' powers manifest.

Ryan and Erica,

My son (and his parents) loves Squirrel Girl! He was so excited to take his custom Squirrel Girl lunchbox to school! Thanks for making such an awesome comic we can enjoy as a family!

Krista

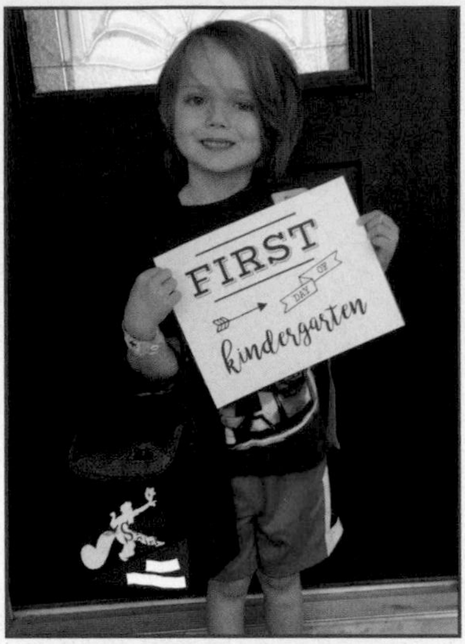
FIRST
DAY OF
kindergarten

RYAN: CUSTOM SQUIRREL GIRL LUNCHBOX! Nicely done. It's super dramatic and looks entirely professional! I would like: seven. And congrats to your son for the first day of kindergarten! I remember on my first day of kindergarten they told us to enter through a certain set of doors because the other doors were for the big kids (grades 1-5). Anyway, on my second day I wandered in through the big kids doors but still found my way there. I thought I'd gotten away with it until the teacher said that she wasn't going to name names but "ONE of us came through the wrong door today." It was my first experience with passive-aggressive feedback! I also remember there being delicious snacks.

ERICA: Ryan, I hope that teacher is seeing this and is ashamed at the arbitrary rules they chose to uphold in order to maintain a social hierarchy based on age. Anyway, that lunchbox is huge! You can fit, like, three lunches in there or any number of desserts you traded up for, amiright, kids?

Hi, Erica and Ryan! A couple of weeks ago, I found out that a Squirrel Girl movie is going to come out! I'm so excited! I'm a huge fan of this smart girl and her little sidekick(s). My Halloween costume this year... is going to be Squirrel Girl! I can't wait.

Once a squirrel, always a squirrel...
Allie A.

RYAN: Please send in pictures of your costume! PLEASE. And you heard something that is ALMOST correc There's no Squirrel Girl movie but the IS a TV show coming out starring he called THE NEW WARRIORS! And doesn't just star Doreen Green – it sta Tippy, too! My excitement on a sca from one to ten is: infinity plus on

ERICA: AH PLEASE SEND US PHOTO OF YOUR COSTUME. I'm writing th after Halloween and maybe yo already did but SEND THEM AGAI

Dear Ryan and Erica,

After reading USG #8 and realizing that m squirrel aversion could be hurting my datin prospects, I've been making an effort to b kinder to my bushy-tailed bros. Perhap a little too kind? Today I made match shortbread and was enjoying an afternoo snack on the fire escape when a fine fluf squirrel dropped by for tea. I threw h a broken chunk of cookie to be sociabl finished my tea, then went back insid About an hour later, I heard a weird noise the kitchen and saw my squirrel buddy ru down the fire escape holding something. I k you not here: My squirrel friend had chewe through the screen on my kitchen windo carefully selected exactly three cooki from the full tray, and skeddadled to th backyard to enjoy her sweet score. I'm st kind of stunned, but also weirdly flattere

I'm enclosing the recipe in case my fello Squirrel Scouts would like to give it try. Thank you for your brilliant wor

INGREDIENTS

1 c all purpose flour
1 T matcha (green tea) powder
1/2 tsp sea salt
1 stick butter
1/4 c confectioner's sugar

DIRECTIONS

1. Sift flour, tea powder, and salt into small bowl; set aside. Place butter in th bowl of an electric mixer fitted with th paddle attachment. Cream on mediu speed until fluffy, 3 to 5 minutes. Ad sugar; continue to beat until very light color and fluffy, about 2 minutes more. Ad flour mixture; combine on low, scrapi sides of bowl with a spatula if necessa until flour is just incorporated and dou sticks together when squeezed with finge

2. Place a piece of parchment on a cle surface; dust with flour. Roll dough

/4-inch thickness; chill in refrigerator r freezer until firm, about 30 minutes.

. Preheat oven to 350 degrees. Line a aking sheet with parchment. Cut chilled ough with 2-inch cutters. Bake until rm and barely starting to color, 10 to 5 minutes, rotating halfway through. ool completely on wire rack; store in an irtight container for up to 3 to 4 weeks.

Your fan,
Lily

YAN: I AM SO EXCITED THAT WE'RE HARING SQUIRREL-APPROVED HORTBREAD COOKIE RECIPES HERE IOW. I have no other comments xcept that these sound delicious, nd you should advertise them as The Cat-Burglar Squirrel's Choice."

RICA: I'm not going to lie, this is giving ie flashbacks to the time when I was a id and my parents and I stopped at a each in Maine (beaches in Maine are ll piles of large rocks next to the ocean) nd had lunch. We were spotted by a ingle seagull, who proceeded to find all f his terrible friends and they chased s off to try to get our sandwiches. S. In my experience, feeding vild animals sets them into a renzy that I don't understand. P.S. This is how I was bitten by a squirrel. P.P.S. Yes, I was bitten by a squirrel or real, but did you know that HOWARD HE DUCK writer Chip Zdarsky was itten by a duck? There's a photo.

i Erica and Ryan!

uge Norwegian fan here. I've been a fan of QUIRREL GIRL for the past year, and honestly, ou guys make the funniest comics I've ever ead. Thank you guys so much for bringing quirrel Girl back for our generation to enjoy.

his summer I visited Marysville, Kansas, nd let me tell you--that is one town oreen Green would love. They call it e Black Squirrel City because of an olated community of Black Squirrels ving there. They are everywhere! The quirrels are said to be escapees from a aveling circus, and could most certainly e of help to our beloved Squirrel Girl and ppy-Toe, should they ever cross paths.

ie city of Marysville have really embraced e squirrels and even use them as a symbol r their city. (There is a fine of $25 for arming one, which I think is great.) You an even go squirrel hunting, where you go l over the city looking for all the squirrel atues located next to shops, corporations nd tourist attractions. (Of course I had to o it, and take pictures with every one of em). My friend Chloe actually made two of em, which makes it even cooler! Sadly she adn't heard of THE UNBEATABLE SQUIRREL RL, so I had to show hear and some other iends what they were missing out on.

I would also recommend that Squirrel Girl visit Norway in the future. We may not have the most evil bad guys, but we do have lots of trees, nuts and adorable squirrels, and would make for an excellent vacation destination for a hero taking a break to eat some nuts (or she could kick butts there, entirely up to you).

Here is a picture of me with Chief the Squirrel, a hardworking squirrel helping to build farming equipment in the city.

Lots of love, and best wishes while continuing to make this amazing comic.

Maren Lovise Øby
Trondheim, Norway

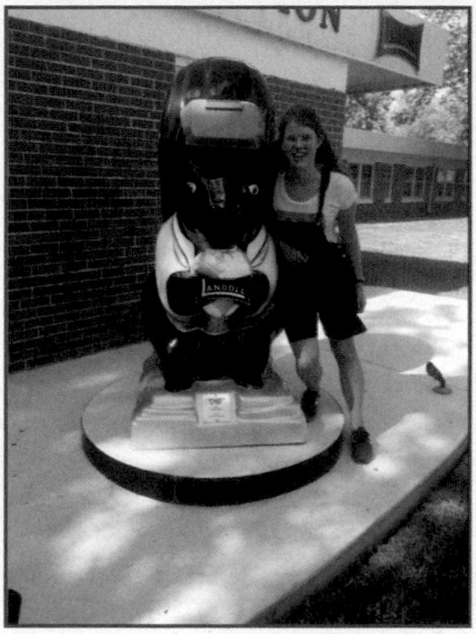

RYAN: I have always wanted to visit Norway, and with this I think we could call it a business trip! Right, Erica? It's very important that we go see squirrels that have escaped from a travelling circus and been so amazing that the town started building statues for them. I feel that this is...mandatory?? Also I figured they'd be tiny statues until I saw you and Chief the Farming Equipment Squirrel, and now I'm even more amazed. So great!

ERICA: We can add these to the list along with the squirrel gardens in Japan. I have already been to the Squirrel Nut Company and have spotted the elusive albino squirrel in town that has its own Facebook page people update with the latest sightings, so I'm halfway there with squirrel landmarks, I think!

Dear readers, our Squirrel Squad is growing! Allow us to introduce Avery, adorable nephew of our very own Ryan North. Look at that grin. What a charmer. And already a squirrel lover! (All right, all right, he MAY have had a little help setting up those blocks.)

See you next month, squirrel fans!

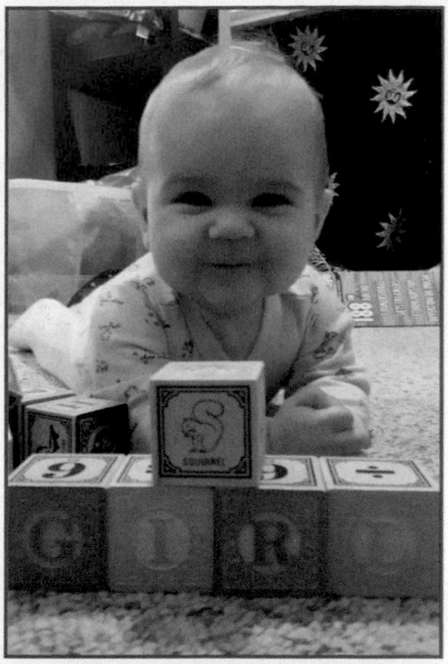

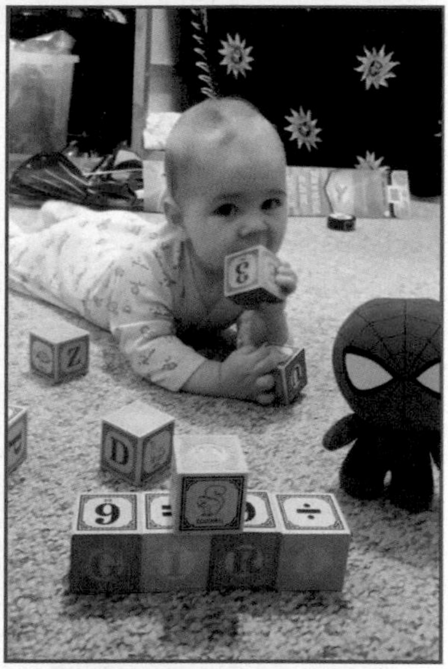

Next Issue:

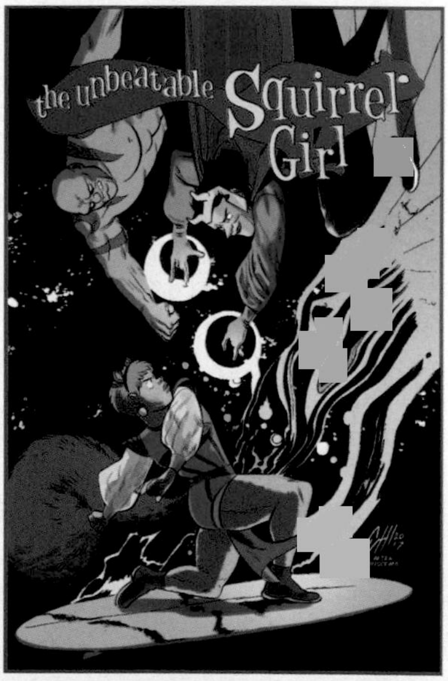
the unbeatable Squirrel Girl

Attention, Squirrel Scouts! Make sure to check out our production blog, **unbeatablesquirrelgirl.tumblr.com**, where we post behind-the-scenes stuff on how the book gets made, along with all sorts of cool things *you* make: fan art, cosplay, whatever!

TIPPY-TOE'S GUIDE TO SQUIRREL GIRL

CARD 001 of ∞

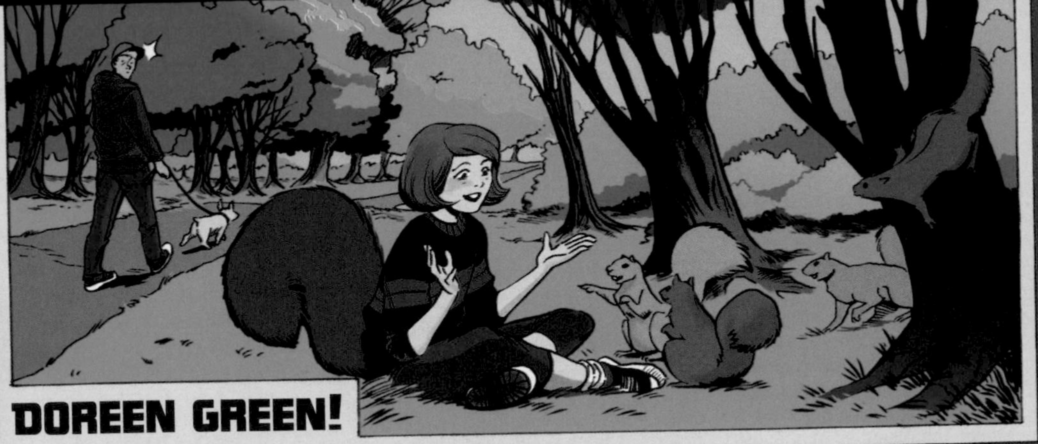
DOREEN GREEN!

Doreen was born with the ability to **communicate** with squirrels. How cool is that? What? You don't think it's cool? I mean, it's cooler than being born with the ability to communicate with sloths. Though I'd totally read an Unwakeable Sloth Girl comic. Any-old-who, the squirrels convinced Doreen to use her powers to help people! And you know what? She **did**! You're **welcome**!

Fun Fact: Did you know Squirrels are the smartest animals in the universe? Well, now you do. Because it's a fact. Also a fact? Nuts are all that matter in life. Nuts. You heard it here first. Tell your friends!

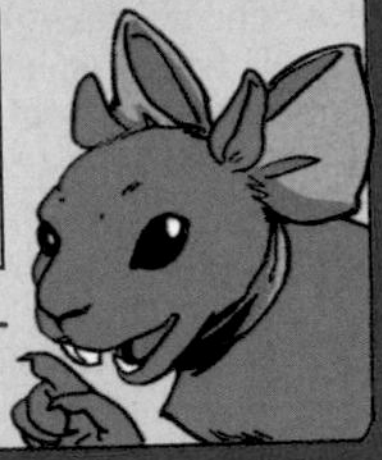

TIPPY-TOE'S GUIDE TO SQUIRREL GIRL

CARD 002 of ∞

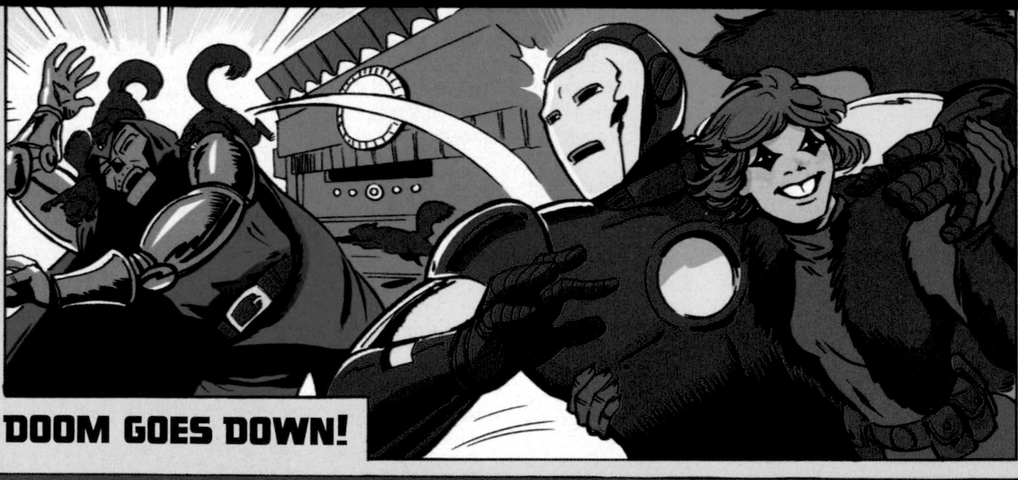
DOOM GOES DOWN!

In Squirrel Girl's first adventure, she totally **saved** her idol Iron Man from Dr. Doom and **proved** she belonged on the big stage! Look out, Avengers, here comes Squirrel Girl!

Fun Fact: Squirrel Girl never did make the Avengers. But she did make the Great Lake Avengers, the 8th or 16th best Avengers squad, where she met me, Tippy-Toe, her partner-in-justice. Also, the real hero of this comic. Seriously, check the wiki--I just updated it while you were reading this.

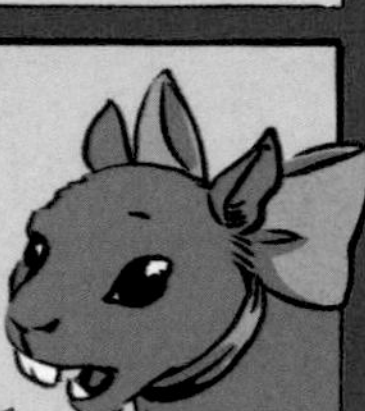

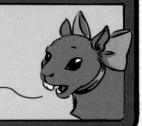

TIPPY-TOE'S GUIDE TO SQUIRREL GIRL

CARD 217 of ∞

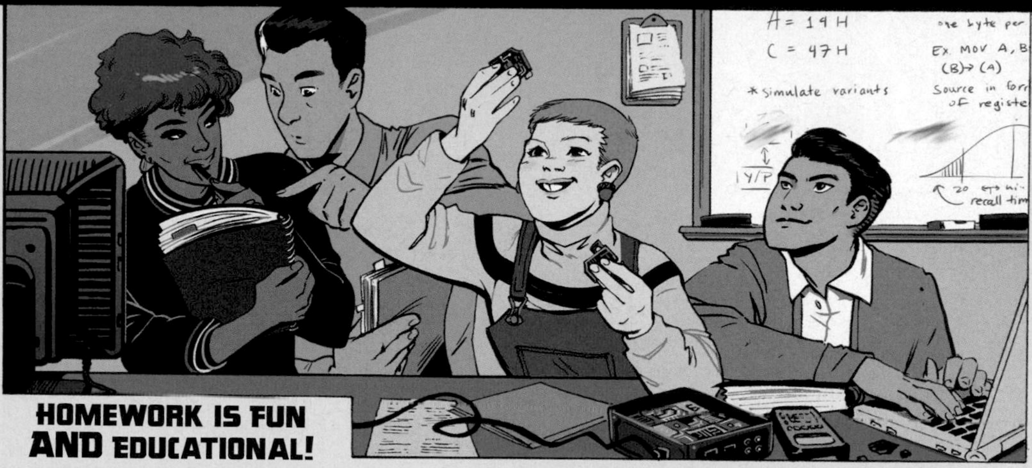
HOMEWORK IS FUN AND EDUCATIONAL!

Unlike most super heroes (for some reason), Doreen has actually grown **and** grown up...and also gone to college! She's a total genius and not just because she can talk to squirrels, but because she can do math and science stuff. So, when she's not busy saving the world from boredom and alien invasions, Doreen is a student of life **and** computer science!

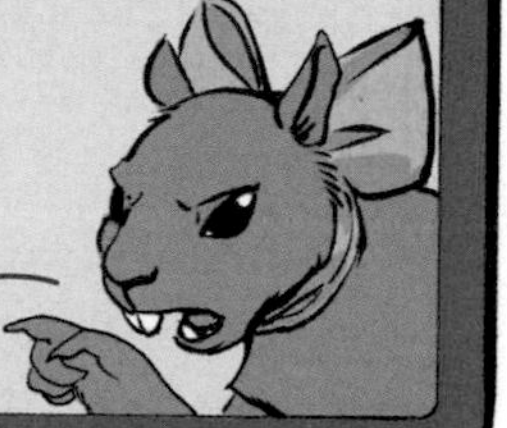

Fun Fact: I'm still bummed she didn't major in squirrels, but maybe you will? Also, stay in school, kids! Like, seriously, when you're done reading this, do your homework. I'm not kidding. Go. Now.

TIPPY-TOE'S GUIDE TO SQUIRREL GIRL

CARD 237 of ∞

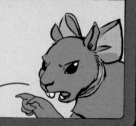

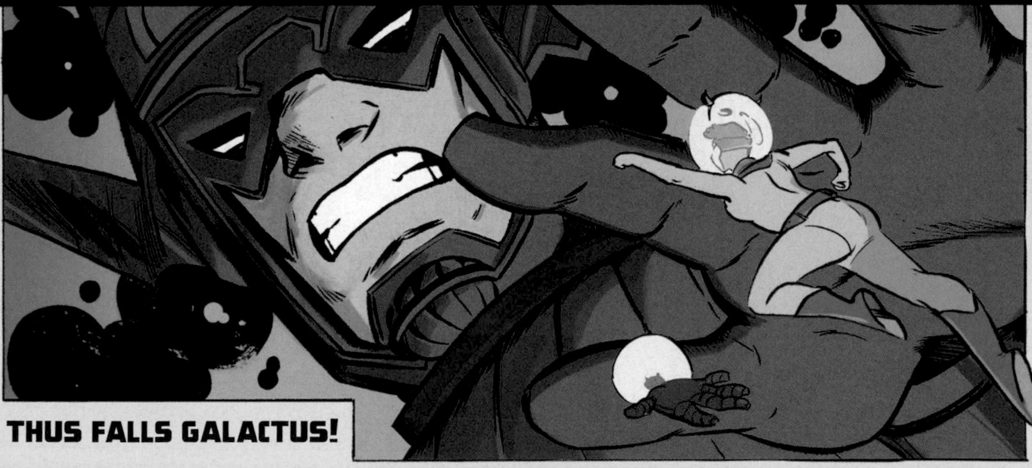
THUS FALLS GALACTUS!

It usually takes a whole bunch of heroes to take down Galactus, purple fanatic and part-time planet eater--but not Squirrel Girl. She crushed this menace with nothing more than her moxie and her adorable sidekick: me! You're welcome, Earth!

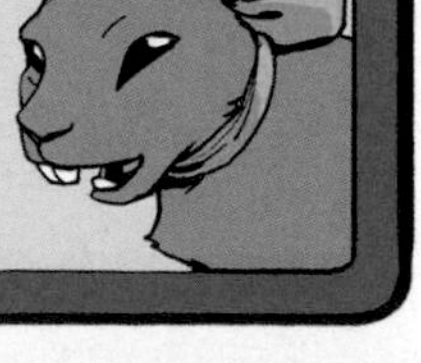

Fun Fact: Did you know Galactus is lactose intolerant? Dude can eat a planet but not a pizza. We all have our crosses to bear.

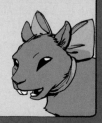

TIPPY-TOE'S GUIDE TO SQUIRREL GIRL

CARD 1138 of ∞

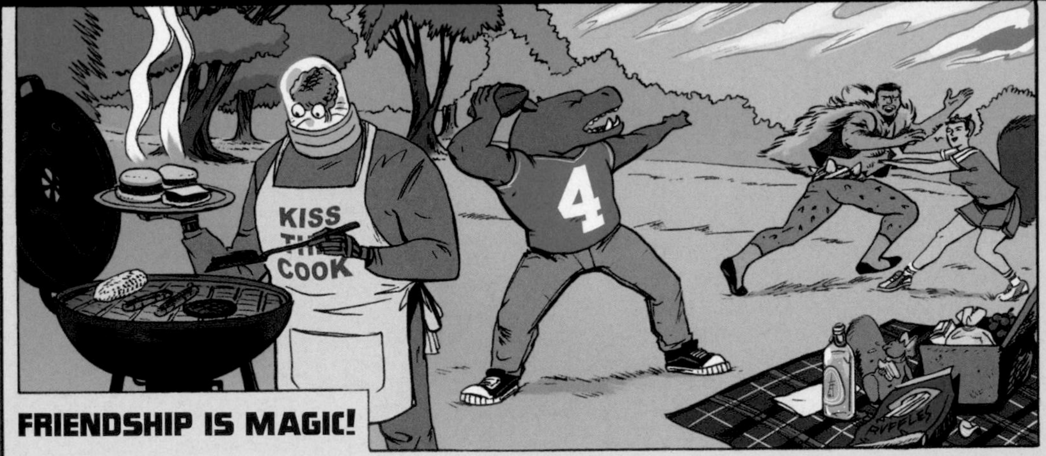
KISS THE COOK
4
FRIENDSHIP IS MAGIC!

It's not all punching, kicking and hoarding nuts, though--along the way Squirrel Girl has made friends. And enemies. She's so delightful, she sometimes turns enemies into friends. Because, c'mon, she's awesome. Who doesn't love Squirrel Girl? No really, who? Give me names.

Fun Fact: Despite being a former member of Hydra as well as a raging nihilist, Brain Drain makes a mean veggie burger.

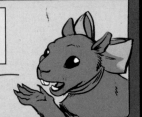

TIPPY-TOE'S GUIDE TO SQUIRREL GIRL

CARD 1984 of ∞

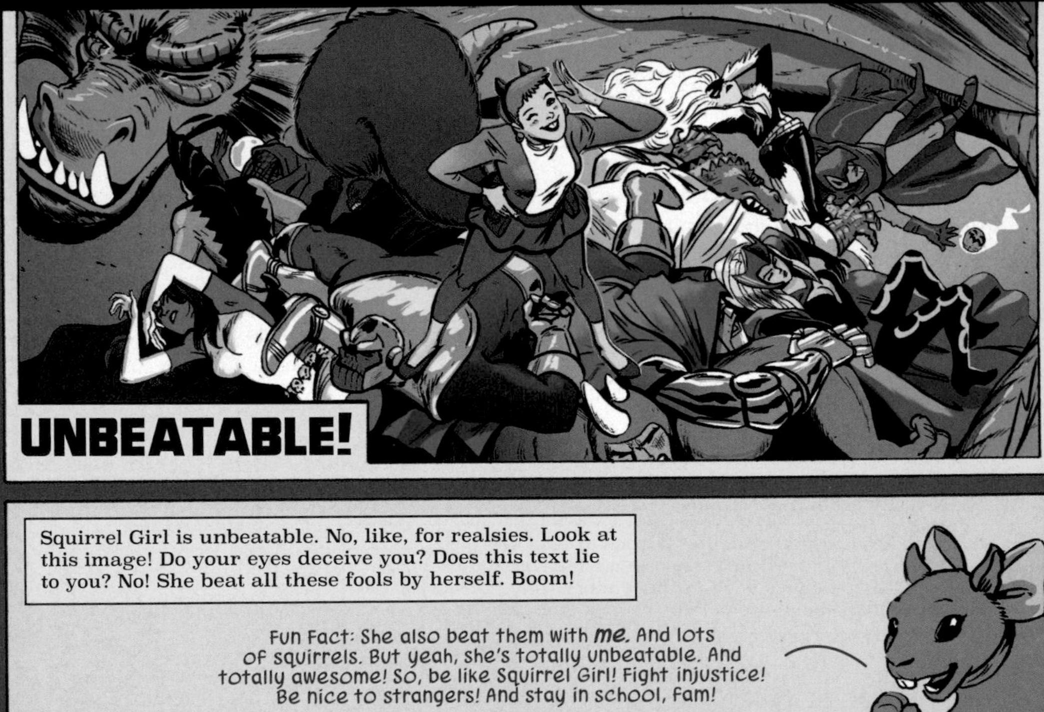
UNBEATABLE!

Squirrel Girl is unbeatable. No, like, for realsies. Look at this image! Do your eyes deceive you? Does this text lie to you? No! She beat all these fools by herself. Boom!

Fun Fact: She also beat them with *me.* And lots of squirrels. But yeah, she's totally unbeatable. And totally awesome! So, be like Squirrel Girl! Fight injustice! Be nice to strangers! And stay in school, Fam!

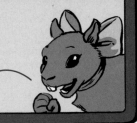

Robbie Thompson: Writer   Veronica Fish: Artist   VC's Travis Lanham: Letterer   Kathleen Wisneski: Assistant Editor   Darren Shan: Editc

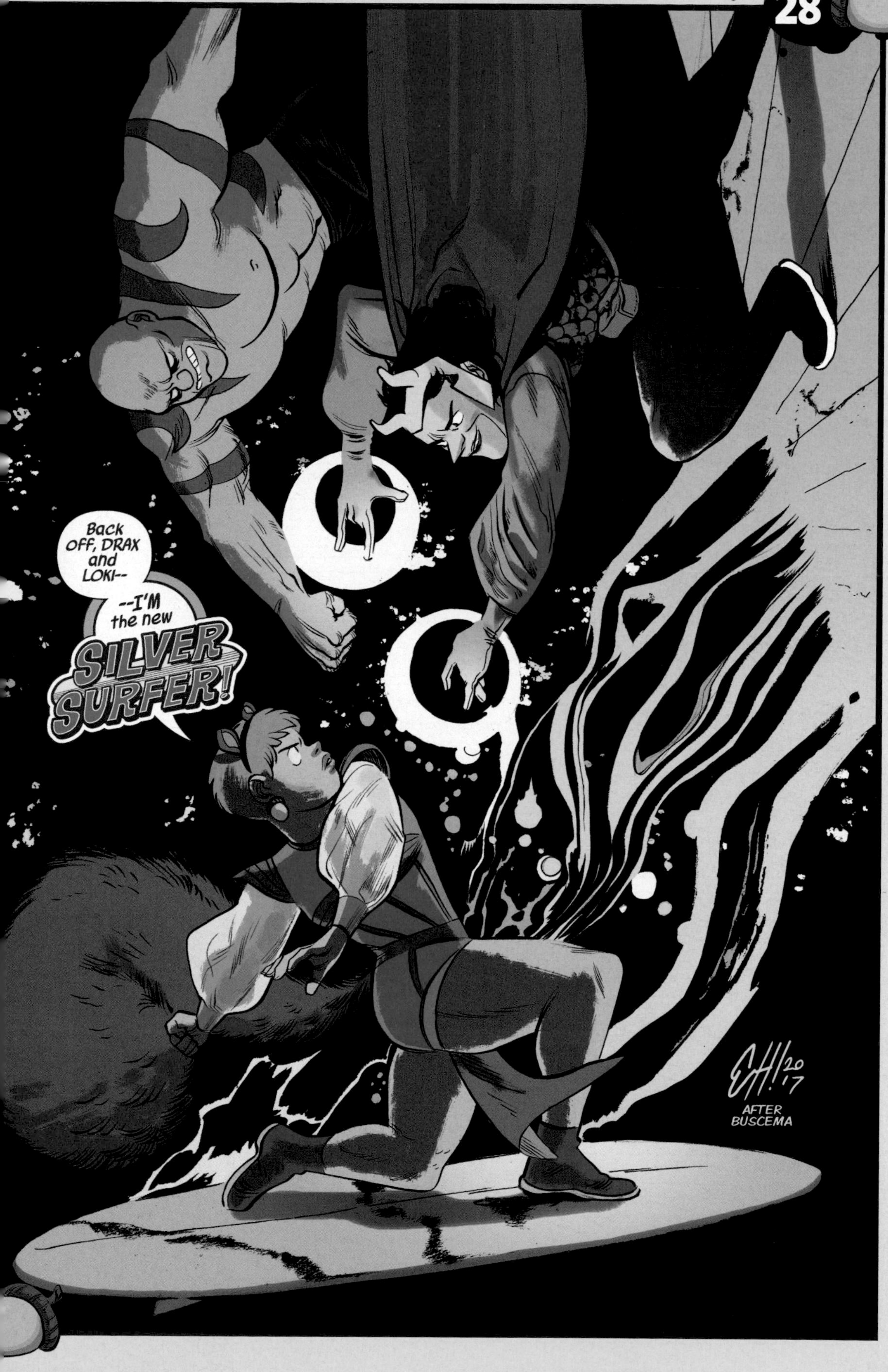
Back off, DRAX and LOKI--
--I'M the new SILVER SURFER!
EH! 2017
AFTER BUSCEMA

Doreen Green isn't just a second-year computer science student: she secretly also has all the powers of both squirrel an girl! She uses her amazing abilities to fight crime and be as awesome as possible. You know her as...The Unbeatable Squirrel Gir Find out what she's been up to, with...

Squirrel Girl *in a nutshell*

Squirrel Girl @unbeatablesg
EVERYONE! NANCY "@sewwiththeflo" WHITEHEAD AND TIPPY "@yoitstippytoe" TOE HAVE DISAPPEARED!!!

Squirrel Girl @unbeatablesg
uh, in unrelated incidents of course

Squirrel Girl @unbeatablesg
just two completely unrelated disappearances that I am now investigating

Squirrel Girl @unbeatablesg
ANYWAY PLEASE LET ME KNOW IF YOU SEE A COOL LADY NAMED NANCY OR A COOL SQUIRREL IN A PINK BOW NAMED TIPPY-TOE

xKravenTheHunterx @unshavenkraven
@unbeatablesg I will be on the hunt for them, Belka. You have my eyes and ears.

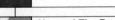

Tony Stark @starkmantony
@unbeatablesg And my repulsor beams.

Howard The Duck @imhowatrd
@unbeatablesg and ym feathre hands & in ur facee atititude

Squirrel Girl @unbeatablesg
@imhowatrd @starkmantony @unshavenkraven thanks pals <3

Squirrel Girl @unbeatablesg
UPDATE! I think maybe Nancy's cat saw something! Who do I know who can speak to cats? @akapatsy lookin at you

HELLCAT! @akapatsy
@unbeatablesg I can't talk to cats, Squirrel Girl.

Squirrel Girl @unbeatablesg
@akapatsy uh excuse me you dress like a cat and have cat-themed powers such as for instance cool cat ears

HELLCAT! @akapatsy
@unbeatablesg That's just part of my costume. I wear fake animal ears for important fashion reasons

Squirrel Girl @unbeatablesg
@akapatsy *clasps you by the shoulders and looks you in the eye* we're not so different, you and i

Squirrel Girl @unbeatablesg
UPDATE! I visited Doctor Strange (who is lowkey Loki now? haha WHAT EVEN IS REALITY) and Loki says Nancy and Tippy are on the other side of the galaxy! :0

Squirrel Girl @unbeatablesg
So I guess that's where we're headed!!!

Squirrel Girl @unbeatablesg
UPDATE! SINCE LOKI IS SORCERER SUPREME NOW THE DREAD DORMAMMU JUMPED US BOTH!!

Squirrel Girl @unbeatablesg
I SHOULD REALLY FOCUS ON THIS FIGHT NOW INSTEAD OF MANAGING MY #SOCIAL #MEDIA #PRESENCE!! I'LL UPDATE YOU ALL LATER, IT'S JUST I REALLY NEED TO FOCUS ON THIS LIFE-OR-DEATH FIGHT RN!

Squirrel Girl @unbeatablesg
YOU KNOW YOUR GIRL LOVES BEING #ONLINE BUT YOU KNOW I LOVE BEING ALIVE **EVEN MORE**

search!

#dreaddormammu
#abracadabra
#greatsquirrelmigration
#trustworthyface

This is just SOME of what Doreen's been posting--all these handles are real! Follow **@unbeatablesg** for more!

When we last left Squirrel Girl and Loki, they were fighting the Dread Dormammu on the Cosmic Plane...

It's my first **week** being Sorcerer Supreme and Strange's *most powerful* villain shows up? Honestly, how is *that* fair??

Maybe that's okay! Maybe this will go really well!

It absolutely has not been going well.

SMACK

Gah!

KA-POW

We can't reason with him, we can't punch him, and every spell you cast--

By **Balthakk's** Bolt and the Flames of the **Faltine!**

SP-TING

--he deflects back at us! Stop doing that, Loki!

I thought Dormammu was lying when he said he could do this all day!

I would've lied about that! 100%!!

ZZZZT

It's kinda my whole deal! I'm not that complicated! I do one thing really really well, and that thing just happens to be lying!

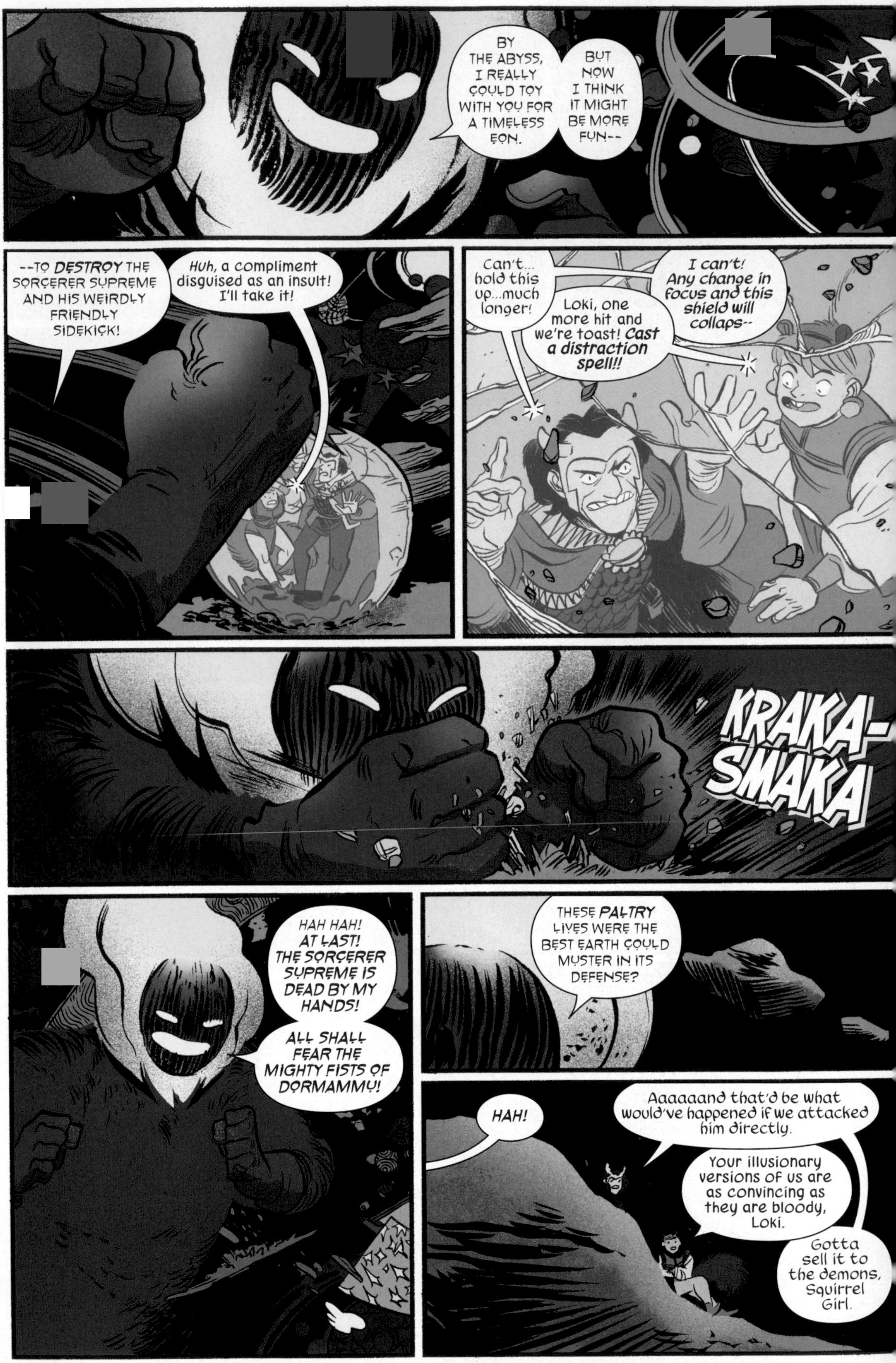
BY THE ABYSS, I REALLY COULD TOY WITH YOU FOR A TIMELESS EON.
BUT NOW I THINK IT MIGHT BE MORE FUN--
--TO DESTROY THE SORCERER SUPREME AND HIS WEIRDLY FRIENDLY SIDEKICK!
Huh, a compliment disguised as an insult! I'll take it!
Can't... hold this up...much longer!
I can't! Any change in focus and this shield will collaps--
Loki, one more hit and we're toast! Cast a distraction spell!!
KRAKA-SMAKA
HAH HAH! AT LAST! THE SORCERER SUPREME IS DEAD BY MY HANDS!
ALL SHALL FEAR THE MIGHTY FISTS OF DORMAMMU!
THESE PALTRY LIVES WERE THE BEST EARTH COULD MUSTER IN ITS DEFENSE?
HAH!
Aaaaaand that'd be what would've happened if we attacked him directly.
Your illusionary versions of us are as convincing as they are bloody, Loki.
Gotta sell it to the demons, Squirrel Girl.

Pretty intense in that one panel where it seemed like Squirrel Girl got squished, *huh?*

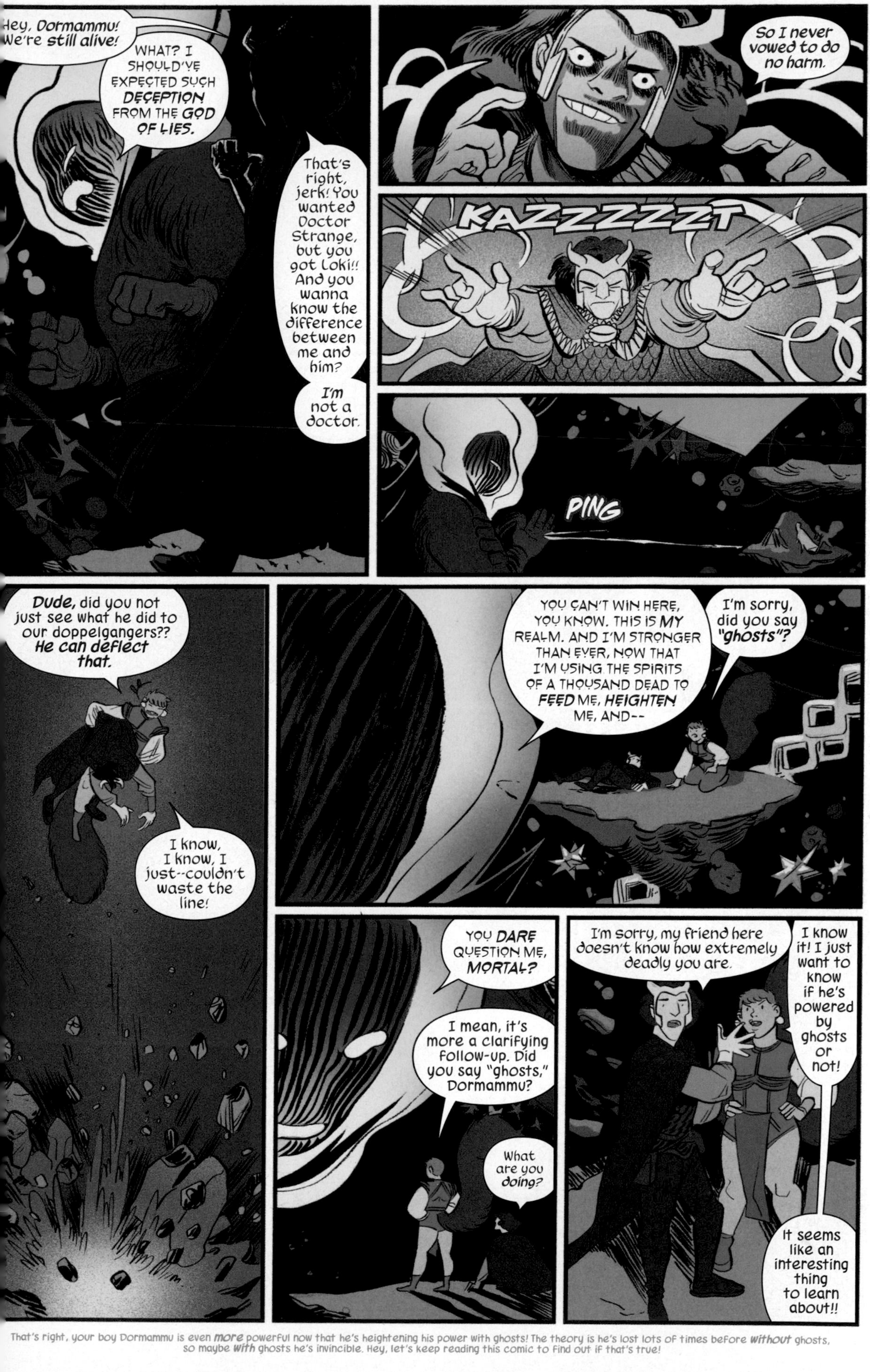
Hey, Dormammu! We're still alive!
WHAT? I SHOULD'VE EXPECTED SUCH DECEPTION FROM THE GOD OF LIES.
That's right, jerk! You wanted Doctor Strange, but you got Loki!! And you wanna know the difference between me and him?
I'm not a doctor.
So I never vowed to do no harm.
KAZZZZZZT
PING
Dude, did you not just see what he did to our doppelgangers?? He can deflect that.
I know, I know, I just--couldn't waste the line!
YOU CAN'T WIN HERE, YOU KNOW. THIS IS MY REALM. AND I'M STRONGER THAN EVER, NOW THAT I'M USING THE SPIRITS OF A THOUSAND DEAD TO FEED ME, HEIGHTEN ME, AND--
I'm sorry, did you say "ghosts"?
YOU DARE QUESTION ME, MORTAL?
I mean, it's more a clarifying follow-up. Did you say "ghosts," Dormammu?
What are you doing?
I'm sorry, my friend here doesn't know how extremely deadly you are.
I know it! I just want to know if he's powered by ghosts or not!
It seems like an interesting thing to learn about!!

That's right, your boy Dormammu is even *more* powerful now that he's heightening his power with ghosts! The theory is he's lost lots of times before *without* ghosts, so maybe *with* ghosts he's invincible. Hey, let's keep reading this comic to find out if that's true!

ALL SOULS IN THIS FALLEN REALM INCREASE MY POWER, YOU INQUISITIVE WHELP.

So when you say "all souls," that *can't* be just humans. Are we talking aliens?

Obviously we're talking aliens.

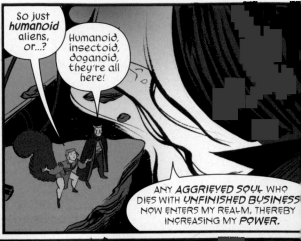

So just *humanoid* aliens, or...?

Humanoid, insectoid, doganoid, they're all here!

ANY *AGGRIEVED SOUL* WHO DIES WITH *UNFINISHED BUSINESS* NOW ENTERS MY REALM, THEREBY INCREASING MY *POWER.*

Just what I thought. Can we have a minute, please?

CERTAINLY. YOU CAN HAVE ALL THE TIME YOU WANT...

...IN YOUR GRAVES!

Loki!! Stop him!

I can't! His fire spell is too powerful, I--

SWOOF

And *that's* what would've happened if I hadn't used most of my magic building up *two* layers of illusionary deceptions.

Daaaang. Good call, my man.

Probably a little less intense in that one panel where it seemed like Squirrel Girl got squished a second time, *huh.*

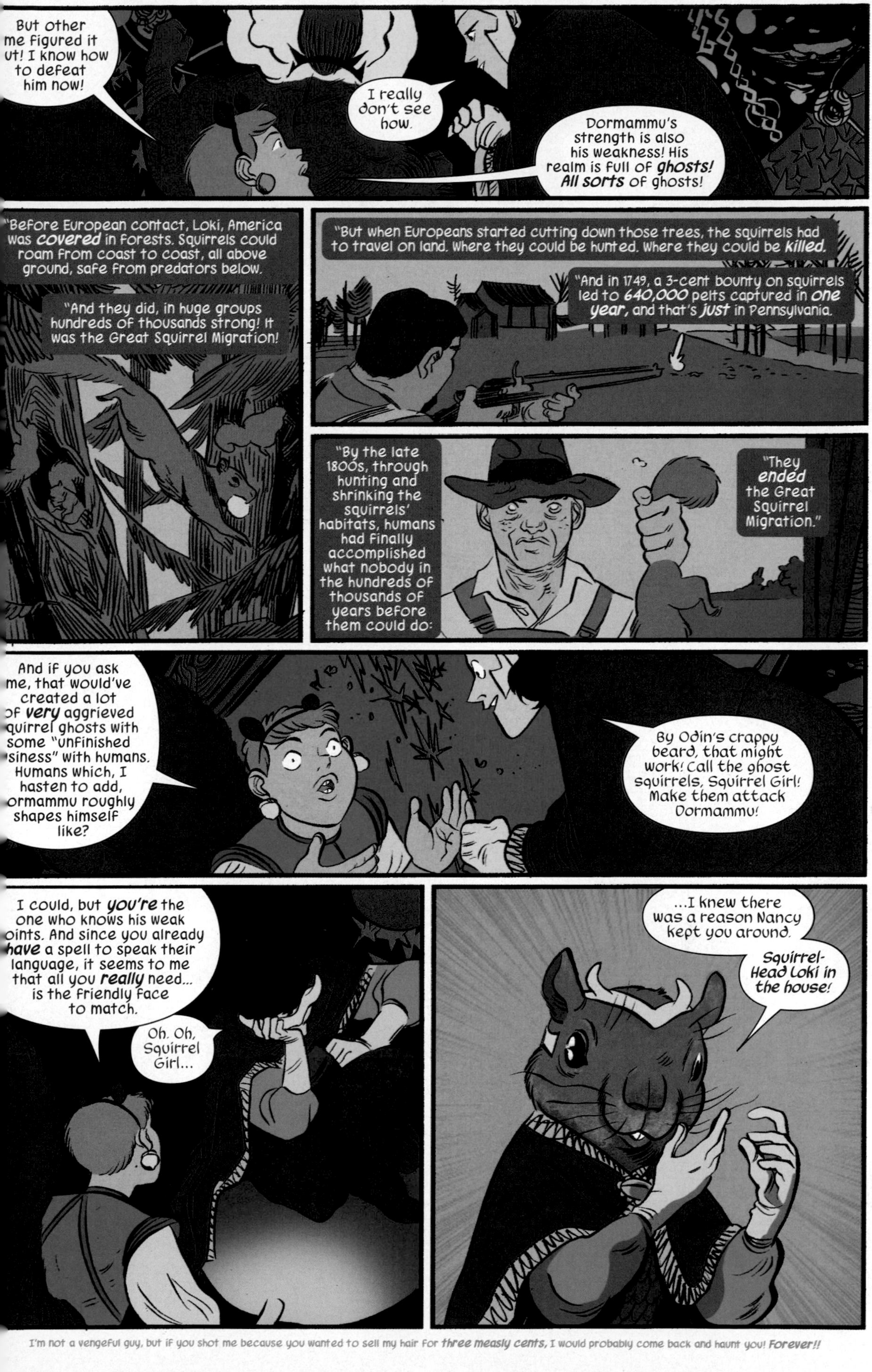
But other me figured it ut! I know how to defeat him now!
I really don't see how.
Dormammu's strength is also his weakness! His realm is full of ghosts! All sorts of ghosts!
"Before European contact, Loki, America was covered in forests. Squirrels could roam from coast to coast, all above ground, safe from predators below.
"And they did, in huge groups hundreds of thousands strong! It was the Great Squirrel Migration!
"But when Europeans started cutting down those trees, the squirrels had to travel on land. Where they could be hunted. Where they could be killed.
"And in 1749, a 3-cent bounty on squirrels led to 640,000 pelts captured in one year, and that's just in Pennsylvania.
"By the late 1800s, through hunting and shrinking the squirrels' habitats, humans had finally accomplished what nobody in the hundreds of thousands of years before them could do:
"They ended the Great Squirrel Migration."
And if you ask me, that would've created a lot of very aggrieved quirrel ghosts with some "unfinished siness" with humans. Humans which, I hasten to add, ormammu roughly shapes himself like?
By Odin's crappy beard, that might work! Call the ghost squirrels, Squirrel Girl! Make them attack Dormammu!
I could, but you're the one who knows his weak oints. And since you already have a spell to speak their language, it seems to me that all you really need... is the friendly face to match.
Oh. Oh, Squirrel Girl...
...I knew there was a reason Nancy kept you around.
Squirrel-Head Loki in the house!

I'm not a vengeful guy, but if you shot me because you wanted to sell my hair for *three measly cents*, I would probably come back and haunt you! *Forever!!*

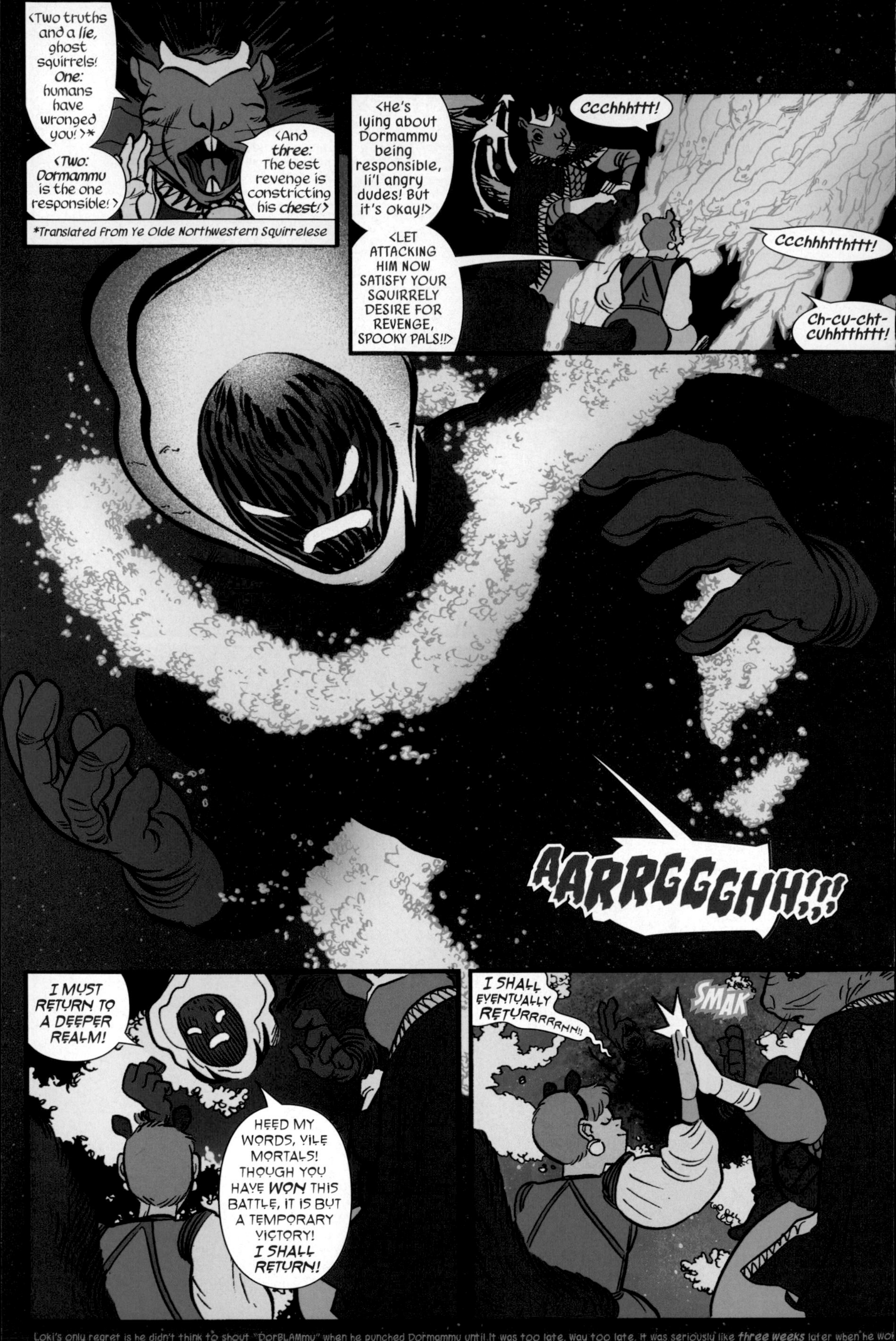

<Two truths and a *lie*, ghost squirrels! *One:* humans have wronged you!>*
<*Two:* Dormammu is the one responsible!>
<And *three:* The best revenge is constricting his *chest!*>
*Translated From Ye Olde Northwestern Squirrelese
<He's lying about Dormammu being responsible, li'l angry dudes! But it's okay!>
<LET ATTACKING HIM NOW SATISFY YOUR SQUIRRELY DESIRE FOR REVENGE, SPOOKY PALS!!>
Ccchhhttt!
Ccchhhtthttt!
Ch-cu-cht-cuhhtthhttt!
AARRGGGHH!!!
I MUST RETURN TO A DEEPER REALM!
HEED MY WORDS, VILE MORTALS! THOUGH YOU HAVE *WON* THIS BATTLE, IT IS BUT A TEMPORARY VICTORY! *I SHALL RETURN!*
I SHALL EVENTUALLY RETURRRRRRNN!!
SMAK

Loki's only regret is he didn't think to shout "DorBLAMmu" when he punched Dormammu until it was too late. Way too late. It was seriously like **three weeks** later when he wo up in the middle of the night and finally realized he could've said that zinger. Dang. Sorry, Loki.

Okay, that was *great.* We saved our dimension *and* gave a bunch of angry squirrel ghosts some closure. I really *am* a pretty supreme sorcerer, huh?

Hey. We did good, Loki.

Now, about sending me to Nancy...

Right! About that. Slight change of plans:

I'mma come too now.

What?!

You heard Dormammu! We've got at *least* a few weeks before he's back. I can take an afternoon off. Only I can't teleport myself, so we're gonna need a ship.

A spaceship? You're gonna summon a *spaceship?*

Sure, why not? What's the point of being Earth's #1 magical protector if you don't get a sweet ride out of it once in a while?

But we won't find one here. Come, let's return to our normal plane of existence!

Let's. Thanks, Loki.

You know what? I might keep this head. Diggin' the whiskers.

Goodbye, ghost squirrels! If Dormammu comes back, eat him for me!

<NO, don't *eat* him, ghost squirrels! Just hassle him in effective but ultimately nonfatal ways!>

<My head is bigger than hers, ghost squirrels! You should definitely listen to me!!>

Fun Fact: Loki doesn't *actually* need a ship! Can you blame him for lying? Yes, absolutely. But the truth is, he *could* magic himself and Squirrel Girl over right away, but he likes road trips and would really like to go on one. And can you blame him? Again, the answer is yes, you definitely can blame him, but we're working with what we've got here.

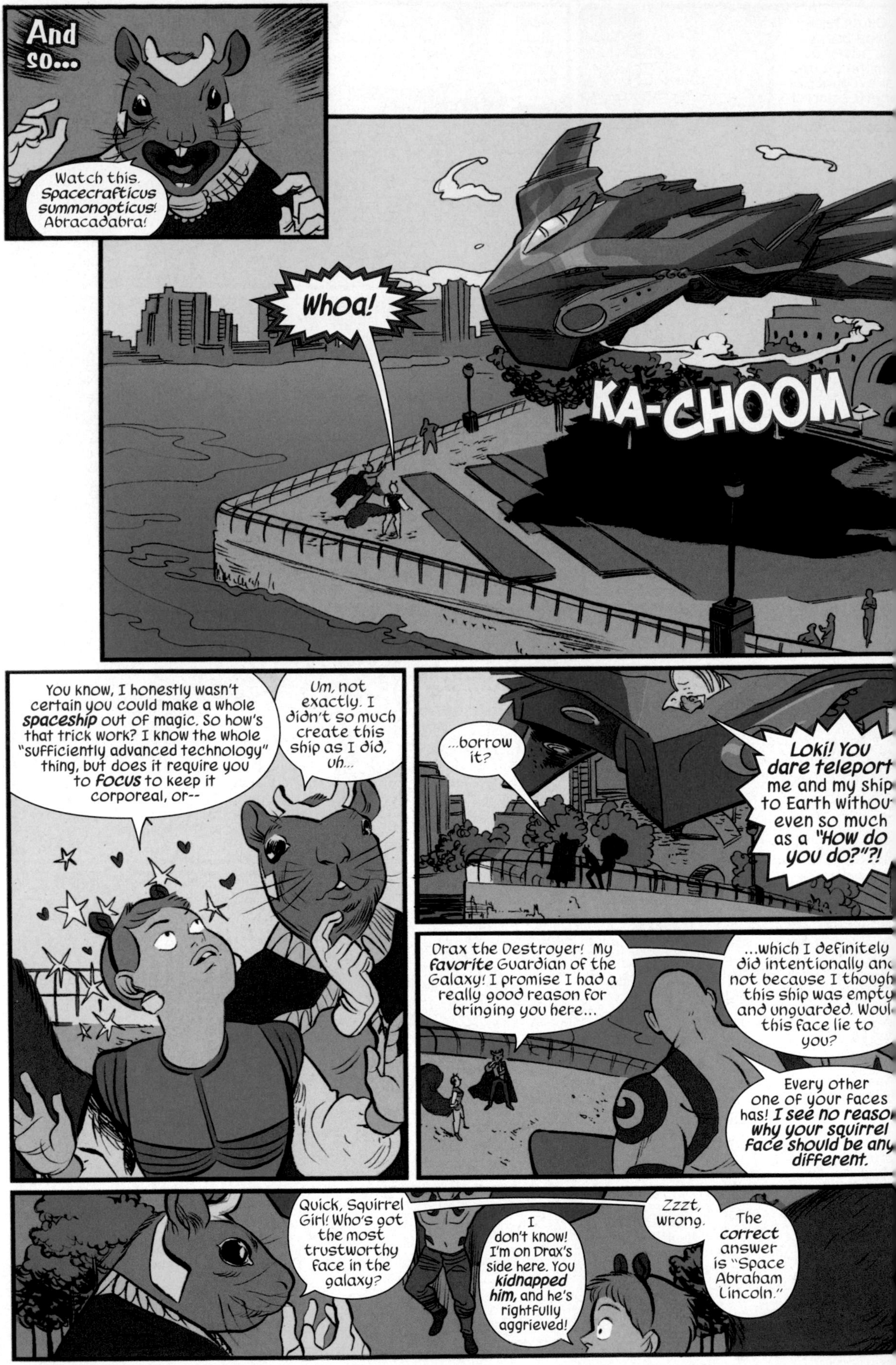
And so...
Watch this. Spacecrafticus summonopticus! Abracadabra!
Whoa!
KA-CHOOM
You know, I honestly wasn't certain you could make a whole spaceship out of magic. So how's that trick work? I know the whole "sufficiently advanced technology" thing, but does it require you to FOCUS to keep it corporeal, or--
Um, not exactly. I didn't so much create this ship as I did, uh...
...borrow it?
Loki! You dare teleport me and my ship to Earth withou even so much as a "How do you do?"?!
Drax the Destroyer! My favorite Guardian of the Galaxy! I promise I had a really good reason for bringing you here...
...which I definitely did intentionally an not because I though this ship was empty and unguarded. Woul this face lie to you?
Every other one of your faces has! I see no reaso why your squirrel face should be any different.
Quick, Squirrel Girl! Who's got the most trustworthy face in the galaxy?
I don't know! I'm on Drax's side here. You kidnapped him, and he's rightfully aggrieved!
Zzzt, wrong.
The correct answer is "Space Abraham Lincoln."

DID YOU KNOW: You hold in your hands the *only* comic this month that has Space Abraham Lincoln in it! It seems weird, right? When you write you can invent whatever you wan *everyone* could put Space Abraham Lincoln into their comics just by writing "And on *this* page, who should appear but, you guessed it, *Space Abraham Lincoln.*" Why aren't t

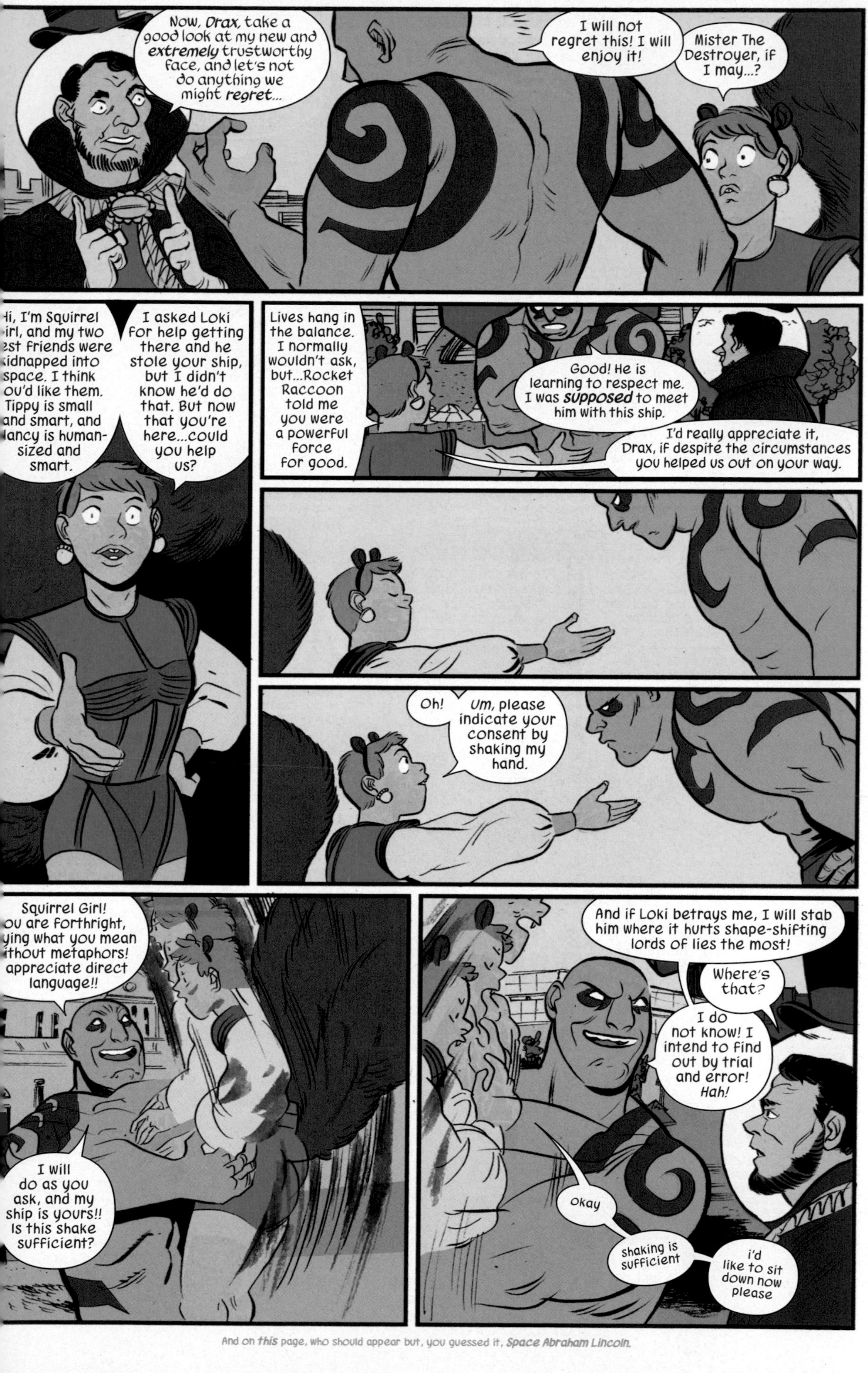
Now, Drax, take a good look at my new and *extremely* trustworthy face, and let's not do anything we might *regret*...
I will not regret this! I will enjoy it!
Mister The Destroyer, if I may...?
i, I'm Squirrel irl, and my two est friends were idnapped into space. I think ou'd like them. Tippy is small and smart, and ancy is human-sized and smart.
I asked Loki for help getting there and he stole your ship, but I didn't know he'd do that. But now that you're here...could you help us?
Lives hang in the balance. I normally wouldn't ask, but...Rocket Raccoon told me you were a powerful force for good.
Good! He is learning to respect me. I was *supposed* to meet him with this ship.
I'd really appreciate it, Drax, if despite the circumstances you helped us out on your way.
Oh!
Um, please indicate your consent by shaking my hand.
Squirrel Girl! ou are forthright, ying what you mean ithout metaphors! appreciate direct language!!
I will do as you ask, and my ship is yours!! Is this shake sufficient?
And if Loki betrays me, I will stab him where it hurts shape-shifting lords of lies the most!
Where's that?
I do not know! I intend to find out by trial and error! *Hah!*
Okay
Shaking is sufficient
i'd like to sit down now please

And on *this* page, who should appear but, you guessed it, *Space Abraham Lincoln.*

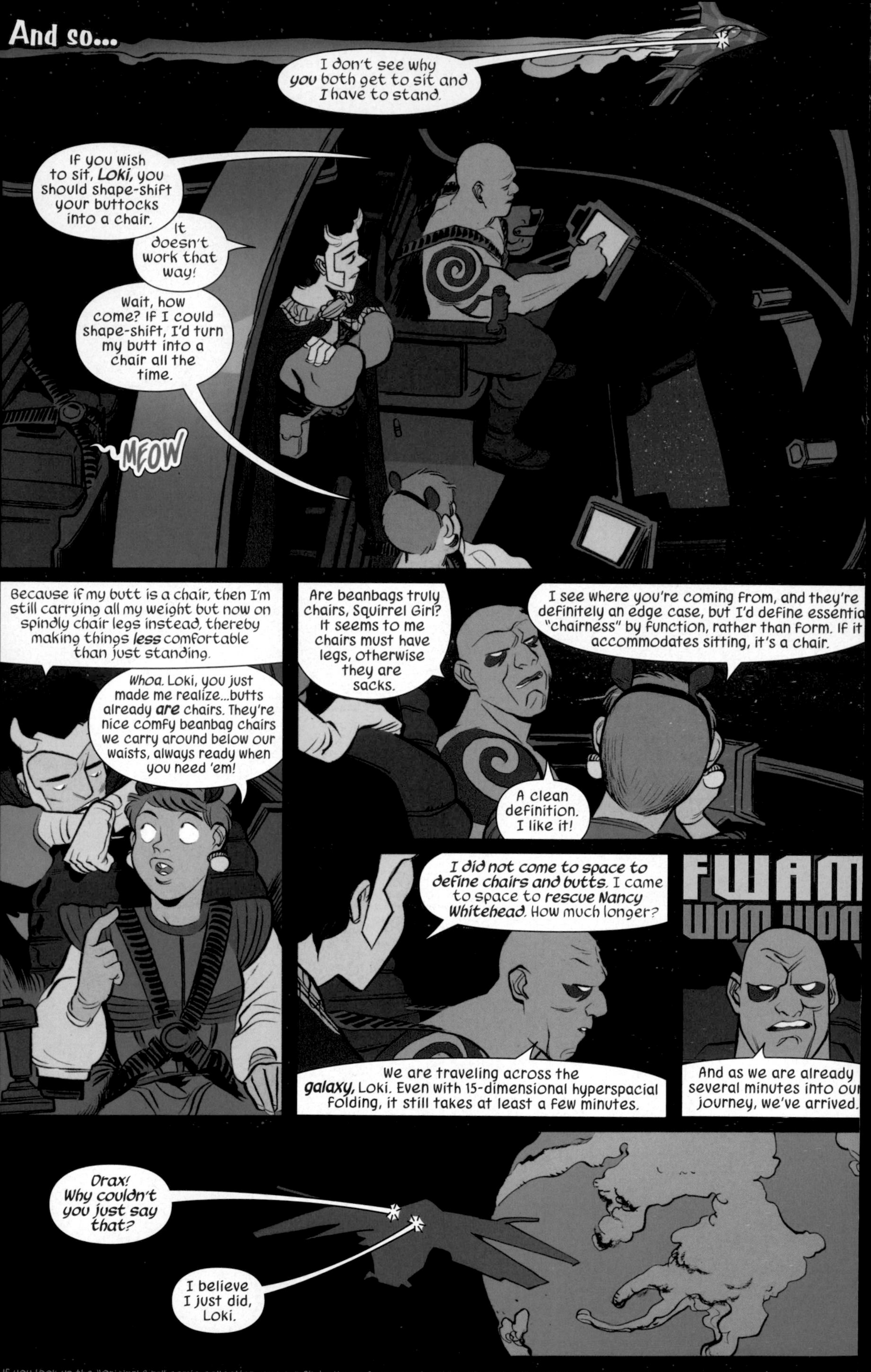
And so...
I don't see why *you* both get to sit and *I* have to stand.
If you wish to sit, **Loki,** you should shape-shift your buttocks into a chair.
It doesn't work that way!
Wait, how come? If I could shape-shift, I'd turn my butt into a chair all the time.
MEOW
Because if my butt is a chair, then I'm still carrying all my weight but now on spindly chair legs instead, thereby making things *less* comfortable than just standing.
Whoa. Loki, you just made me realize...butts already *are* chairs. They're nice comfy beanbag chairs we carry around below our waists, always ready when you need 'em!
Are beanbags truly chairs, Squirrel Girl? It seems to me chairs must have legs, otherwise they are sacks.
I see where you're coming from, and they're definitely an edge case, but I'd define essentia "chairness" by function, rather than form. If it accommodates sitting, it's a chair.
A clean definition. I like it!
I did not come to space to define chairs and butts. I came to space to *rescue Nancy Whitehead.* How much longer?
We are traveling across the *galaxy,* Loki. Even with 15-dimensional hyperspacial folding, it still takes at least a few minutes.
FWAM
WOM WOM
And as we are already several minutes into our journey, we've arrived.
Orax! Why couldn't you just say that?
I believe I just did, Loki.

If you look up the "Original Sins" comic collection, you can find a Young Avengers story I wrote where Marvel Boy asks Hulkling a very similar question vis-a-vis shape-shiftir and butts as chairs. Apparently my writerly trademark is constantly wondering why shape-shifters don't turn into chairs all the time. I'm...fine with this?

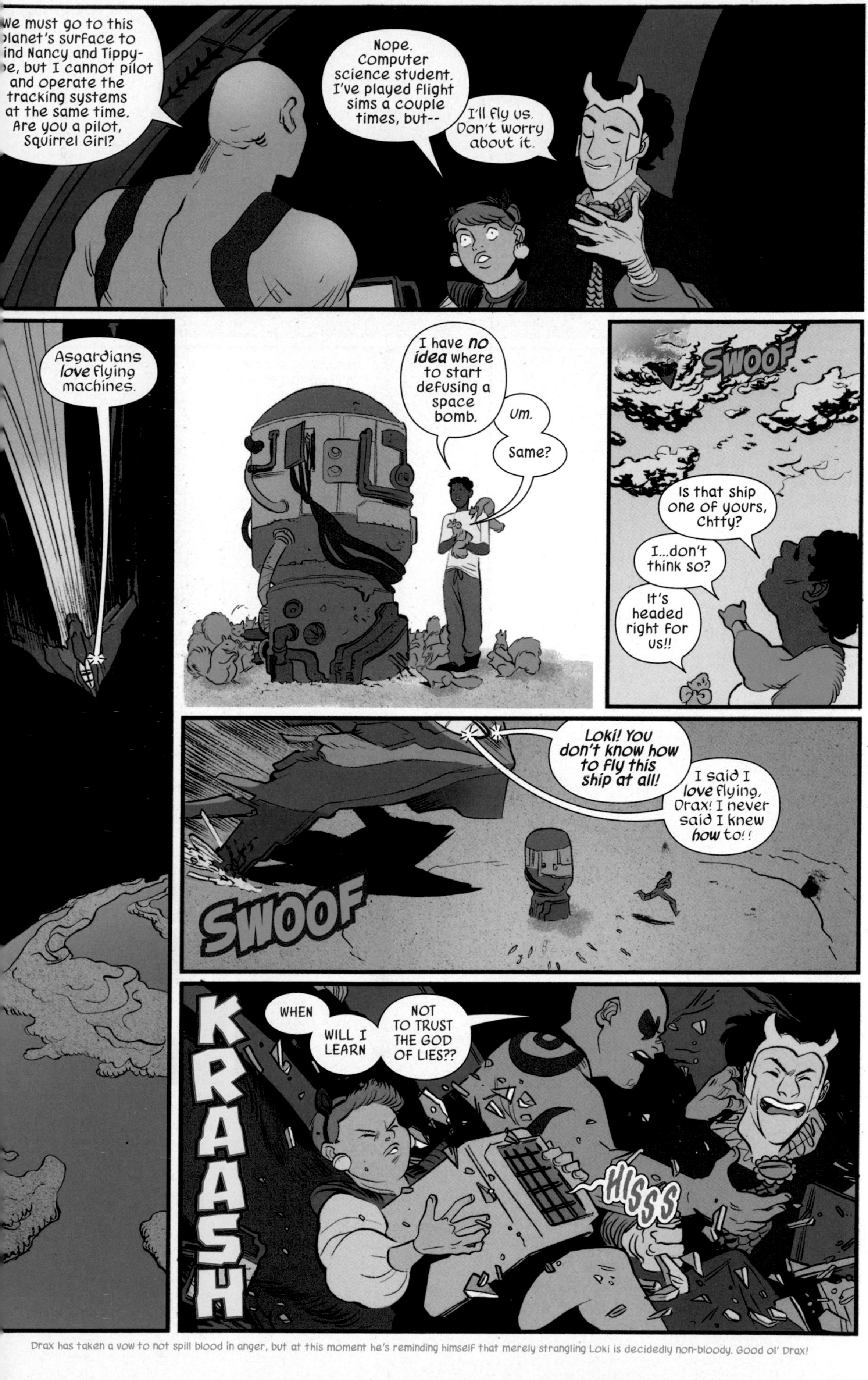
We must go to this lanet's surface to ind Nancy and Tippy-oe, but I cannot pilot and operate the tracking systems at the same time. Are you a pilot, Squirrel Girl?
Nope. Computer science student. I've played flight sims a couple times, but--
I'll fly us. Don't worry about it.
Asgardians *love* flying machines.
I have *no idea* where to start defusing a space bomb.
Um.
Same?
SWOOF
Is that ship one of yours, Chtty?
I...don't think so?
It's headed right for us!!
Loki! You don't know how to fly this ship at all!
I said I *love* flying, Drax! I never said I knew *how* to!!
SWOOF
KRAASH
WHEN
WILL I LEARN
NOT TO TRUST THE GOD OF LIES??
HISSS

Drax has taken a vow to not spill blood in anger, but at this moment he's reminding himself that merely strangling Loki is decidedly non-bloody. Good ol' Drax!

Nancy! Tippy!

Squirrel Girl!

And Mew!

And you destroyed that stupid bomb too!!

Also, Loki's here too! Everyone's favorite! Good ol' Loki!

Loki! My #1 Asgardian Cat Thor guy!

Nancy! My #1 Midgardian cat-owning gal!

Also, Drax the Destroyer is here! I have quickly observed, and am now eager to share, the traditional greeting of your friend group!!

I hate to interrupt, Space Strangers, but your crash landing unwittingly revealed something startling

These bomb parts aren't metal, they're spray-painted *plywood*! The bomb the Silver Surfer and his friends left here...

...is a *total fake.*

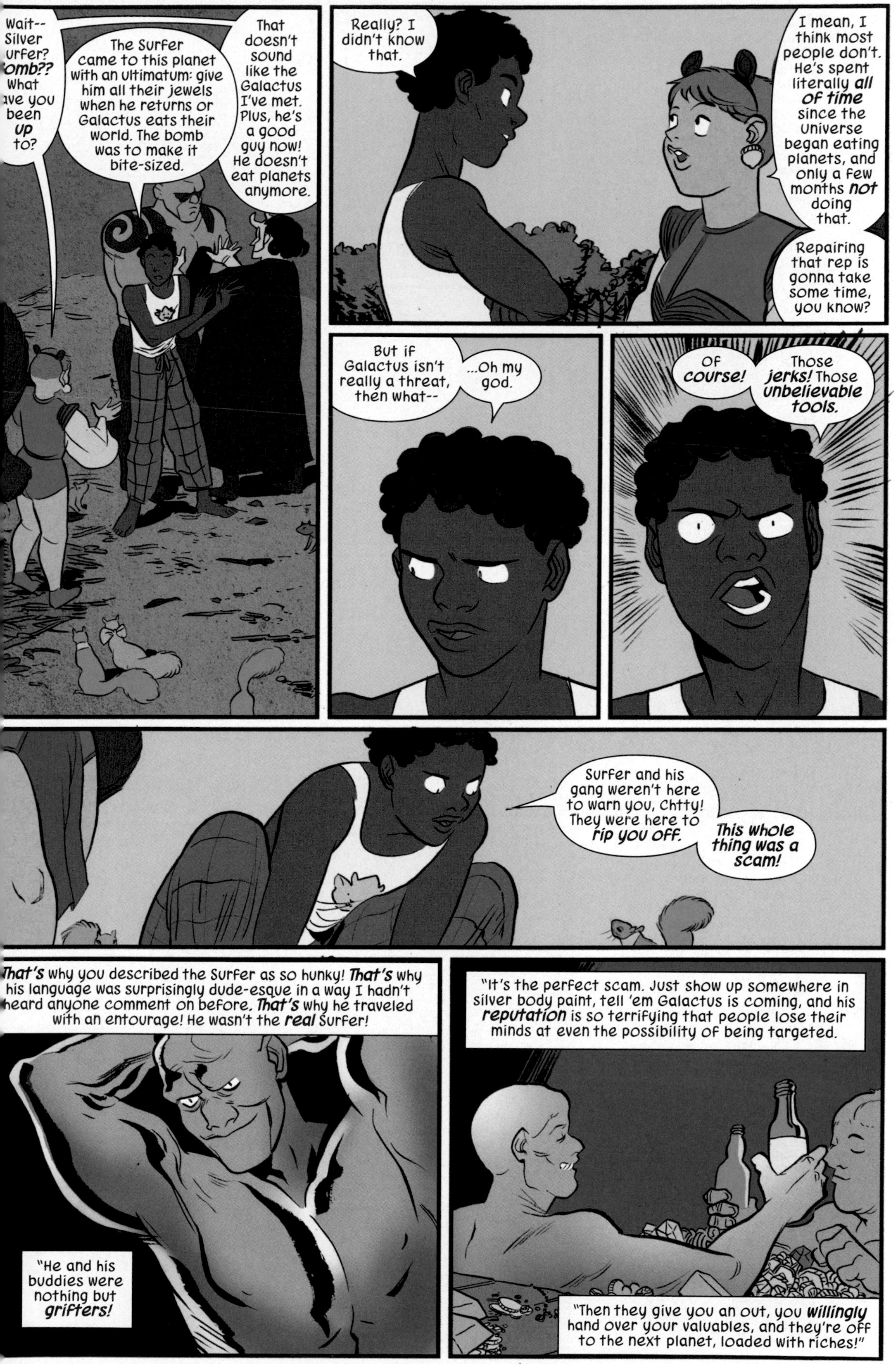
Wait-- Silver Surfer? Bomb?? What have you been up to?
The Surfer came to this planet with an ultimatum: give him all their jewels when he returns or Galactus eats their world. The bomb was to make it bite-sized.
That doesn't sound like the Galactus I've met. Plus, he's a good guy now! He doesn't eat planets anymore.
Really? I didn't know that.
I mean, I think most people don't. He's spent literally all of time since the universe began eating planets, and only a few months not doing that.
Repairing that rep is gonna take some time, you know?
But if Galactus isn't really a threat, then what--
...Oh my god.
Of course!
Those jerks! Those unbelievable tools.
Surfer and his gang weren't here to warn you, Chtty! They were here to rip you off.
This whole thing was a scam!
That's why you described the Surfer as so hunky! That's why his language was surprisingly dude-esque in a way I hadn't heard anyone comment on before. That's why he traveled with an entourage! He wasn't the real Surfer!
"He and his buddies were nothing but grifters!
"It's the perfect scam. Just show up somewhere in silver body paint, tell 'em Galactus is coming, and his reputation is so terrifying that people lose their minds at even the possibility of being targeted.
"Then they give you an out, you willingly hand over your valuables, and they're off to the next planet, loaded with riches!"

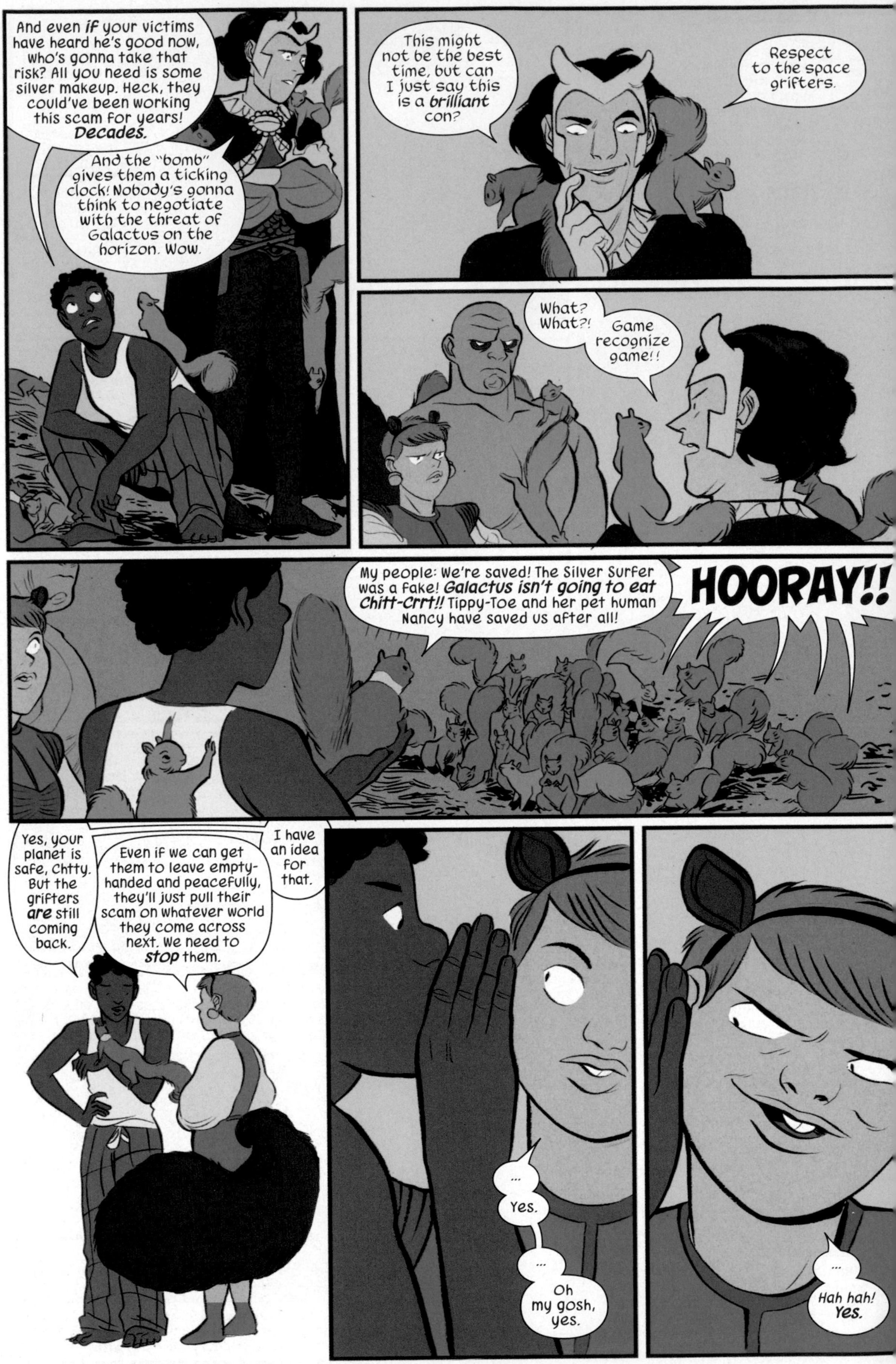
And even *if* your victims have heard he's good now, who's gonna take that risk? All you need is some silver makeup. Heck, they could've been working this scam for years! **Decades.**
And the "bomb" gives them a ticking clock! Nobody's gonna think to negotiate with the threat of Galactus on the horizon. Wow.
This might not be the best time, but can I just say this is a *brilliant* con?
Respect to the space grifters.
What? What?!
Game recognize game!!
My people: We're saved! The Silver Surfer was a fake! *Galactus isn't going to eat Chitt-Crrt!!* Tippy-Toe and her pet human Nancy have saved us after all!
HOORAY!!
Yes, your planet is safe, Chtty. But the grifters *are* still coming back.
Even if we can get them to leave empty-handed and peacefully, they'll just pull their scam on whatever world they come across next. We need to *stop* them.
I have an idea for that.
...
Yes.
...
Oh my gosh, yes.
...
Hah hah! *Yes.*

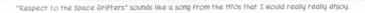

"Respect to the Space Grifters" sounds like a song from the 1970s that I would really really enjoy.

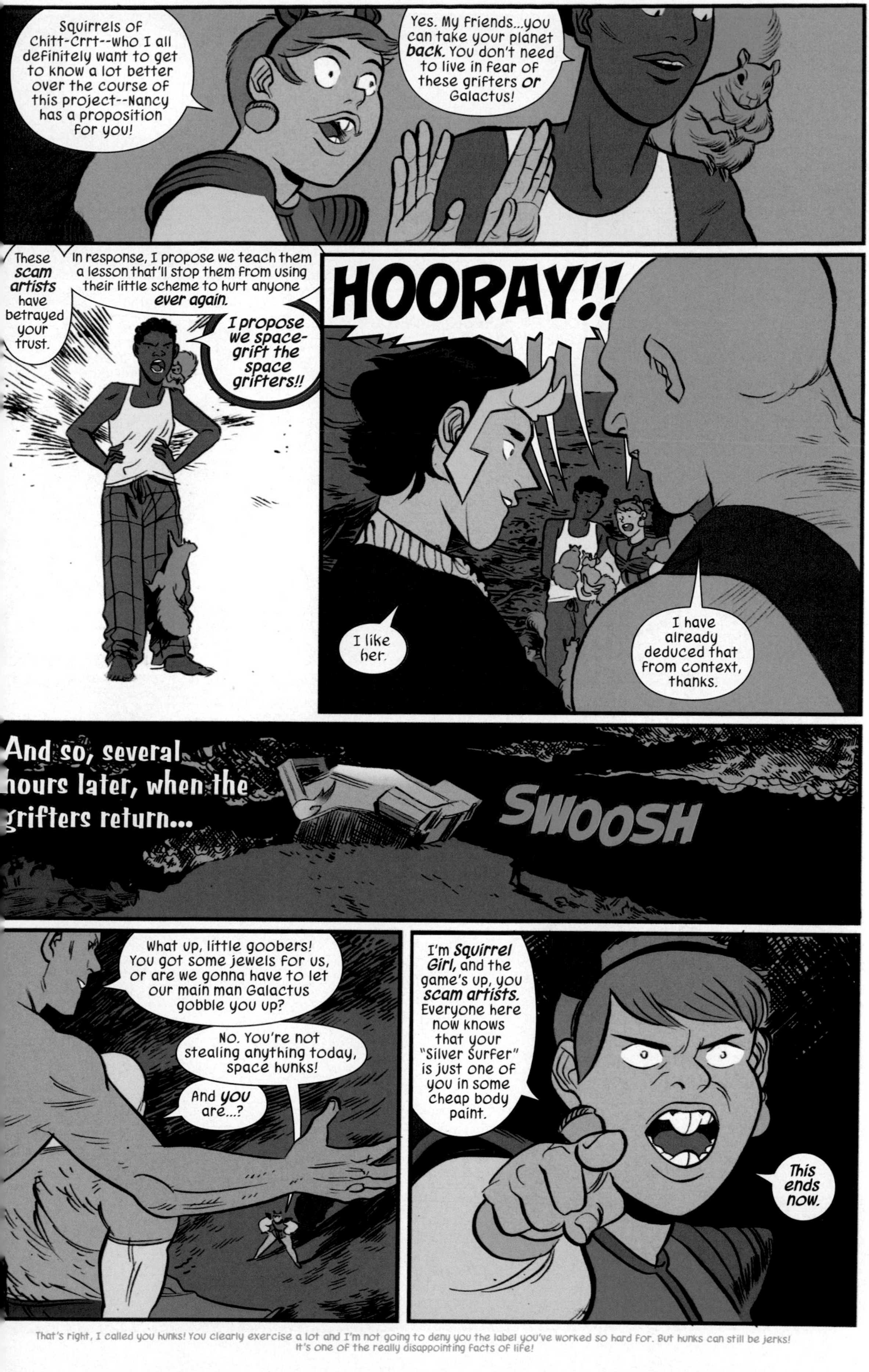
Squirrels of Chitt-Crrt--who I all definitely want to get to know a lot better over the course of this project--Nancy has a proposition for you!
Yes. My friends...you can take your planet **back**. You don't need to live in fear of these grifters **or** Galactus!
These **scam artists** have betrayed your trust.
In response, I propose we teach them a lesson that'll stop them from using their little scheme to hurt anyone **ever again.**
I propose we space-grift the space grifters!!
HOORAY!!
I like her.
I have already deduced that from context, thanks.
And so, several hours later, when the grifters return...
SWOOSH
What up, little goobers! You got some jewels for us, or are we gonna have to let our main man Galactus gobble you up?
No. You're not stealing anything today, space hunks!
And **you** are...?
I'm **Squirrel Girl**, and the game's up, you **scam artists.** Everyone here now knows that your "Silver Surfer" is just one of you in some cheap body paint.
This ends now.

That's right, I called you hunks! You clearly exercise a lot and I'm not going to deny you the label you've worked so hard for. But hunks can still be jerks! It's one of the really disappointing facts of life!

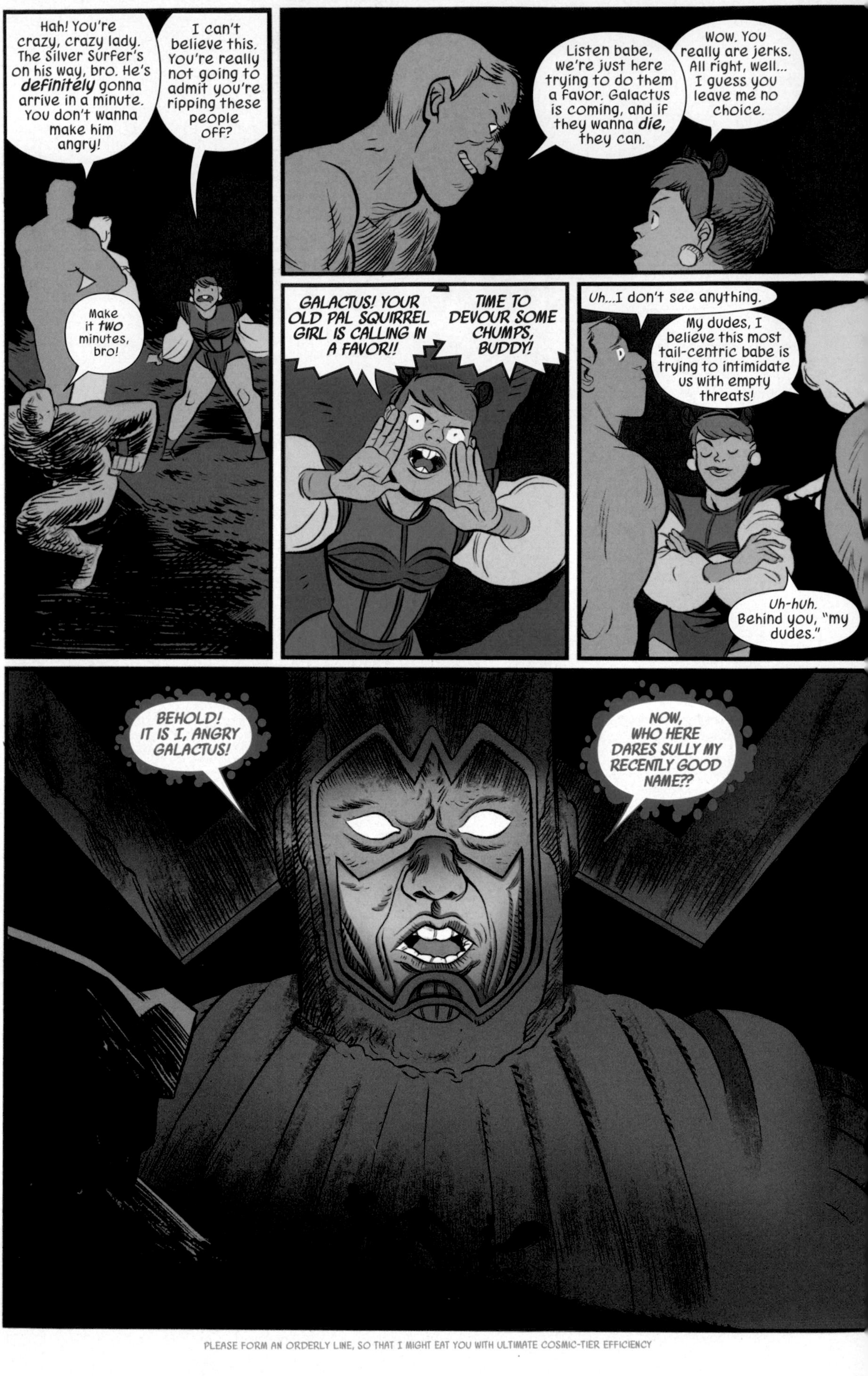
Hah! You're crazy, crazy lady. The Silver Surfer's on his way, bro. He's *definitely* gonna arrive in a minute. You don't wanna make him angry!
I can't believe this. You're really not going to admit you're ripping these people off?
Make it *two* minutes, bro!
Listen babe, we're just here trying to do them a favor. Galactus is coming, and if they wanna *die,* they can.
Wow. You really are jerks. All right, well... I guess you leave me no choice.
GALACTUS! YOUR OLD PAL SQUIRREL GIRL IS CALLING IN A FAVOR!!
TIME TO DEVOUR SOME CHUMPS, BUDDY!
Uh...I don't see anything.
My dudes, I believe this most tail-centric babe is trying to intimidate us with empty threats!
Uh-huh. Behind you, "my dudes."
BEHOLD! IT IS I, ANGRY GALACTUS!
NOW, WHO HERE DARES SULLY MY RECENTLY GOOD NAME??

PLEASE FORM AN ORDERLY LINE, SO THAT I MIGHT EAT YOU WITH ULTIMATE COSMIC-TIER EFFICIENCY

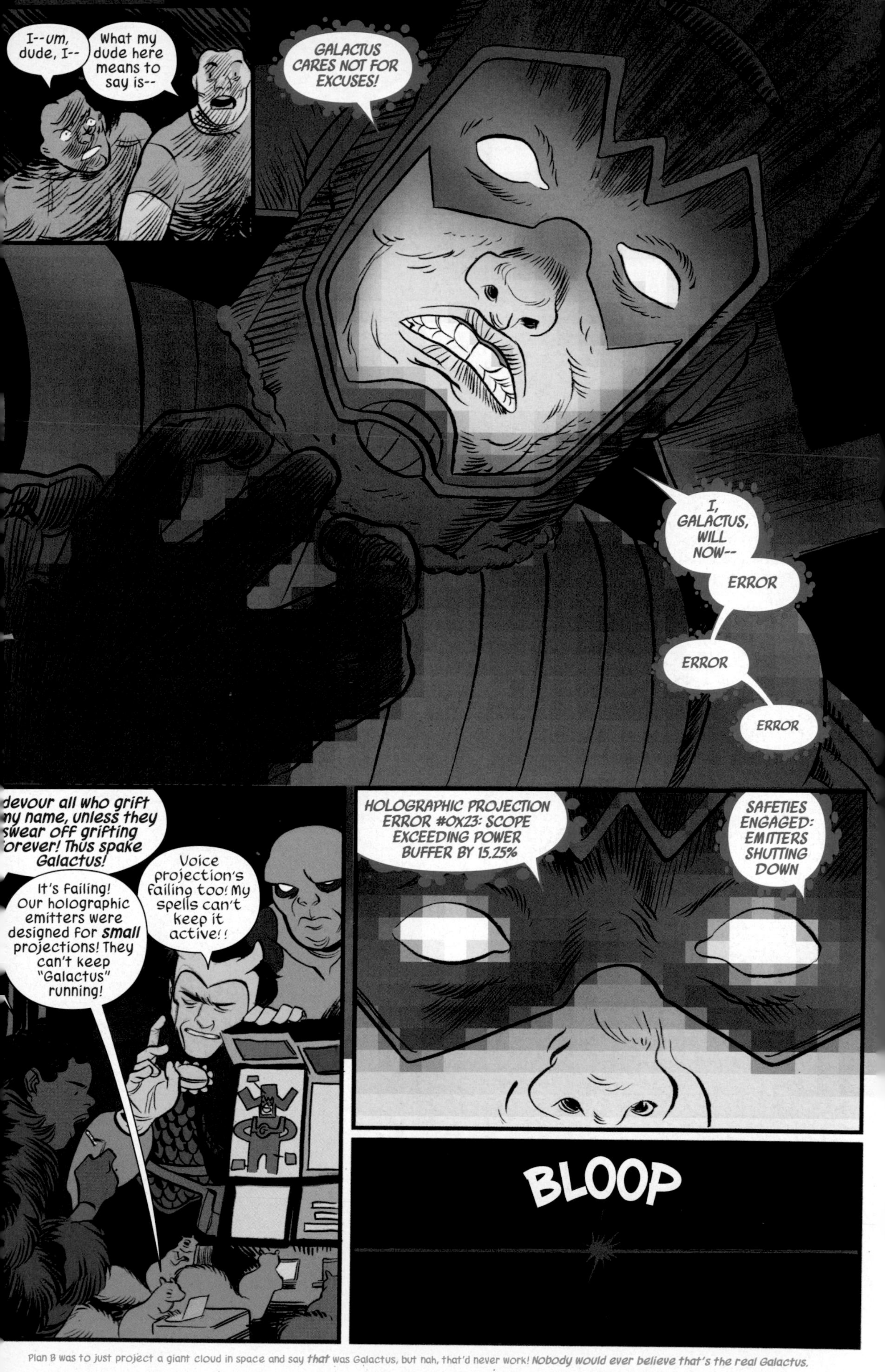
I--um, dude, I--
What my dude here means to say is--
GALACTUS CARES NOT FOR EXCUSES!
I, GALACTUS, WILL NOW--
ERROR
ERROR
ERROR
devour all who grift ny name, unless they swear off grifting orever! Thus spake Galactus!
It's failing! Our holographic emitters were designed for *small* projections! They can't keep "Galactus" running!
Voice projection's failing too! My spells can't keep it active!!
HOLOGRAPHIC PROJECTION ERROR #0X23: SCOPE EXCEEDING POWER BUFFER BY 15.25%
SAFETIES ENGAGED: EMITTERS SHUTTING DOWN
BLOOP

Plan B was to just project a giant cloud in space and say *that* was Galactus, but nah, that'd never work! *Nobody would ever believe that's the real Galactus.*

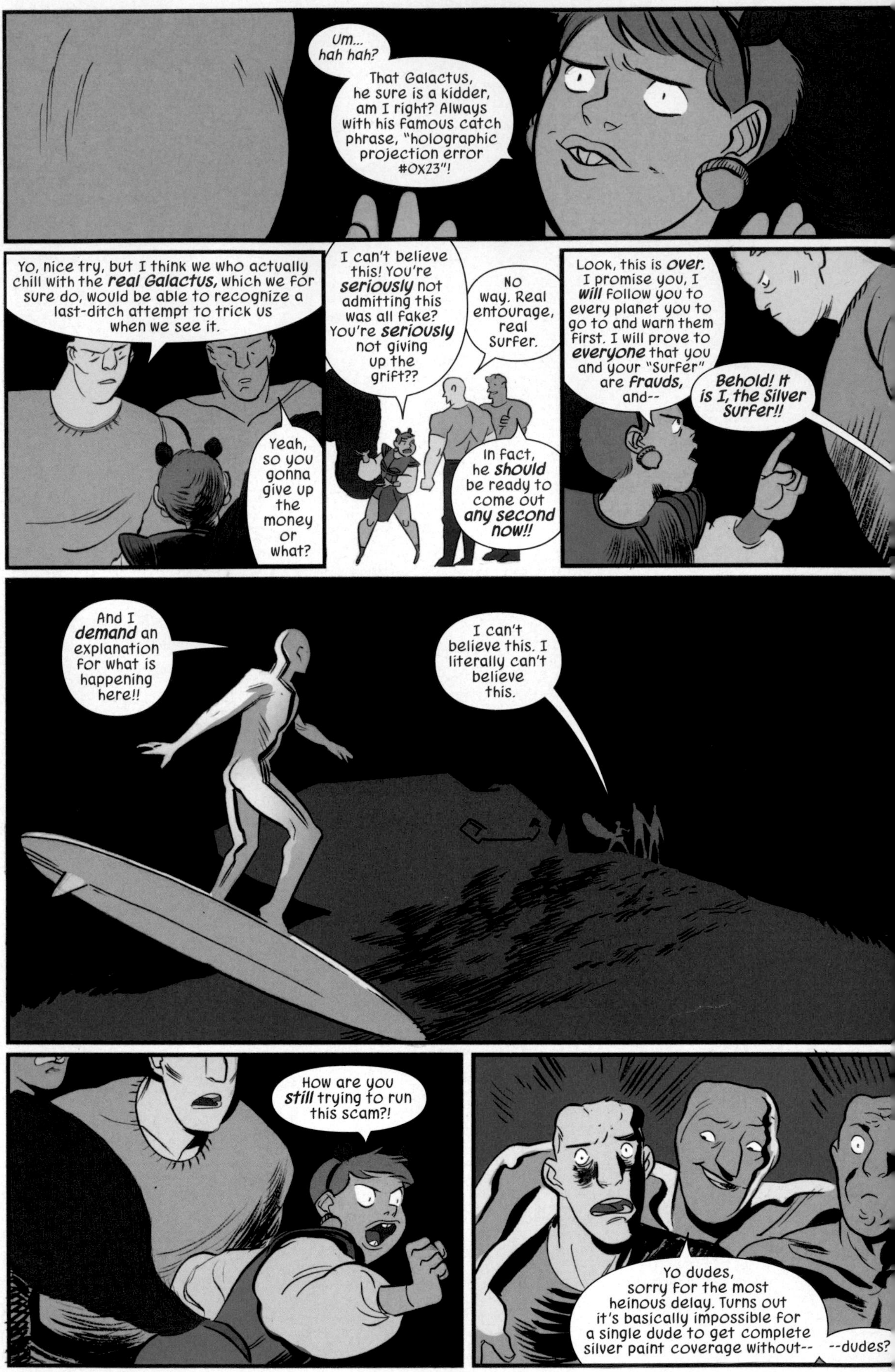
Um... hah hah?
That Galactus, he sure is a kidder, am I right? Always with his famous catch phrase, "holographic projection error #OX23"!
Yo, nice try, but I think we who actually chill with the real Galactus, which we for sure do, would be able to recognize a last-ditch attempt to trick us when we see it.
Yeah, so you gonna give up the money or what?
I can't believe this! You're seriously not admitting this was all fake? You're seriously not giving up the grift??
No way. Real entourage, real Surfer.
In fact, he should be ready to come out any second now!!
Look, this is over. I promise you, I will follow you to every planet you to go to and warn them first. I will prove to everyone that you and your "Surfer" are frauds, and--
Behold! It is I, the Silver Surfer!!
And I demand an explanation for what is happening here!!
I can't believe this. I literally can't believe this.
How are you still trying to run this scam?!
Yo dudes, sorry for the most heinous delay. Turns out it's basically impossible for a single dude to get complete silver paint coverage without--
--dudes?

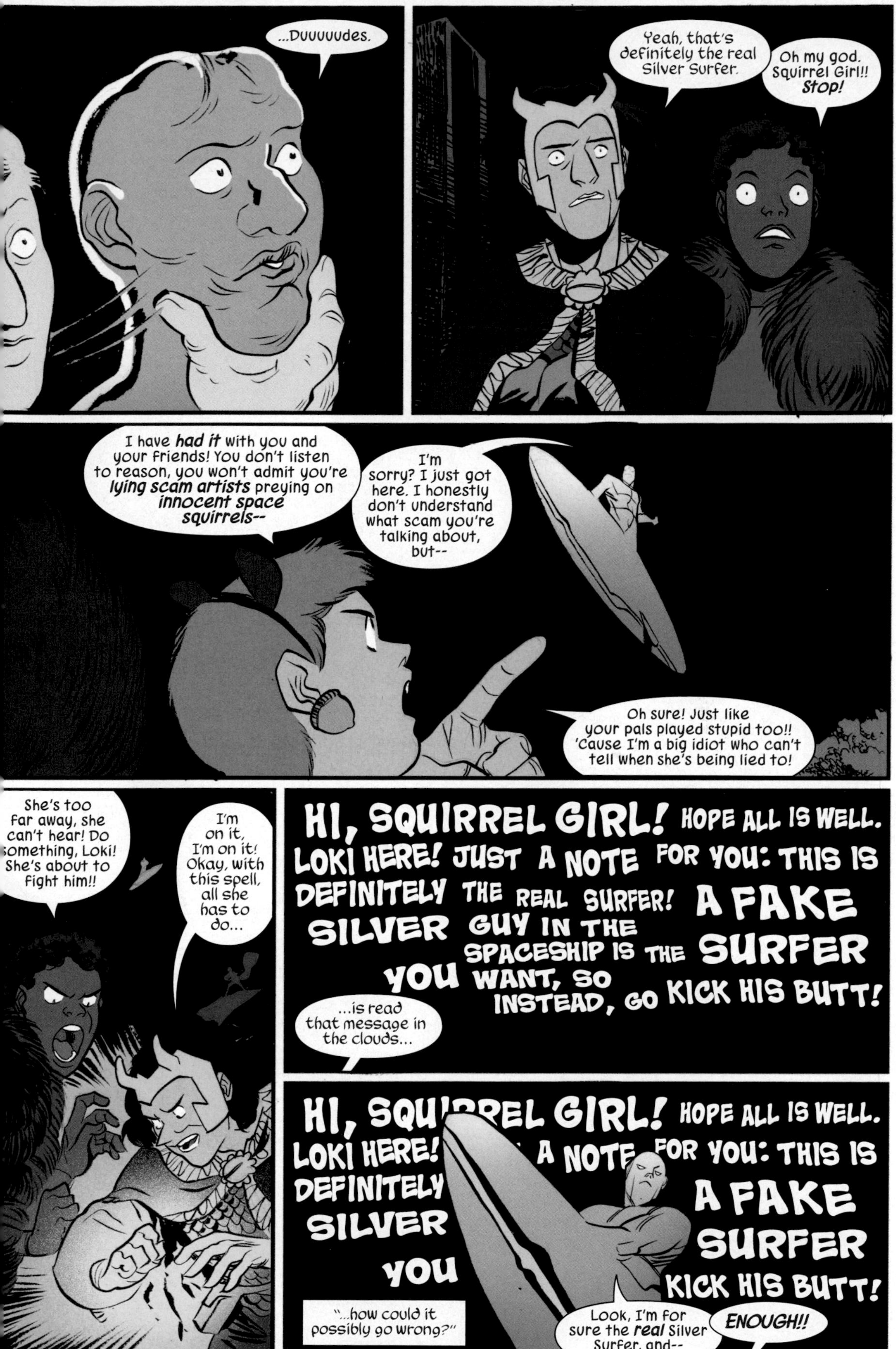
...Duuuuudes.
Yeah, that's definitely the real Silver Surfer.
Oh my god. Squirrel Girl!! *Stop!*
I have ***had it*** with you and your friends! You don't listen to reason, you won't admit you're ***lying scam artists*** preying on ***innocent space squirrels***--
I'm sorry? I just got here. I honestly don't understand what scam you're talking about, but--
Oh sure! Just like your pals played stupid too!! 'Cause I'm a big idiot who can't tell when she's being lied to!
She's too far away, she can't hear! Do something, Loki! She's about to fight him!!
I'm on it, I'm on it! Okay, with this spell, all she has to do...
HI, SQUIRREL GIRL! HOPE ALL IS WELL. LOKI HERE! JUST A NOTE FOR YOU: THIS IS DEFINITELY THE REAL SURFER! A FAKE SILVER GUY IN THE SPACESHIP IS THE SURFER YOU WANT, SO INSTEAD, GO KICK HIS BUTT!
...is read that message in the clouds...
HI, SQU RREL GIRL! HOPE ALL IS WELL. LOKI HERE! A NOTE FOR YOU: THIS IS DEFINITELY SILVER A FAKE SURFER YOU KICK HIS BUTT!
"...how could it possibly go wrong?"
Look, I'm for sure the ***real*** Silver Surfer, and--
ENOUGH!!

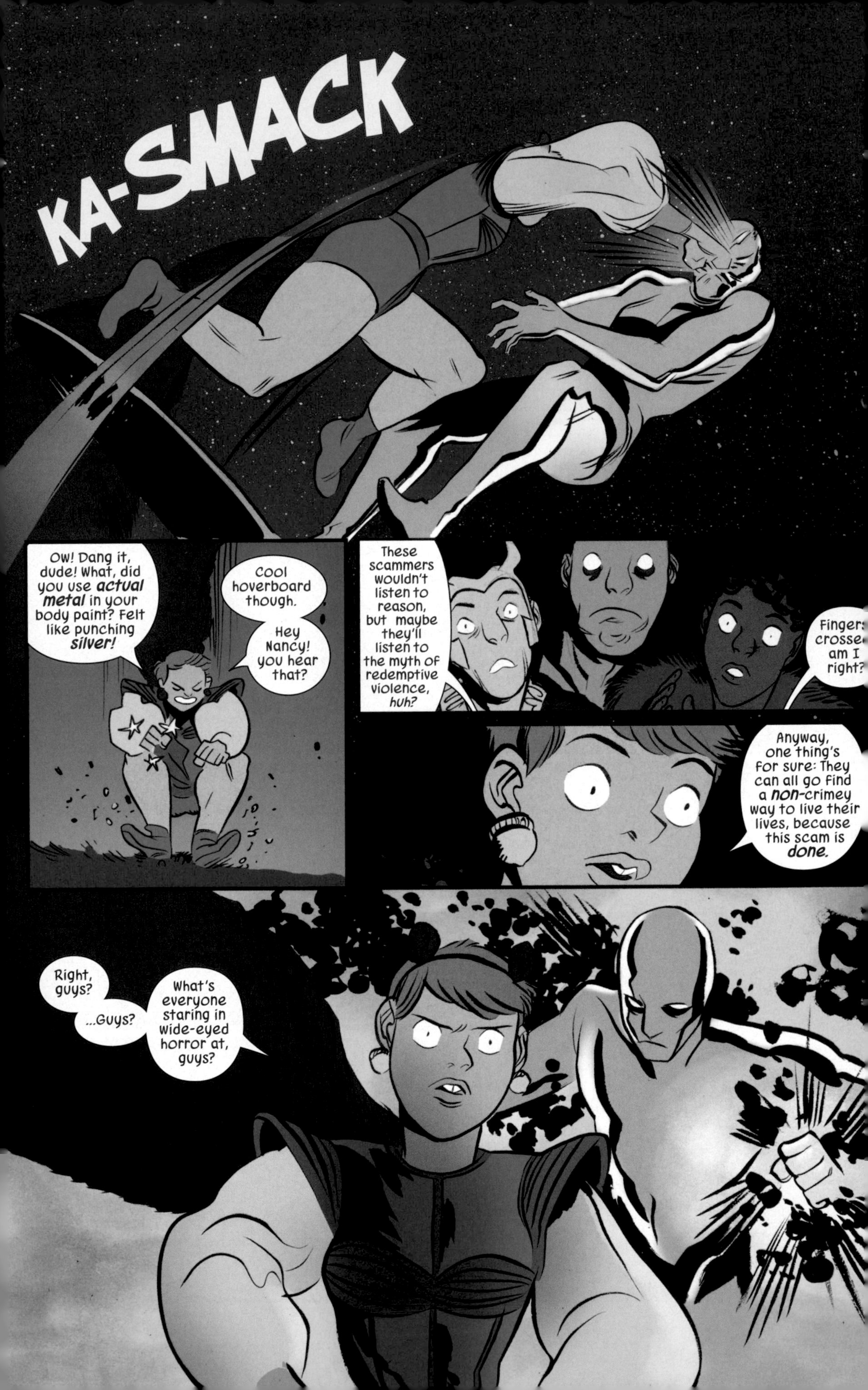
KA-SMACK
Ow! Dang it, dude! What, did you use actual metal in your body paint? Felt like punching silver!
Cool hoverboard though.
Hey Nancy! you hear that?
These scammers wouldn't listen to reason, but maybe they'll listen to the myth of redemptive violence, huh?
Finger crosse am I right?
Anyway, one thing's for sure: They can all go find a non-crimey way to live their lives, because this scam is done.
Right, guys?
...Guys?
What's everyone staring in wide-eyed horror at, guys?

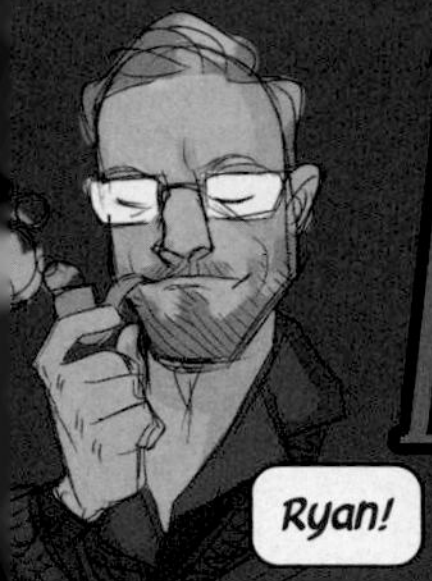
Ryan!

Letters From Nuts

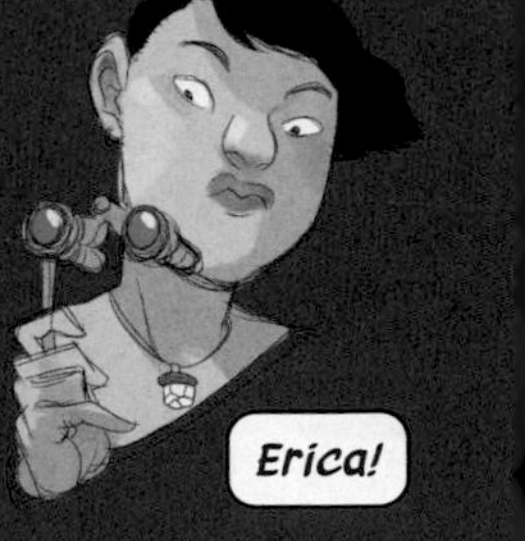
Erica!

Send letters to mheroes@marvel.com or 135 W 50th St, 7th Floor, New York, NY 10020 (Please mark "OKAY TO PRINT")

ello Erica and Ryan,

ophie has been looking forward to dressing s Squirrel Girl at New York Comic Con for long time now. We even made Deadpool ards! Anyway, Soph was CRAZY excited o meet Erica this year and pick up this henomenal sketch of Squirrel Girl and our og Esther, who had just passed away. I now it meant an awful lot to her (and to ne as well). She actually went home that ay and pretended to be a Marvel artist aking commissions to sketch super heroes!

hank you both so much for this comic. When she was two, Sophie started to xpress an interest in super heroes (which vas great for me), but got discouraged y the lack of female characters she vas exposed to. I picked SQUIRREL GIRL ecause I heard it was a good all-ages title. y the end of issue one it was clear that I ad a new favorite comic, and the next thing knew, I also had a pull list for the first time n over 20 years. More importantly, I have ad something wonderful to share with my aughter before bed for the past three years.

You guys are awesome. Stay nuts.

Jay and Sophie

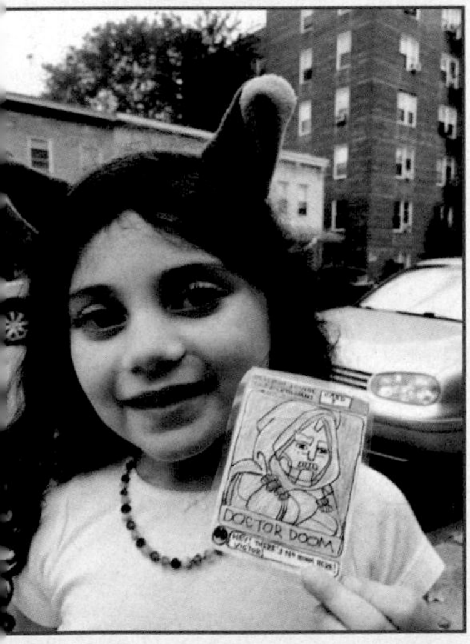
DOCTOR DOOM

RYAN: Hi Jay and Sophie, I'm really sorry o hear about your loss. Erica showed ne a snapshot of the picture she drew f Esther, and let me tell you: I know a ood dog when I see one. Soph, your ostume is awesome, and I love that ou have the cards too--amazing! And ay, congrats on the pull list! It's great hat you trust us to put together a cool omic for you and your Soph, and I really appreciate it! I really like signing books at shows too because it's fun, and you get to meet nice people and then write your name all over their stuff. Normally this is frowned upon! But not at signings.

ERICA: I still have the photo of Esther you gave me for reference! I literally just saw it in my convention stuff this week. It was an honor to do that piece, and I'm glad it inspired Sophie.

My two daughters and I are big fans of Squirrel Girl! She is so fun to read about! We love her style! We laugh out loud together reading it! This is a picture done by my oldest daughter Helen. She is 10 years old.

Sincerely,
Jacqueline
Oregon

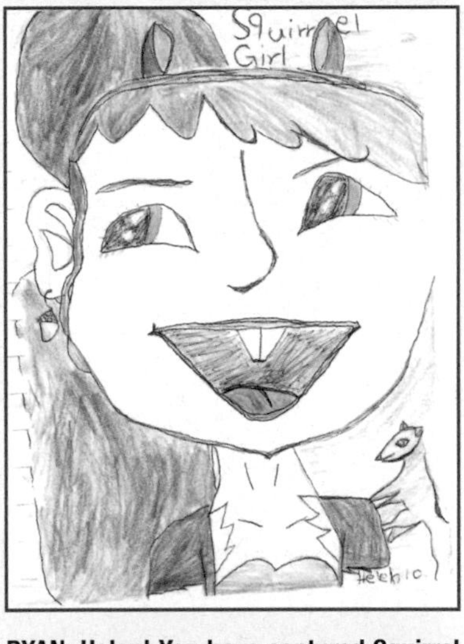
Squirrel Girl

RYAN: Helen! You have captured Squirrel Girl's attitude perfectly. I LOVE IT. Jacqueline, I also love Doreen's style: That's all Erica's work, but it makes me want to be a more fashionable person in real life. For example, I recently bought an '80s-style calculator watch, so now I am at the extreme heights of both fashion AND calculation. Erica can back me up on this!!

ERICA: Ryan, no comment.

Fellow nuts,

Congrats on the Eisner Award! And while it's inarguable that THE UNBEATABLE SQUIRREL GIRL is a great comic for teens, I must say that it's also a pretty darned good one for statistics professors in their late thirties. I hope this book survives long enough to experience many, many relaunches!

Stephen Davidson
Danville, VA

RYAN: Aw, thanks, Stephen! Yeah, I see the categories as not being exclusive: They're for teens but also everyone else (including the non-teens featured earlier IN THIS VERY LETTERS PAGE). Knowing that we have stats professors reading this, I'll have to be careful not to put in any incorrect stats information! I promise to achieve this goal 95% of the time, 19 times out of 20.

ERICA: What are the odds we'll make it that far? I'm actually asking. I've...never taken a statistics class.

Ryan, Erica, and Rico,

Hello again! It's Hazel the Radford University Squirrel! It's been a while since you last heard from me way back in USG #11 when I wrote in to tell you about meeting Erica at HeroesCon 2016 with my ol' pal Professor Scott (as you can see, I still have the Tippy-Toe button Erica drew for me). A lot has happened since then.

First of all, I am now a college graduate! After many years of hard work, I have finally graduated from Radford with a Bachelor of Arts in Nuciferous Studies. It was a tough nut to crack, but I finally made it with help from good friends like Professor Scott.

After much deliberation, I decided to pursue my master's and to leave RU behind, so I packed up and headed to Longwood University. They're a smaller school but they have an excellent Acorn Studies program. They also host the Virginia Children's Book Festival every fall. There's even a full day dedicated to comics and super heroes! You had better bet I'm going to be there telling all the kids about UNBEATABLE SQUIRREL GIRL!

Oh, I almost forgot the best part! When I arrived, who should I find but Professor Scott. He had already accepted a position teaching at Longwood and he has agreed to let me stay with him (well, in the tree in his backyard). I had been at Radford a long time, so having a familiar face around to help with the transition is certainly nice (I'm sure Professor Scott appreciates it too---he had been at Radford for over 15 years before taking the job at Longwood).

The nearest comic-book store is a one-hour-drive away, but fortunately, Professor

Scott has a subscription to USG delivered every month (he has other subscriptions too...one of them is something about a Spectacular Spider...but who cares about spiders? But I think it's written by a chipmunk or something...so that's pretty cool). Well, I better get back to my studies! I guess next time you hear from me, I'll be Hazel the Longwood Squirrel!

Stay Nutty, My Friends!

P.S. Professor Scott is planning to be at HeroesCon again next year. Hope you'll all be there; I've already met Rico and Erica, but I would love to meet Ryan!

Hazel
Tree in Professor Scott's Backyard
A Street
Farmville, VA 23901

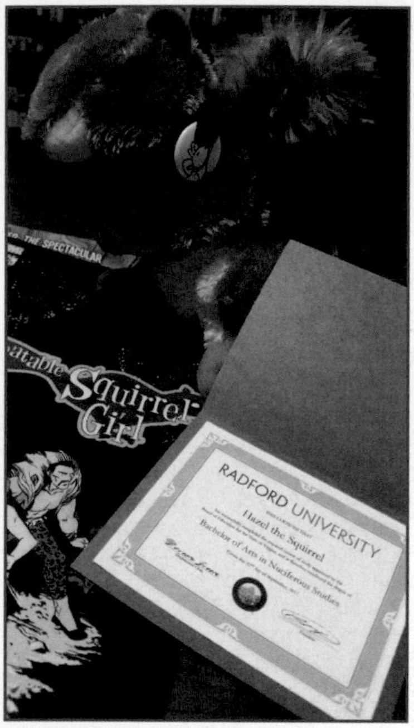
THE SPECTACULAR
Squirrel Girl
RADFORD UNIVERSITY
Hazel the Squirrel

RYAN: YES, follow-up letters from squirrels! PERFECTION. This "Chipmunk Zdarsky" writing SPECTACULAR SPIDER-MAN sounds interesting: I'll have to check it out! Congrats on your degree, and also, tell Prof. Scott congrats on his new gig and that I hope I can meet him one day too!

ERICA: Okay. I'm going to go down a completely different path here. THERE'S A REAL FARMVILLE? As a survivor/ex-employee of gambling-disguised-as-cute-games companies, I'm shook. I'm also curious who named this town. I suspect I know what the main industry was. ANYWAY. Congrats on the new gig and new digs.

My third-grader Kate was Squirrel Girl this year for Halloween (and will be wearing this to Phoenix Comic Con in May!). She wanted to be the glider version from the cover of Vol. 6. Her grandma and I made the costume! She reads the comics over and over and over.

Marjory

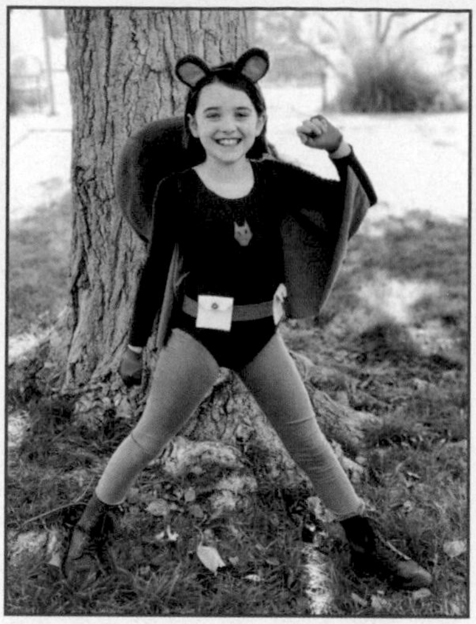

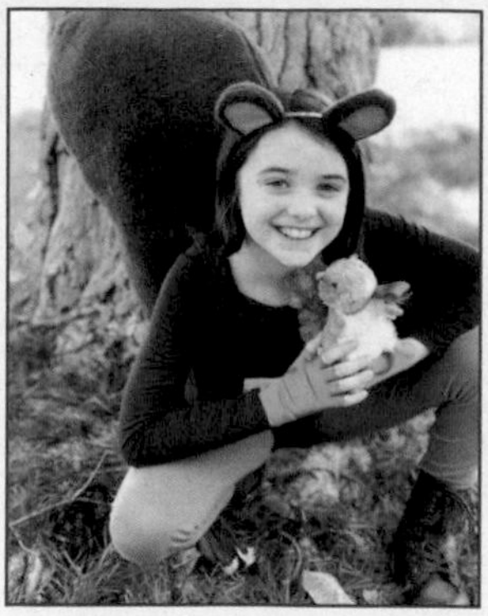

RYAN: KATE! You look amazing. This is not an easy costume to make, so props to you and your mother, Marjory! I love the emblem on the chest and the matching gloves. SO GOOD. And the tail's never easy but it looks like this turned out great!

ERICA: YES. I LOVE IT. It's so good.

Next Issue:

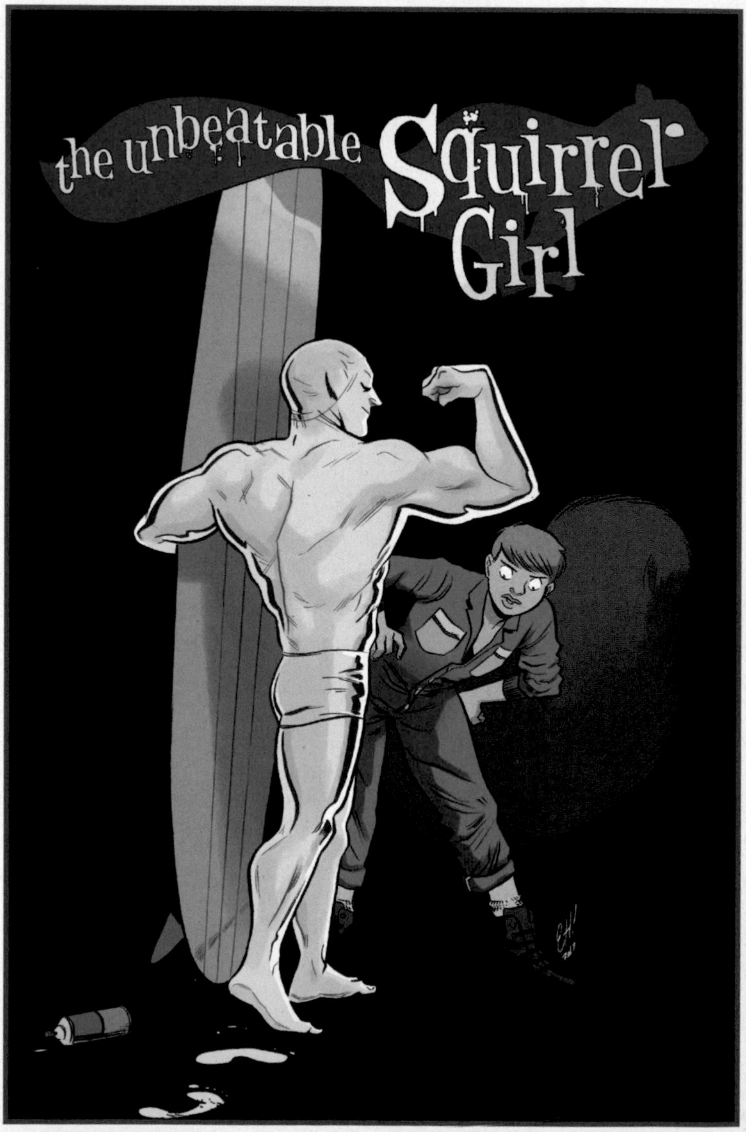
the unbeatable Squirrel Girl

Attention, Squirrel Scouts! Make sure to check out our production blog, **unbeatablesquirrelgirl.tumblr.com**, where we post behind-the-scenes stuff on how the book gets made, along with all sorts of cool things *you* make: fan art, cosplay, whatever!

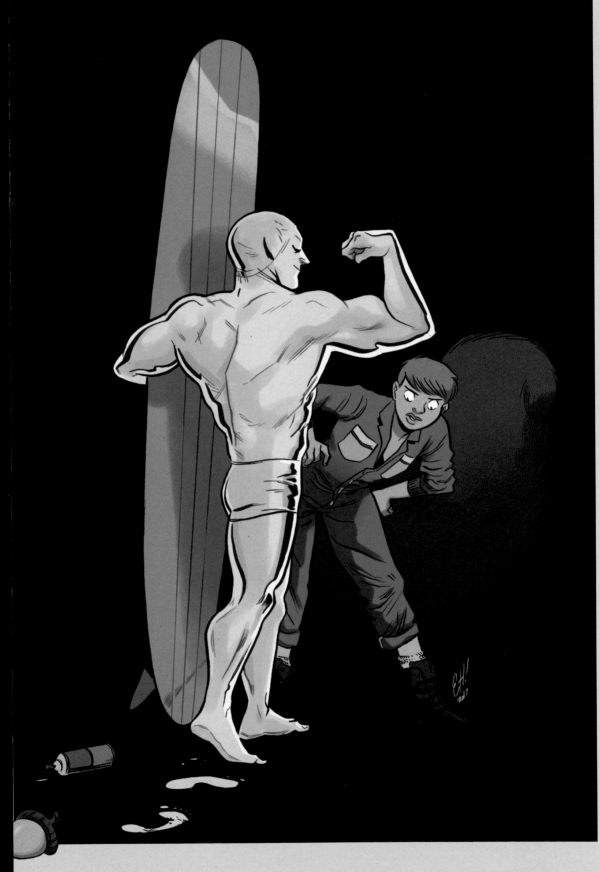

Doreen Green isn't just a second-year computer science student: she secretly also has all the powers of both squirrel and girl! She uses her amazing abilities to fight crime **and** be as awesome as possible. You know her as...*The Unbeatable Squirrel Girl!* Find out what she's been up to, with...

Squirrel Girl *in a nutshell*

Squirrel Girl @unbeatablesg
RT if you'd travel into SPACE HERSELF to rescue your missing friends

Squirrel Girl @unbeatablesg
haha okay wow lots of RTs!! Okay, try this on for size: RT if you'd travel into SPACE HERSELF to rescue your missing friends if they were kidnapped by SPACE SQUIRRELS

Squirrel Girl @unbeatablesg
okay, okay, how about THIS: RT if you'd ever travel into SPACE HERSELF with DRAX, and fight ELDER GODS with LOKI, just to rescue your missing friends who were kidnapped by SPACE SQUIRRELS

Squirrel Girl @unbeatablesg
hmm yes it seems everyone who follows me is a cool person with correct opinions who also tacitly endorses all my decisions

Squirrel Girl @unbeatablesg
i rate this news: EXCELLENT

Spider-Man @aspidercan
@unbeatablesg hey squirrel girl

Squirrel Girl @unbeatablesg
@aspidercan spidey

Spider-Man @aspidercan
@unbeatablesg hey i just wanted to say

Spider-Man @aspidercan
@unbeatablesg one time when i went into space i got a new costume, but then it turned out my new costume was a shapeshifting alien

Spider-Man @aspidercan
@unbeatablesg and THEN the alien turned evil and now he's one of my greatest foes who looks like a bad version of me with a big slimey tongue

Spider-Man @aspidercan
@unbeatablesg the only moral i learned from this was "be careful what clothes you wear in space" so i now share that lesson with you

Squirrel Girl @unbeatablesg
@aspidercan aw, thank you spider-man!! it's great to know you're looking out for me <3

Squirrel Girl @unbeatablesg
@aspidercan but i'm actually wearing MAGIC SPACE CLOTHES made for me by Loki so I think I'm probably good

Squirrel Girl @unbeatablesg
@aspidercan he made them very "now" for space, apparently my squirrel t-shirt was not high fashion enough for the cosmos

Spider-Man @aspidercan
@unbeatablesg what

Squirrel Girl @unbeatablesg
@aspidercan yeah my cool clothes give me the confidence I need to for instance get into a fistfight with the silver surfer

Spider-Man @aspidercan
@unbeatablesg WHAT

Squirrel Girl @unbeatablesg
@aspidercan SPEAKING OF WHICH, GOTTA GO

Spider-Man @aspidercan
@unbeatablesg squirrel girl

Spider-Man @aspidercan
@unbeatablesg hello

Spider-Man @aspidercan
@unbeatablesg squirrel girl

Spider-Man @aspidercan
@unbeatablesg do you think loki can make me magic space clothes too

search! 🔍

#horsewhinny

#saltahgoth

#ulyaoth

#wunulath

#sheila

This is just SOME of what Doreen's been posting--all these handles are real! Follow **@unbeatablesg** for more!

When we last saw *Squirrel* Girl, she was *fighting* the Silver Surfer--*wielder* of the Power *Cosmic* and former herald *of* Galactus--who she *incorrectly* thinks is the *imposter* who's been *robbing* entire planets!

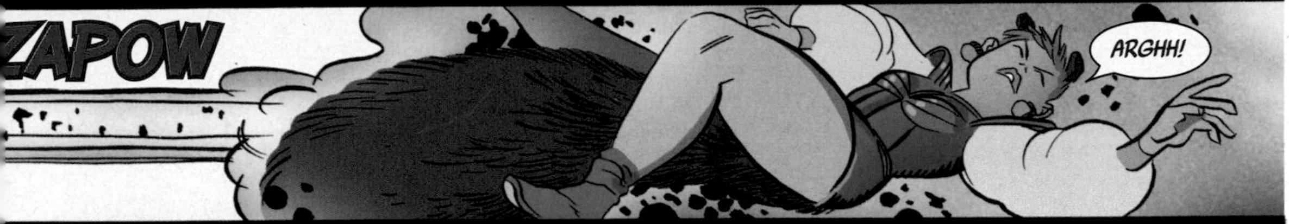
ZAPOW
ARGHH!

It is not going well...

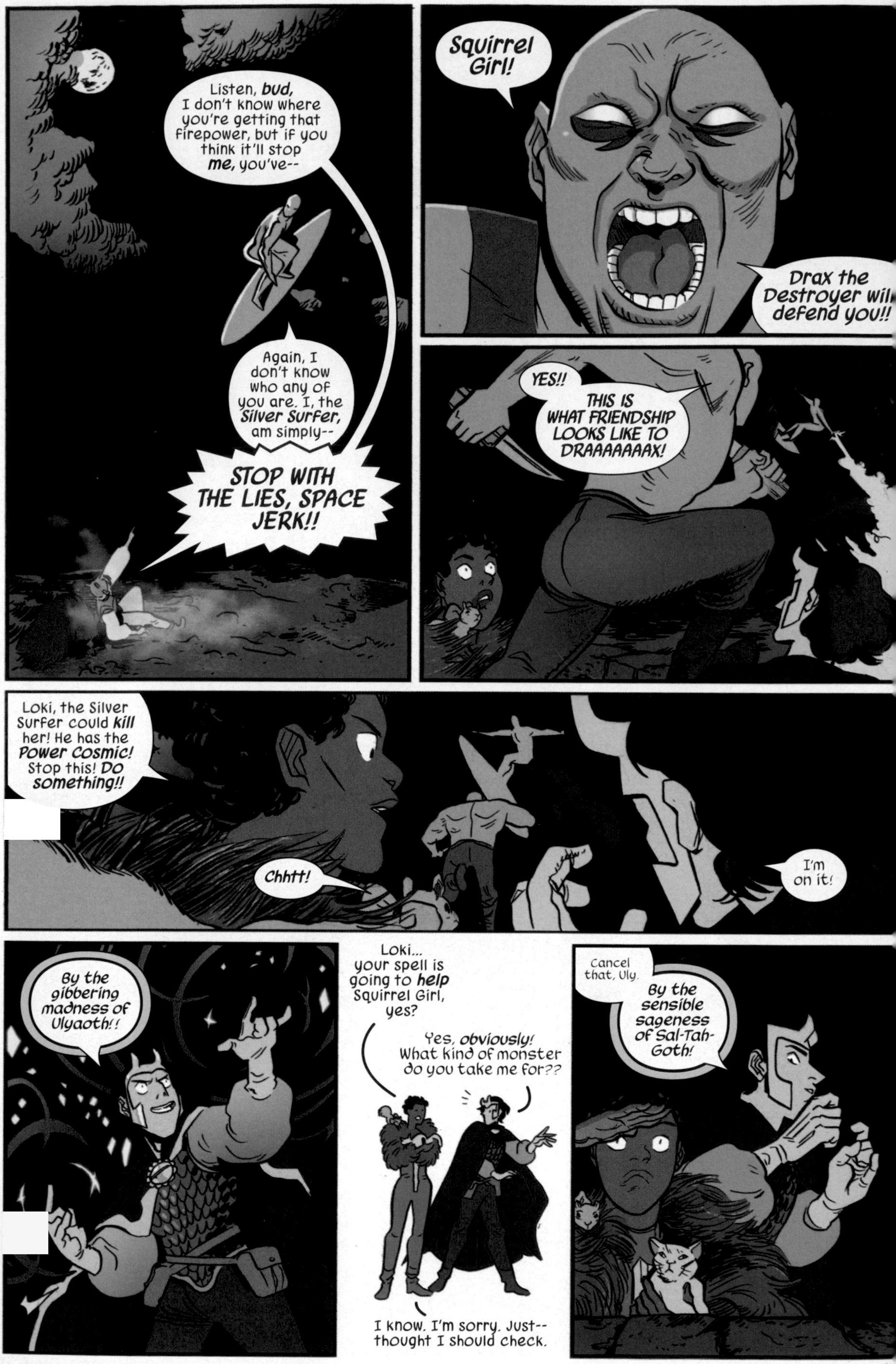
Listen, bud, I don't know where you're getting that firepower, but if you think it'll stop me, you've--
Again, I don't know who any of you are. I, the Silver Surfer, am simply--
STOP WITH THE LIES, SPACE JERK!!
Squirrel Girl!
Drax the Destroyer wil defend you!!
YES!!
THIS IS WHAT FRIENDSHIP LOOKS LIKE TO DRAAAAAAAX!
Loki, the Silver Surfer could kill her! He has the Power Cosmic! Stop this! Do something!!
Chhtt!
I'm on it!
By the gibbering madness of Ulyaoth!!
Loki... your spell is going to help Squirrel Girl, yes?
Yes, obviously! What kind of monster do you take me for??
I know. I'm sorry. Just--thought I should check.
Cancel that, Uly.
By the sensible sageness of Sal-Tah-Goth!

Elsewhere: Ulyaoth is jumping from his chair when he hears Loki's call, but after he cancels it, Ulyaoth just sighs, puts his reading glasses back on, and returns to his book.

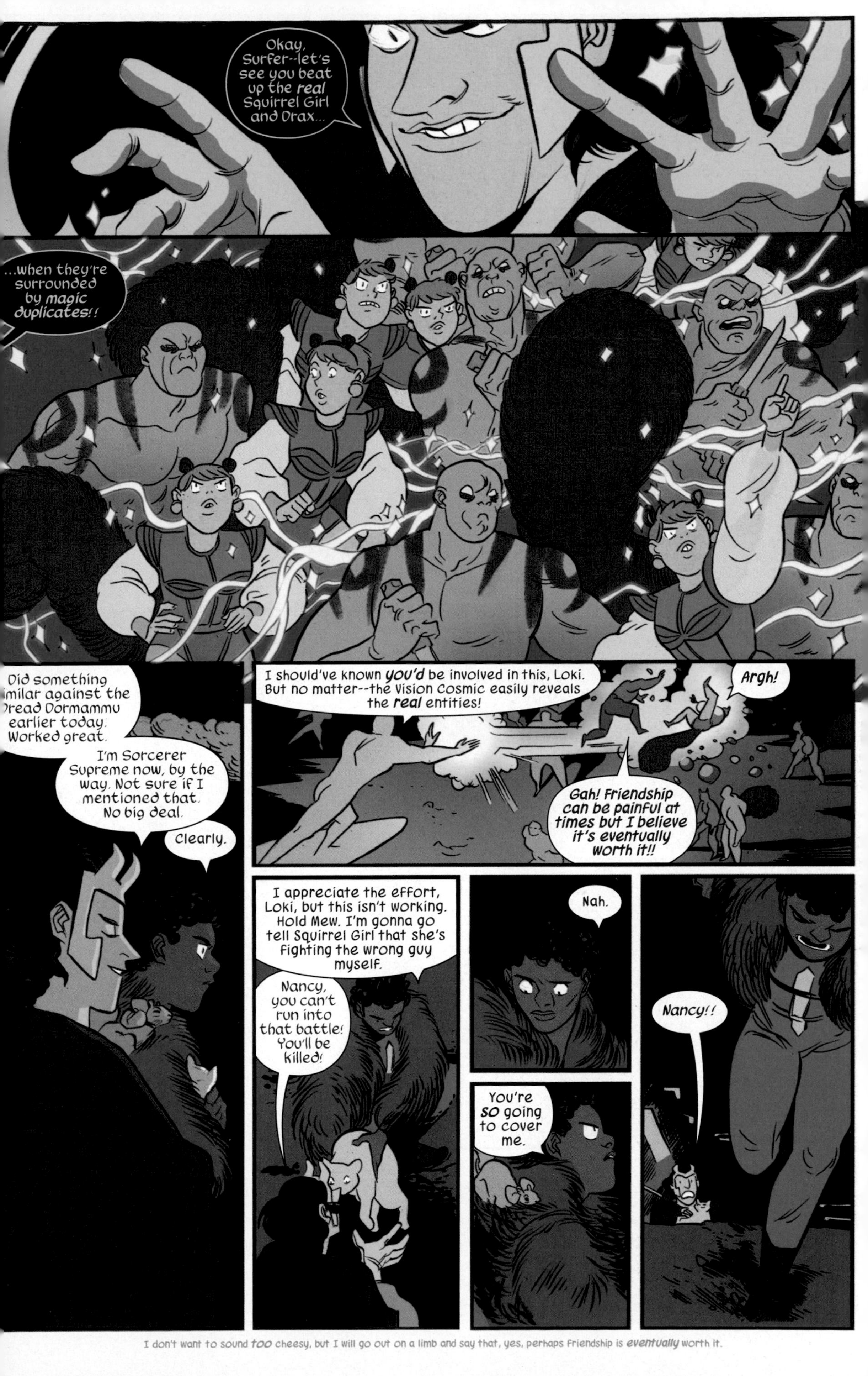
Okay, Surfer--let's see you beat up the *real* Squirrel Girl and Drax...
...when they're surrounded by *magic duplicates!!*
Did something imilar against the Dread Dormammu earlier today. Worked great.
I'm Sorcerer Supreme now, by the way. Not sure if I mentioned that. No big deal.
Clearly.
I should've known *you'd* be involved in this, Loki. But no matter--the Vision Cosmic easily reveals the *real* entities!
Argh!
Gah! Friendship can be painful at times but I believe it's eventually worth it!!
I appreciate the effort, Loki, but this isn't working. Hold Mew. I'm gonna go tell Squirrel Girl that she's fighting the wrong guy myself.
Nancy, you can't run into that battle! You'll be killed!
Nah.
You're *so* going to cover me.
Nancy!!

I don't want to sound *too* cheesy, but I will go out on a limb and say that, yes, perhaps friendship is *eventually* worth it.

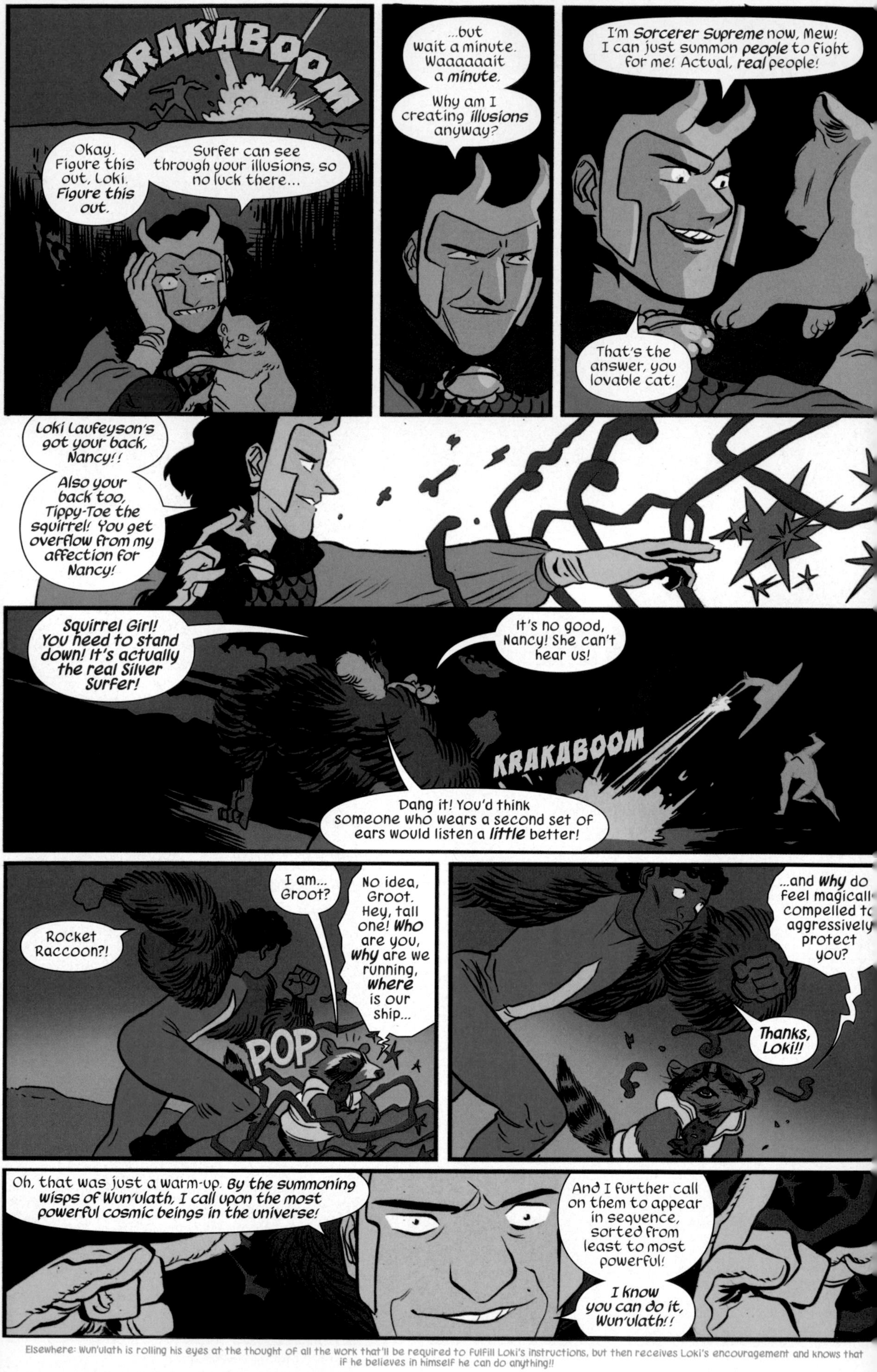
KRAKABOOM
Okay. Figure this out, Loki. Figure this out.
Surfer can see through your illusions, so no luck there...
...but wait a minute. Waaaaaait a minute.
Why am I creating illusions anyway?
I'm Sorcerer Supreme now, Mew! I can just summon people to fight for me! Actual, real people!
That's the answer, you lovable cat!
Loki Laufeyson's got your back, Nancy!!
Also your back too, Tippy-Toe the squirrel! You get overflow from my affection for Nancy!
Squirrel Girl! You need to stand down! It's actually the real Silver Surfer!
It's no good, Nancy! She can't hear us!
KRAKABOOM
Dang it! You'd think someone who wears a second set of ears would listen a little better!
Rocket Raccoon?!
I am... Groot?
No idea, Groot. Hey, tall one! Who are you, why are we running, where is our ship...
POP
...and why do
feel magical
compelled t
aggressively
protect you?
Thanks, Loki!!
Oh, that was just a warm-up. By the summoning wisps of Wun'ulath, I call upon the most powerful cosmic beings in the universe!
And I further call on them to appear in sequence, sorted from least to most powerful!
I know you can do it, Wun'ulath!!

Elsewhere: Wun'ulath is rolling his eyes at the thought of all the work that'll be required to fulfill Loki's instructions, but then receives Loki's encouragement and knows that if he believes in himself he can do anything!!

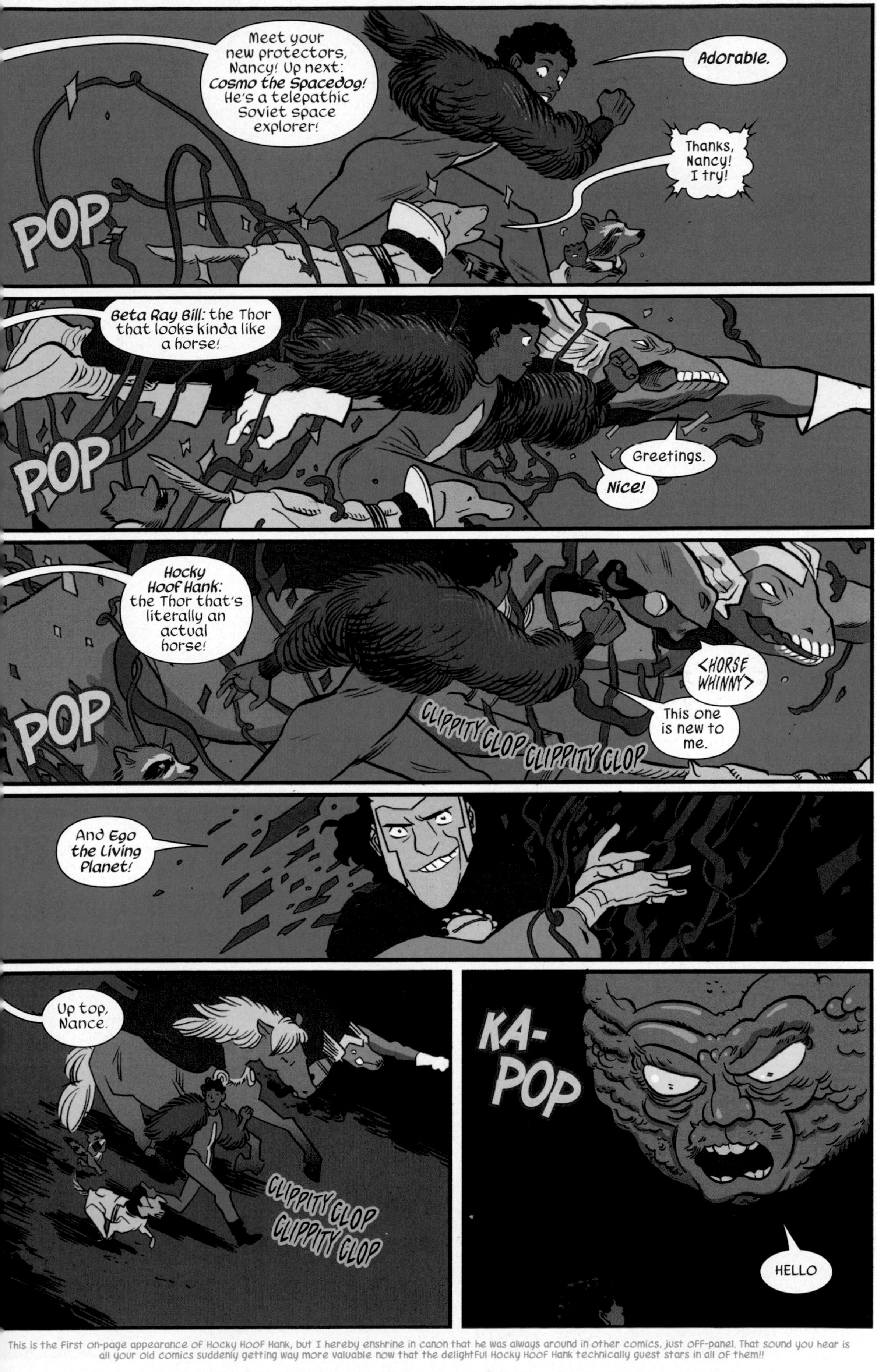
Meet your new protectors, Nancy! Up next: Cosmo the Spacedog! He's a telepathic Soviet space explorer!
Adorable.
Thanks, Nancy! I try!
POP
Beta Ray Bill: the Thor that looks kinda like a horse!
POP
Greetings.
Nice!
Hocky Hoof Hank: the Thor that's literally an actual horse!
POP
<HORSE WHINNY>
This one is new to me.
CLIPPITY CLOP CLIPPITY CLOP
And Ego the Living Planet!
Up top, Nance.
CLIPPITY CLOP CLIPPITY CLOP
KA-POP
HELLO

This is the first on-page appearance of Hocky Hoof Hank, but I hereby enshrine in canon that he was always around in other comics, just off-panel. That sound you hear is all your old comics suddenly getting way more valuable now that the delightful Hocky Hoof Hank technically guest stars in all of them!!

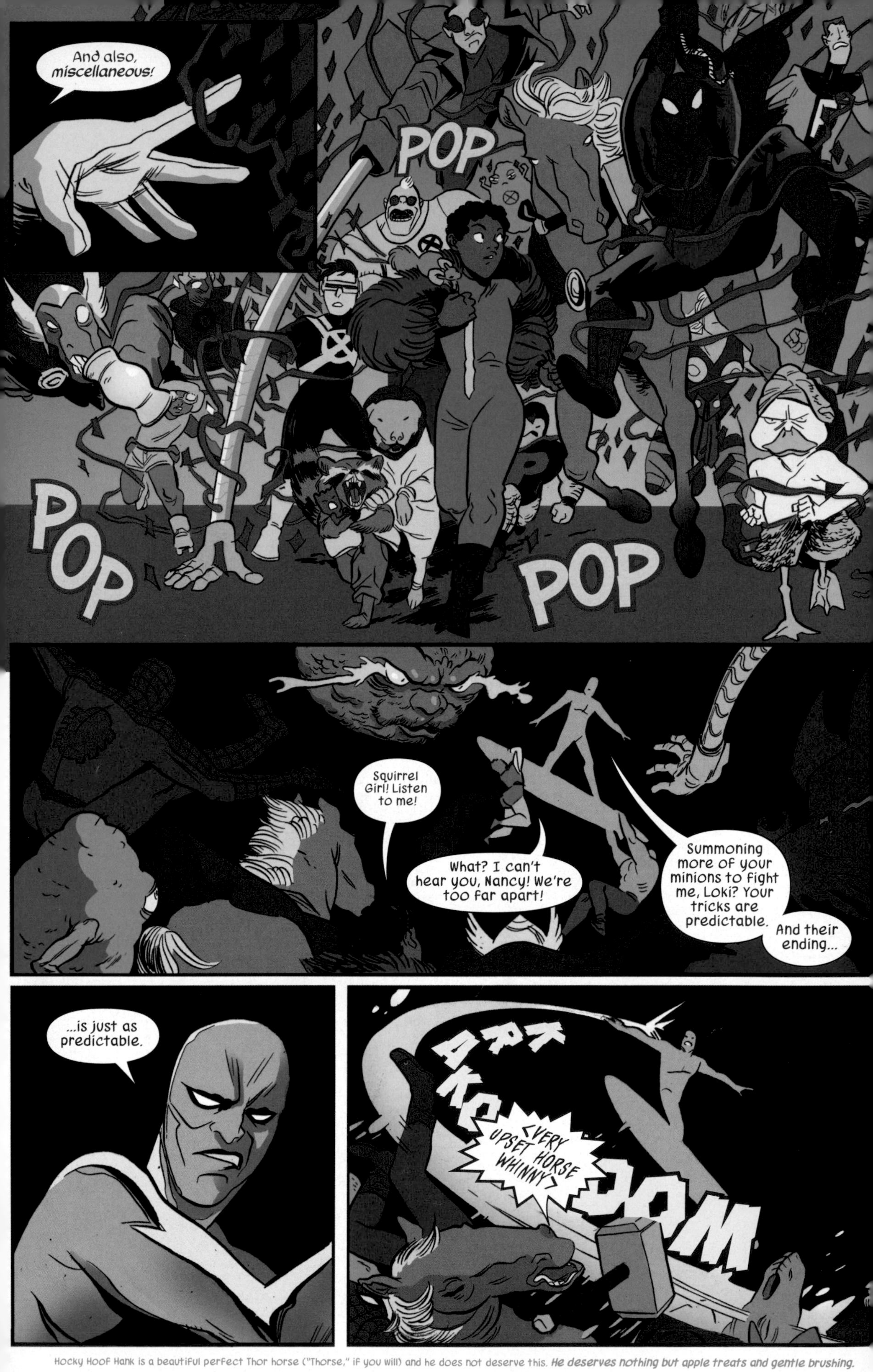
And also, *miscellaneous!*
POP
POP
POP
Squirrel Girl! Listen to me!
What? I can't hear you, Nancy! We're too far apart!
Summoning more of your minions to fight me, Loki? Your tricks are predictable.
And their ending...
...is just as predictable.
KRAKOOOM
<VERY UPSET HORSE WHINNY>

Hocky Hoof Hank is a beautiful perfect Thor horse ("Thorse," if you will) and he does not deserve this. *He deserves nothing but apple treats and gentle brushing.*

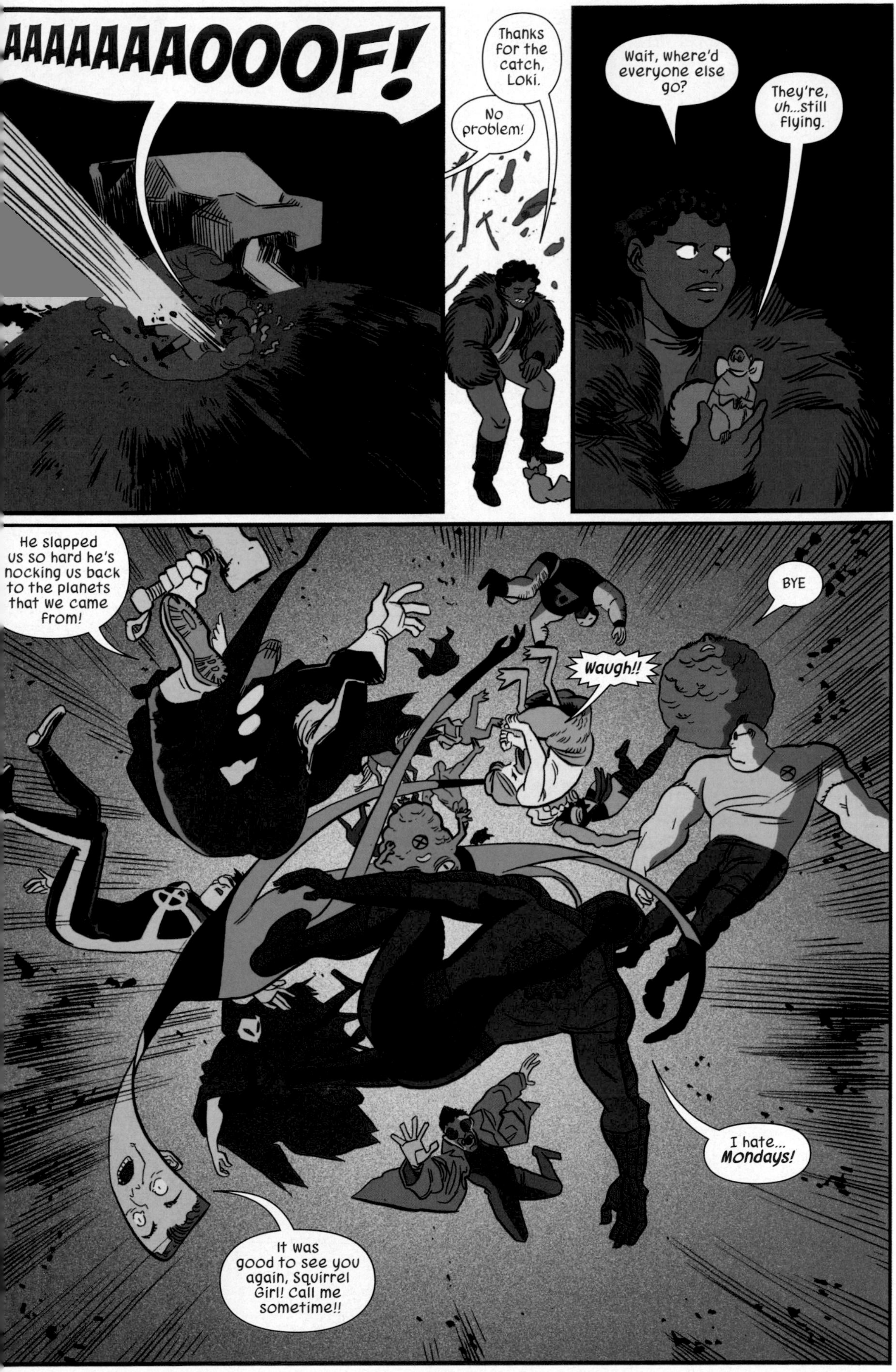
AAAAAAAOOOF!
Thanks for the catch, Loki.
No problem!
Wait, where'd everyone else go?
They're, uh...still flying.
He slapped us so hard he's nocking us back to the planets that we came from!
BYE
Waugh!!
I hate... Mondays!
It was good to see you again, Squirrel Girl! Call me sometime!!

Here is a short *but true* Howard the Duck story: When Howard lands back on Earth in NYC, he finds it's actually nine days after he was first teleported away by Loki. The Silver Surfer literally knocked him into *next week*, and now all his bills are overdue! *He's so mad*, the end!

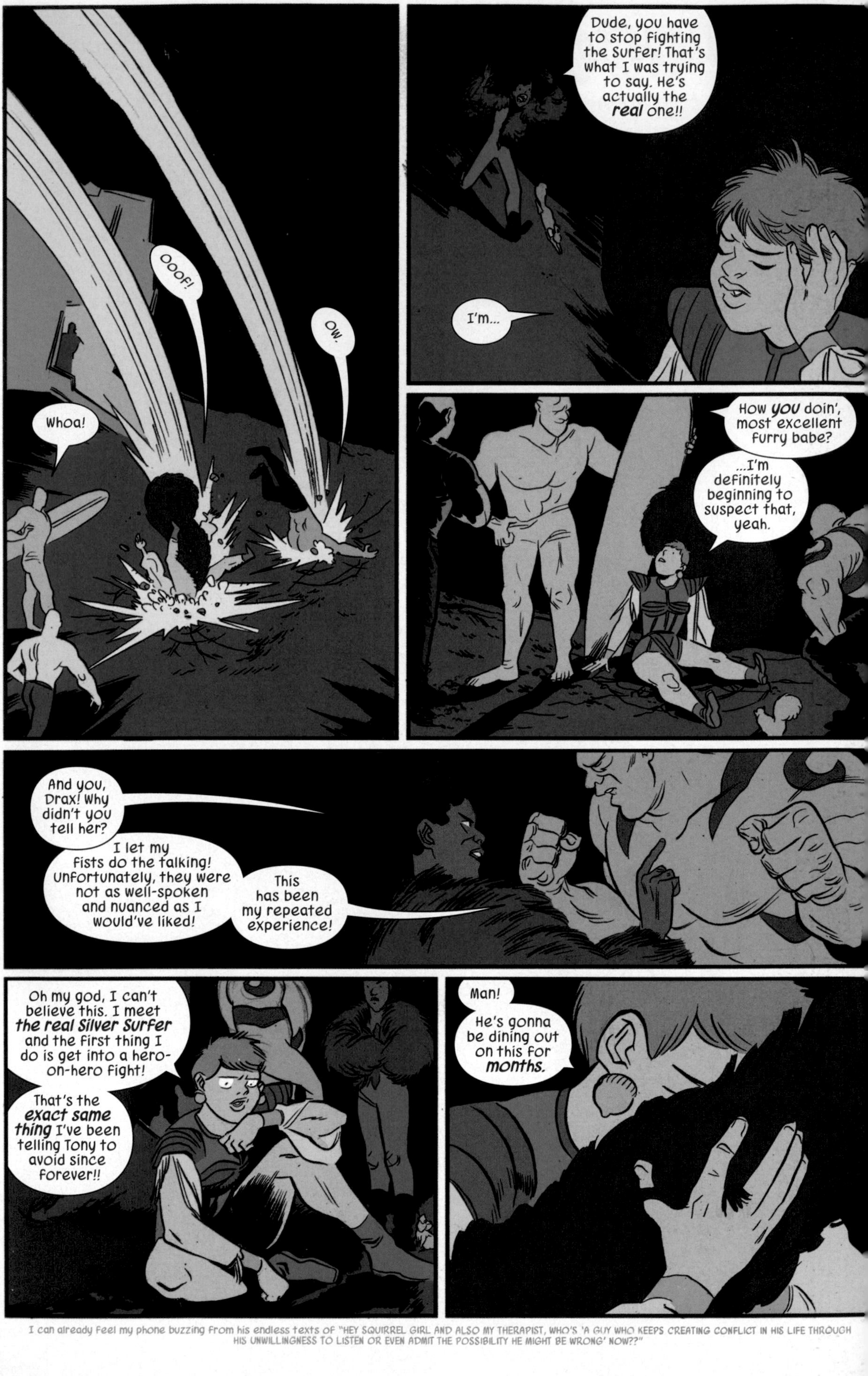
OOOF!
OW.
Whoa!
Dude, you have to stop fighting the Surfer! That's what I was trying to say. He's actually the *real* one!!
I'm...
How *you* doin', most excellent furry babe?
...I'm definitely beginning to suspect that, yeah.
And you, Drax! Why didn't you tell her?
I let my fists do the talking! Unfortunately, they were not as well-spoken and nuanced as I would've liked!
This has been my repeated experience!
Oh my god, I can't believe this. I meet *the real Silver Surfer* and the first thing I do is get into a hero-on-hero fight!
That's the *exact same thing* I've been telling Tony to avoid since forever!!
Man!
He's gonna be dining out on this for *months.*

I can already feel my phone buzzing from his endless texts of "HEY SQUIRREL GIRL AND ALSO MY THERAPIST, WHO'S 'A GUY WHO KEEPS CREATING CONFLICT IN HIS LIFE THROUGH HIS UNWILLINGNESS TO LISTEN OR EVEN ADMIT THE POSSIBILITY HE MIGHT BE WRONG' NOW??"

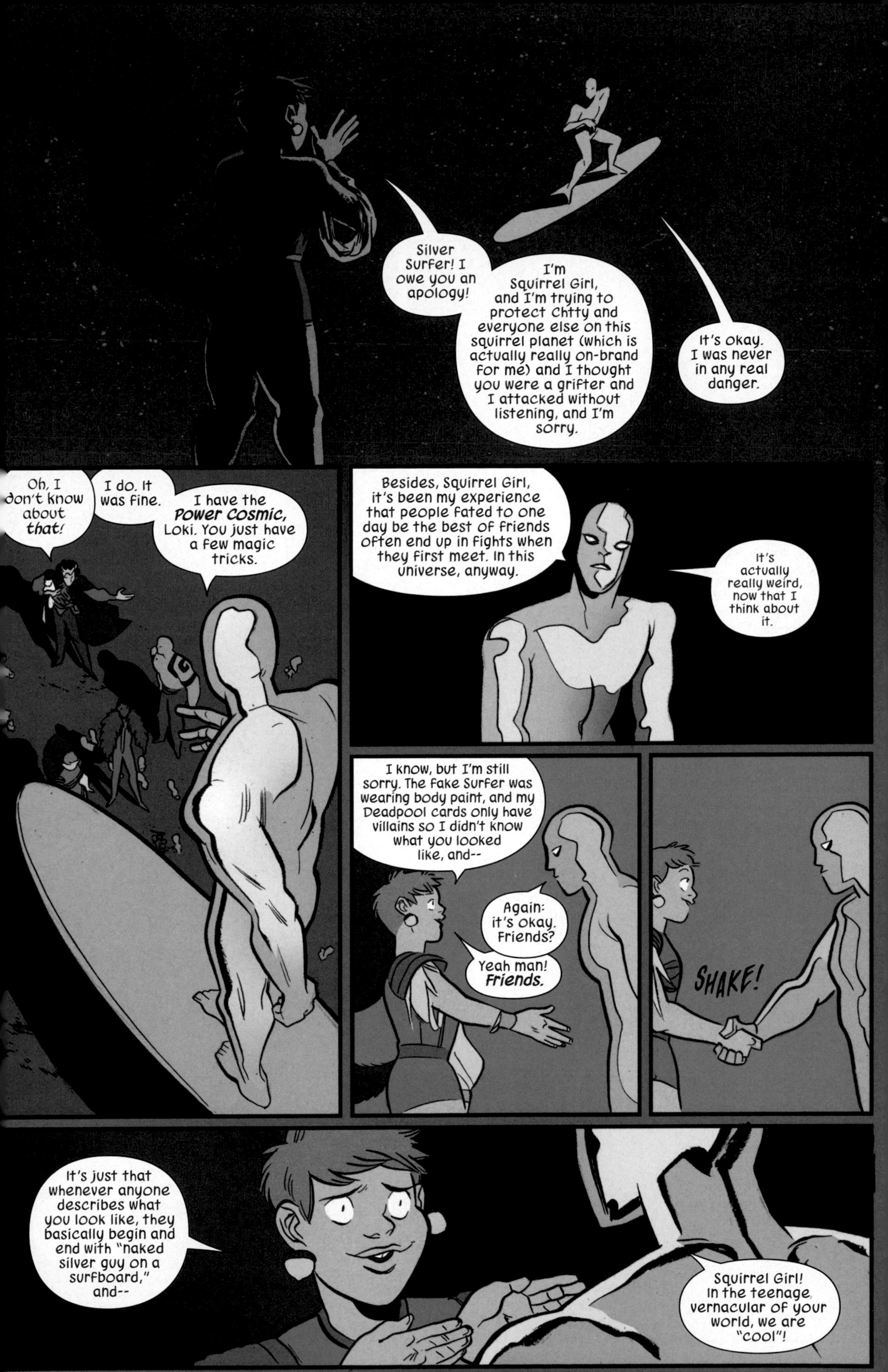
Silver Surfer! I owe you an apology!
I'm Squirrel Girl, and I'm trying to protect Chtty and everyone else on this squirrel planet (which is actually really on-brand for me) and I thought you were a grifter and I attacked without listening, and I'm sorry.
It's okay. I was never in any real danger.
Oh, I don't know about *that!*
I do. It was fine.
I have the ***Power Cosmic,*** Loki. You just have a few magic tricks.
Besides, Squirrel Girl, it's been my experience that people fated to one day be the best of friends often end up in fights when they first meet. In this universe, anyway.
It's actually really weird, now that I think about it.
I know, but I'm still sorry. The fake Surfer was wearing body paint, and my Deadpool cards only have villains so I didn't know what you looked like, and--
Again: it's okay. Friends?
Yeah man! ***Friends.***
SHAKE!
It's just that whenever anyone describes what you look like, they basically begin and end with "naked silver guy on a surfboard," and--
Squirrel Girl! In the teenage vernacular of your world, we are "cool"!

In the teenage vernacular of your world, we are "Totes McGoats lit to the max, daddy-o." Oh no. My cosmic senses tell me that the vernacular of your world has already shifted and left me painfully out of touch! *Again!*

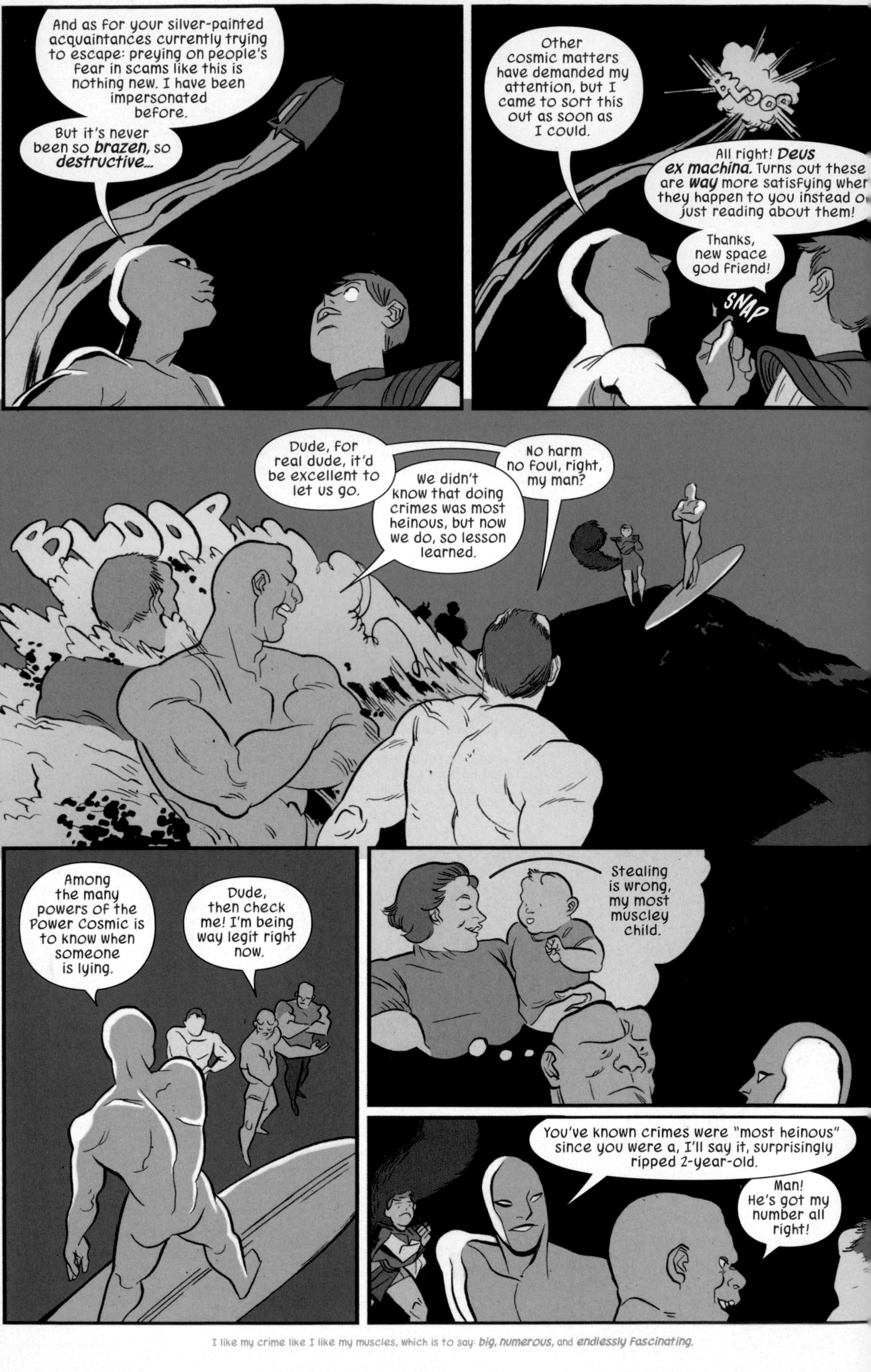
And as for your silver-painted acquaintances currently trying to escape: preying on people's fear in scams like this is nothing new. I have been impersonated before.
But it's never been so **brazen**, so **destructive...**
Other cosmic matters have demanded my attention, but I came to sort this out as soon as I could.
BLOOP
All right! **Deus ex machina.** Turns out these are **way** more satisfying when they happen to you instead of just reading about them!
Thanks, new space god friend!
SNAP
Dude, for real dude, it'd be excellent to let us go.
We didn't know that doing crimes was most heinous, but now we do, so lesson learned.
No harm no foul, right, my man?
BLOOP
Among the many powers of the Power Cosmic is to know when someone is lying.
Dude, then check me! I'm being way legit right now.
Stealing is wrong, my most muscley child.
You've known crimes were "most heinous" since you were a, I'll say it, surprisingly ripped 2-year-old.
Man! He's got my number all right!

I like my crime like I like my muscles, which is to say: *big, numerous,* and *endlessly fascinating.*

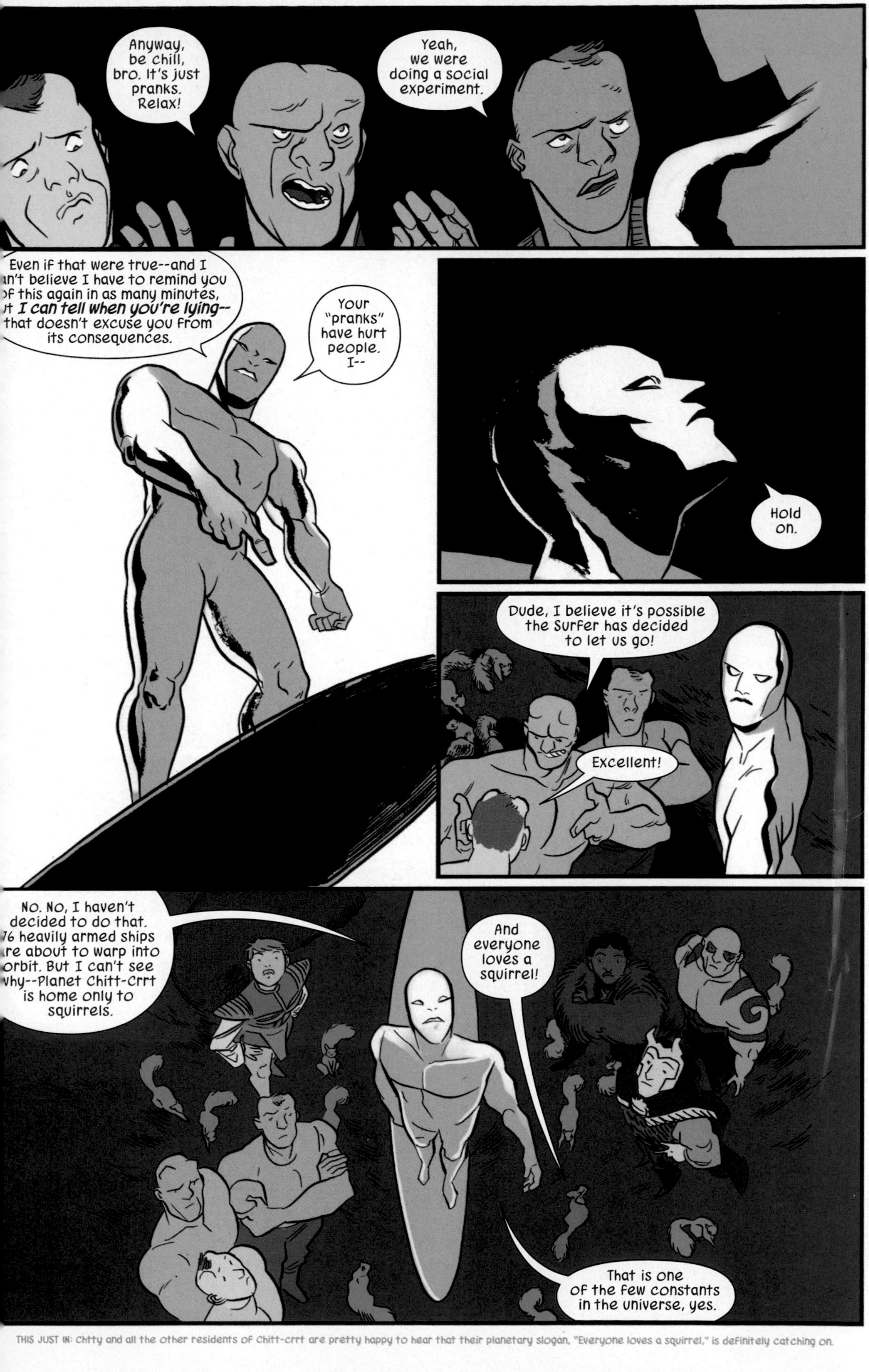
Anyway, be chill, bro. It's just pranks. Relax!
Yeah, we were doing a social experiment.
Even if that were true--and I an't believe I have to remind you of this again in as many minutes, ut *I can tell when you're lying--* that doesn't excuse you from its consequences.
Your "pranks" have hurt people. I--
Hold on.
Dude, I believe it's possible the Surfer has decided to let us go!
Excellent!
No. No, I haven't decided to do that. 76 heavily armed ships re about to warp into orbit. But I can't see why--Planet Chitt-Crrt is home only to squirrels.
And everyone loves a squirrel!
That is one of the few constants in the universe, yes.

THIS JUST IN: Chtty and all the other residents of Chitt-crrt are pretty happy to hear that their planetary slogan, "Everyone loves a squirrel," is definitely catching on.

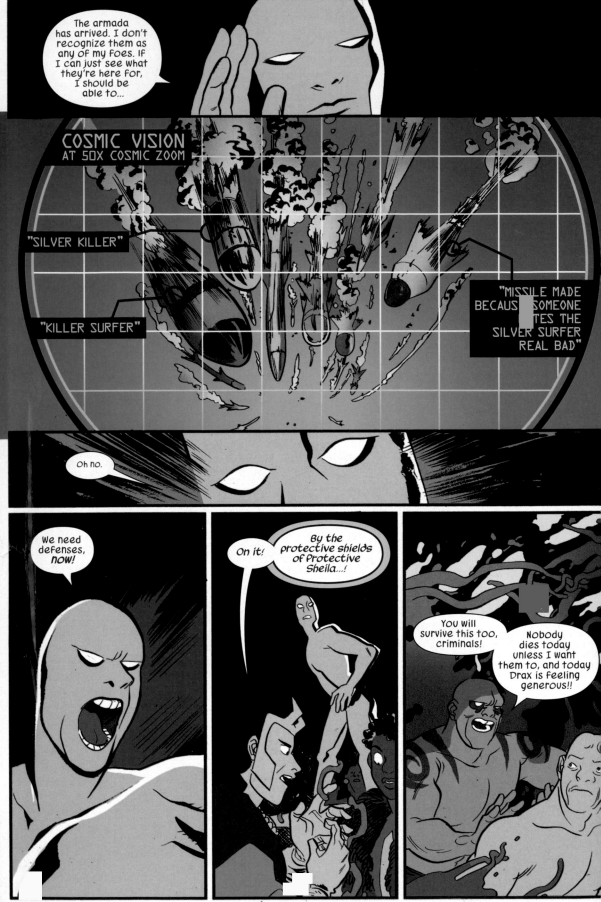

The armada has arrived. I don't recognize them as any of my foes. If I can just see what they're here for, I should be able to...

COSMIC VISION
AT 50X COSMIC ZOOM

"SILVER KILLER"

"KILLER SURFER"

"MISSILE MADE BECAUSE SOMEONE [HA]TES THE SILVER SURFER REAL BAD"

Oh no.

We need defenses, NOW!

On it!

By the protective shields of Protective Sheila...!

You will survive this too, criminals!

Nobody dies today unless I want them to, and today Drax is feeling generous!!

These people helpfully labeled their missiles with what they're thinking, in case the sentiment from firing hundreds of missiles at you isn't coming across clearly.

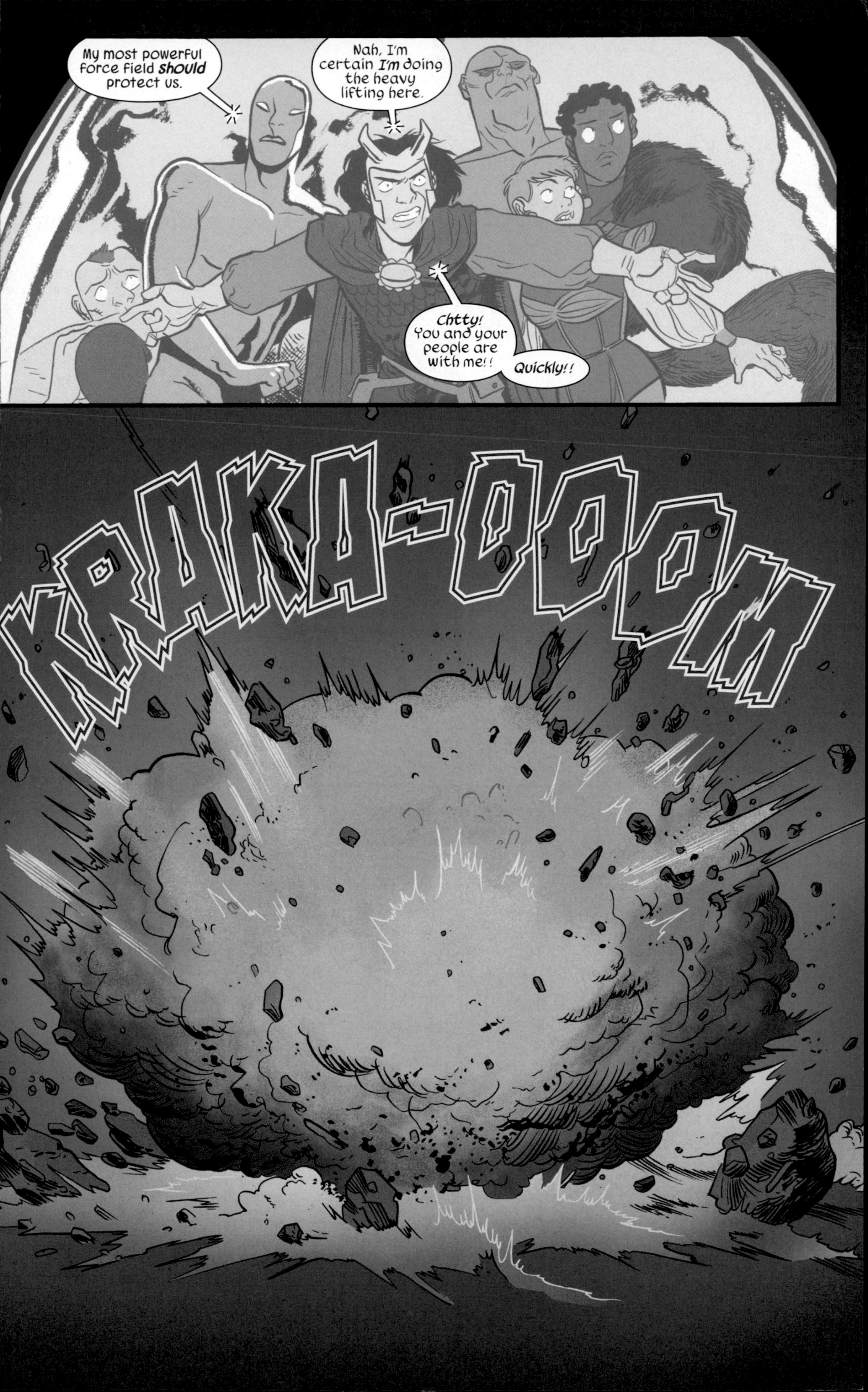
My most powerful force field *SHOULD* protect us.
Nah, I'm certain *I'm* doing the heavy lifting here.
Chtty! You and your people are with me!!
Quickly!!
KRAKA-DOOOM

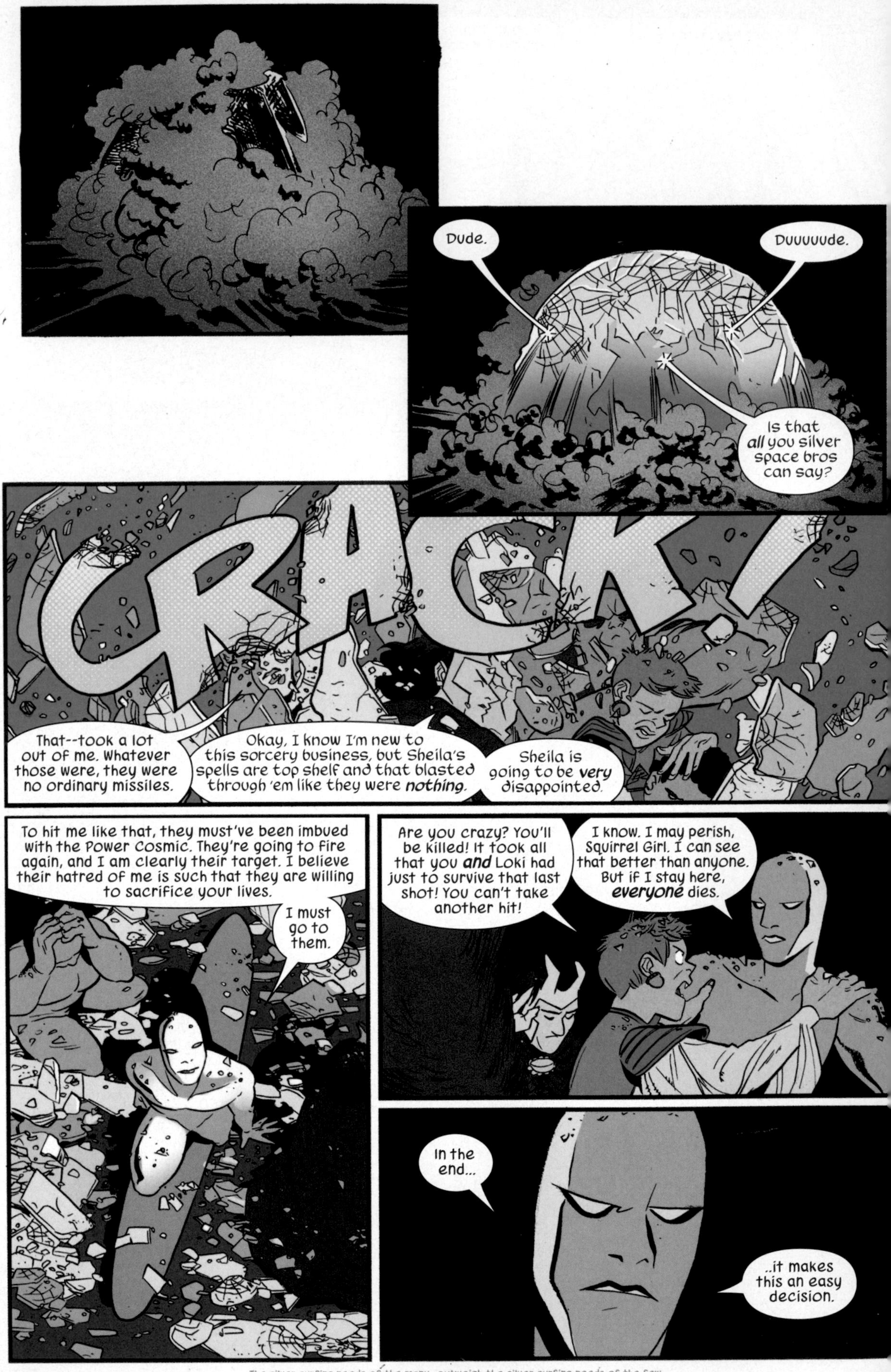
Dude.
Duuuuude.
Is that all you silver space bros can say?
CRACK!
That--took a lot out of me. Whatever those were, they were no ordinary missiles.
Okay, I know I'm new to this sorcery business, but Sheila's spells are top shelf and that blasted through 'em like they were nothing.
Sheila is going to be very disappointed.
To hit me like that, they must've been imbued with the Power Cosmic. They're going to fire again, and I am clearly their target. I believe their hatred of me is such that they are willing to sacrifice your lives.
I must go to them.
Are you crazy? You'll be killed! It took all that you and Loki had just to survive that last shot! You can't take another hit!
I know. I may perish, Squirrel Girl. I can see that better than anyone. But if I stay here, everyone dies.
In the end...
..it makes this an easy decision.

The silver surfing needs of the many...outweigh the silver surfing needs of the few.

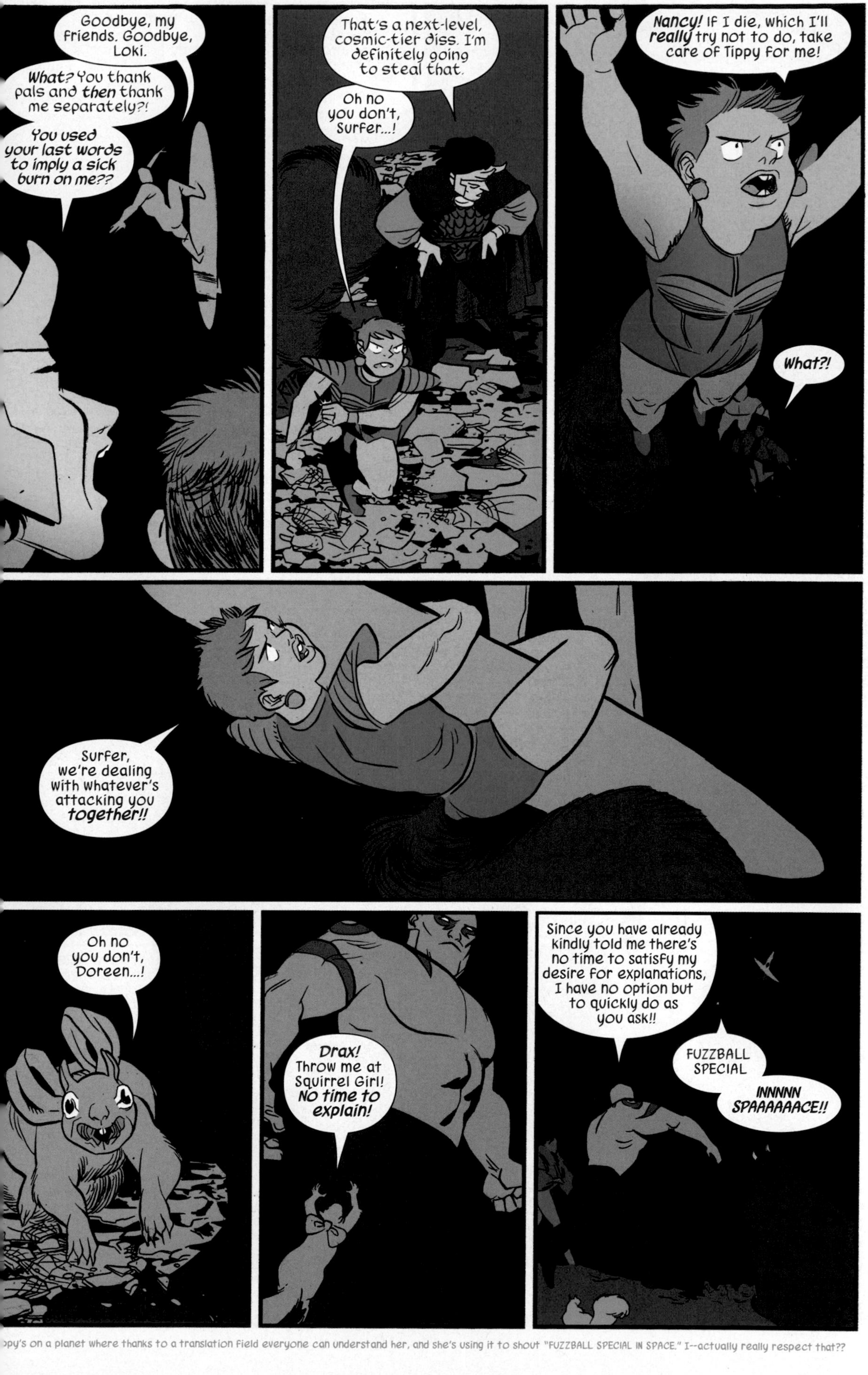
Goodbye, my friends. Goodbye, Loki.
What? You thank pals and then thank me separately?!
You used your last words to imply a sick burn on me??
That's a next-level, cosmic-tier diss. I'm definitely going to steal that.
Oh no you don't, Surfer...!
Nancy! If I die, which I'll really try not to do, take care of Tippy for me!
What?!
Surfer, we're dealing with whatever's attacking you together!!
Oh no you don't, Doreen...!
Drax! Throw me at Squirrel Girl! No time to explain!
Since you have already kindly told me there's no time to satisfy my desire for explanations, I have no option but to quickly do as you ask!!
FUZZBALL SPECIAL
INNNNN SPAAAAAACE!!

ppy's on a planet where thanks to a translation field everyone can understand her, and she's using it to shout "FUZZBALL SPECIAL IN SPACE." I--actually really respect that??

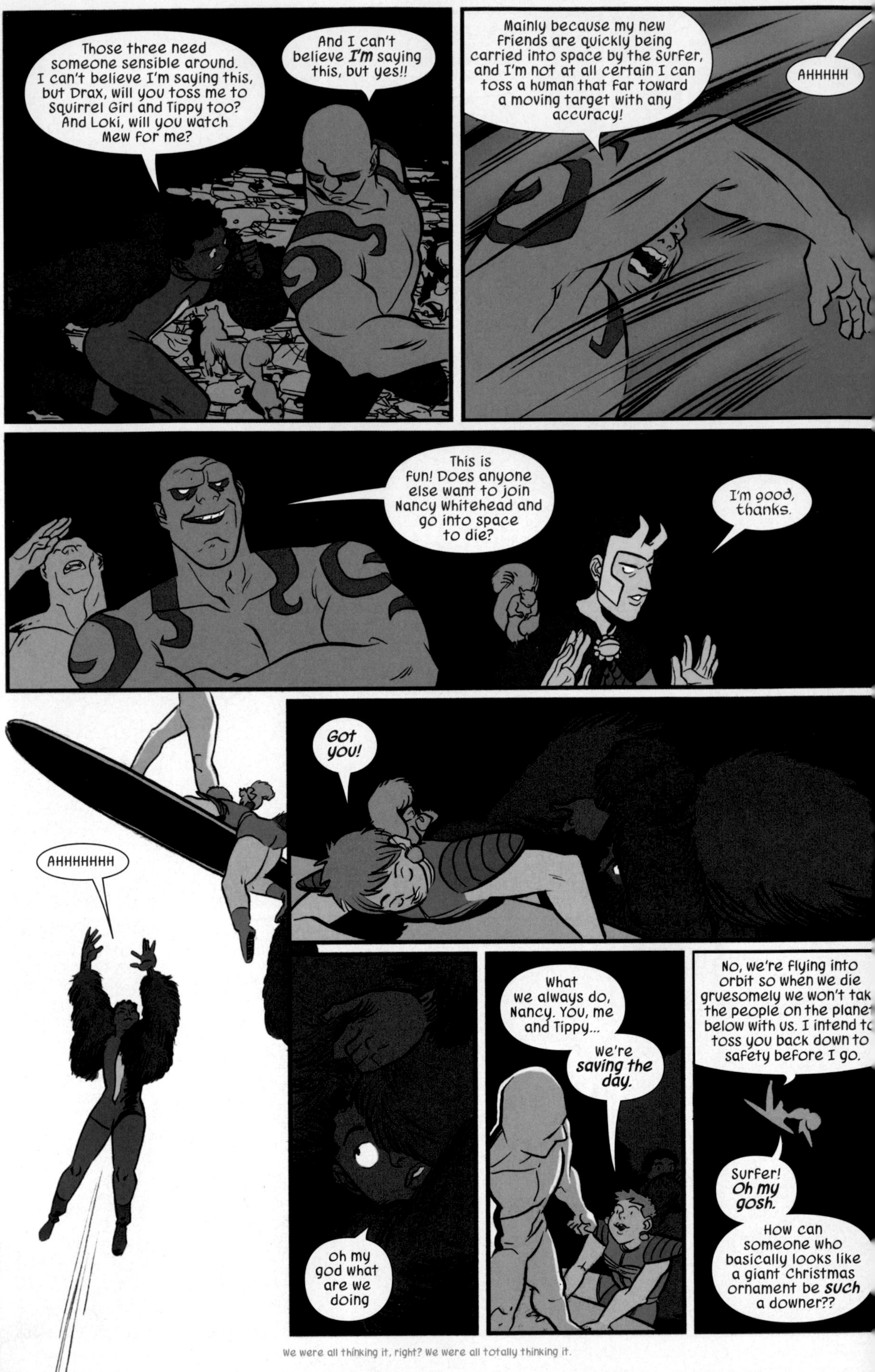
Those three need someone sensible around. I can't believe I'm saying this, but Drax, will you toss me to Squirrel Girl and Tippy too? And Loki, will you watch Mew for me?
And I can't believe *I'm* saying this, but yes!!
Mainly because my new friends are quickly being carried into space by the Surfer, and I'm not at all certain I can toss a human that far toward a moving target with any accuracy!
AHHHHH
This is fun! Does anyone else want to join Nancy Whitehead and go into space to die?
I'm good, thanks.
AHHHHHHH
Got you!
Oh my god what are we doing
What we always do, Nancy. You, me and Tippy...
We're *saving the day.*
No, we're flying into orbit so when we die gruesomely we won't tak the people on the plane below with us. I intend to toss you back down to safety before I go.
Surfer! *Oh my gosh.*
How can someone who basically looks like a giant Christmas ornament be *SUCH* a downer??

We were all thinking it, right? We were all totally thinking it.

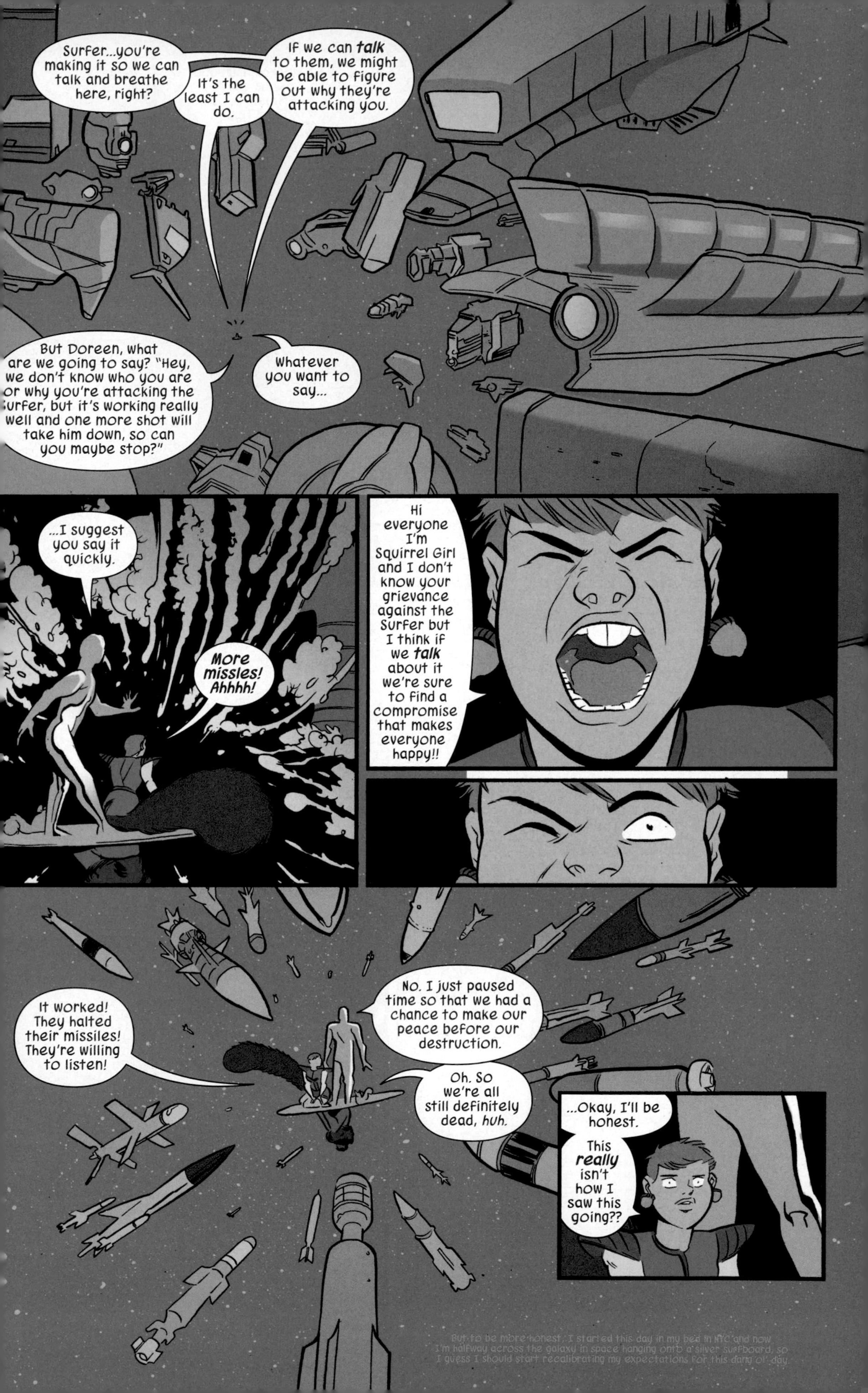
Surfer...you're making it so we can talk and breathe here, right?
It's the least I can do.
If we can *talk* to them, we might be able to figure out why they're attacking you.
But Doreen, what are we going to say? "Hey, we don't know who you are or why you're attacking the Surfer, but it's working really well and one more shot will take him down, so can you maybe stop?"
Whatever you want to say...
...I suggest you say it quickly.
More missles! Ahhhh!
Hi everyone I'm Squirrel Girl and I don't know your grievance against the Surfer but I think if we *talk* about it we're sure to find a compromise that makes everyone happy!!
It worked! They halted their missiles! They're willing to listen!
No. I just paused time so that we had a chance to make our peace before our destruction.
Oh. So we're all still definitely dead, *huh*.
...Okay, I'll be honest.
This *really* isn't how I saw this going??
But to be more honest, I started this day in my bed in NYC and now I'm halfway across the galaxy in space hanging onto a silver surfboard, so I guess I should start recalibrating my expectations for this dang ol' day.

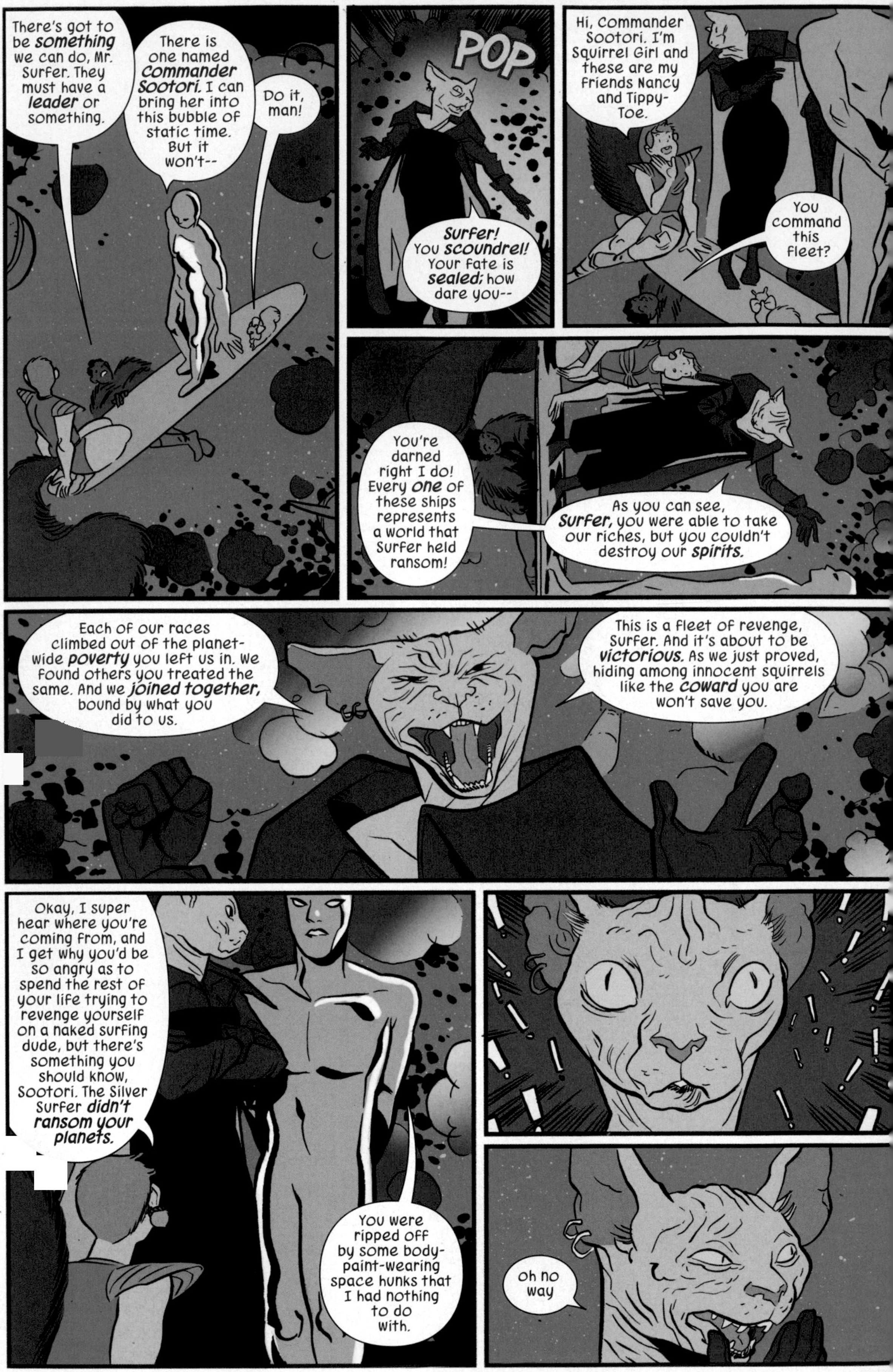
There's got to be something we can do, Mr. Surfer. They must have a leader or something.
There is one named Commander Sootori. I can bring her into this bubble of static time. But it won't--
Do it, man!
POP
Surfer! You scoundrel! Your fate is sealed; how dare you--
Hi, Commander Sootori. I'm Squirrel Girl and these are my friends Nancy and Tippy-Toe.
You command this fleet?
You're darned right I do! Every one of these ships represents a world that Surfer held ransom!
As you can see, Surfer, you were able to take our riches, but you couldn't destroy our spirits.
Each of our races climbed out of the planet-wide poverty you left us in. We found others you treated the same. And we joined together, bound by what you did to us.
This is a fleet of revenge, Surfer. And it's about to be victorious. As we just proved, hiding among innocent squirrels like the coward you are won't save you.
Okay, I super hear where you're coming from, and I get why you'd be so angry as to spend the rest of your life trying to revenge yourself on a naked surfing dude, but there's something you should know, Sootori. The Silver Surfer didn't ransom your planets.
You were ripped off by some body-paint-wearing space hunks that I had nothing to do with.
Oh no way

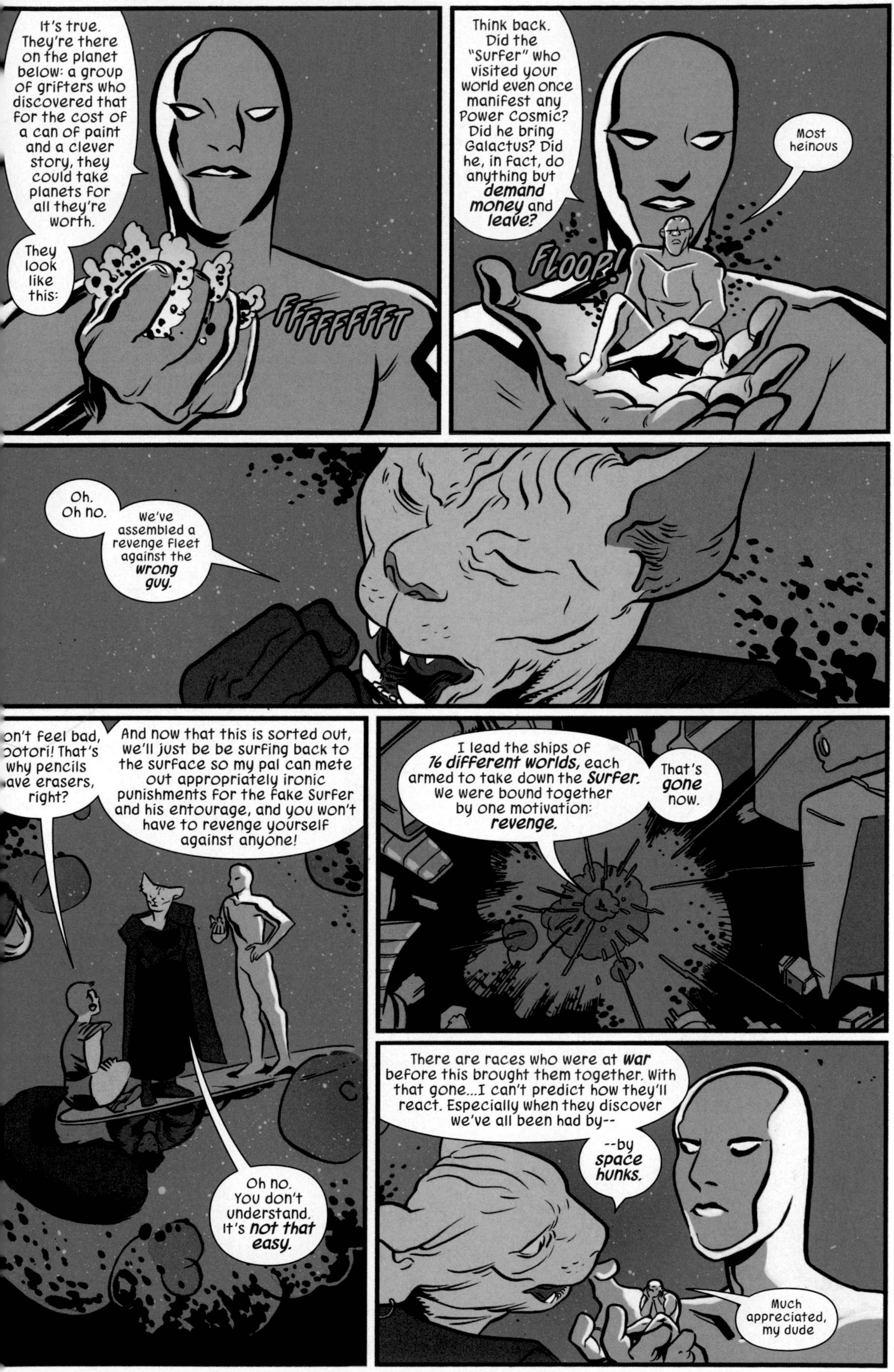
It's true. They're there on the planet below: a group of grifters who discovered that for the cost of a can of paint and a clever story, they could take planets for all they're worth.
They look like this:
FFFFFFFFT
Think back. Did the "Surfer" who visited your world even once manifest any Power Cosmic? Did he bring Galactus? Did he, in fact, do anything but **demand money** and **leave?**
FLOOP!
Most heinous
Oh. Oh no.
We've assembled a revenge fleet against the **wrong guy.**
on't feel bad, ootori! That's why pencils ave erasers, right?
And now that this is sorted out, we'll just be be surfing back to the surface so my pal can mete out appropriately ironic punishments for the fake Surfer and his entourage, and you won't have to revenge yourself against anyone!
Oh no. You don't understand. It's **not that easy.**
I lead the ships of **76 different worlds,** each armed to take down the **Surfer.** We were bound together by one motivation: **revenge.**
That's **gone** now.
There are races who were at **war** before this brought them together. With that gone...I can't predict how they'll react. Especially when they discover we've all been had by--
--by **space hunks.**
Much appreciated, my dude

I'm sorry, I forgot I'm billions of light-years away from Earth, and what I said must've sounded confusing. What I ***meant*** to say was "that's why our strange ***Earth*** pencils have strange ***Earth*** erasers."

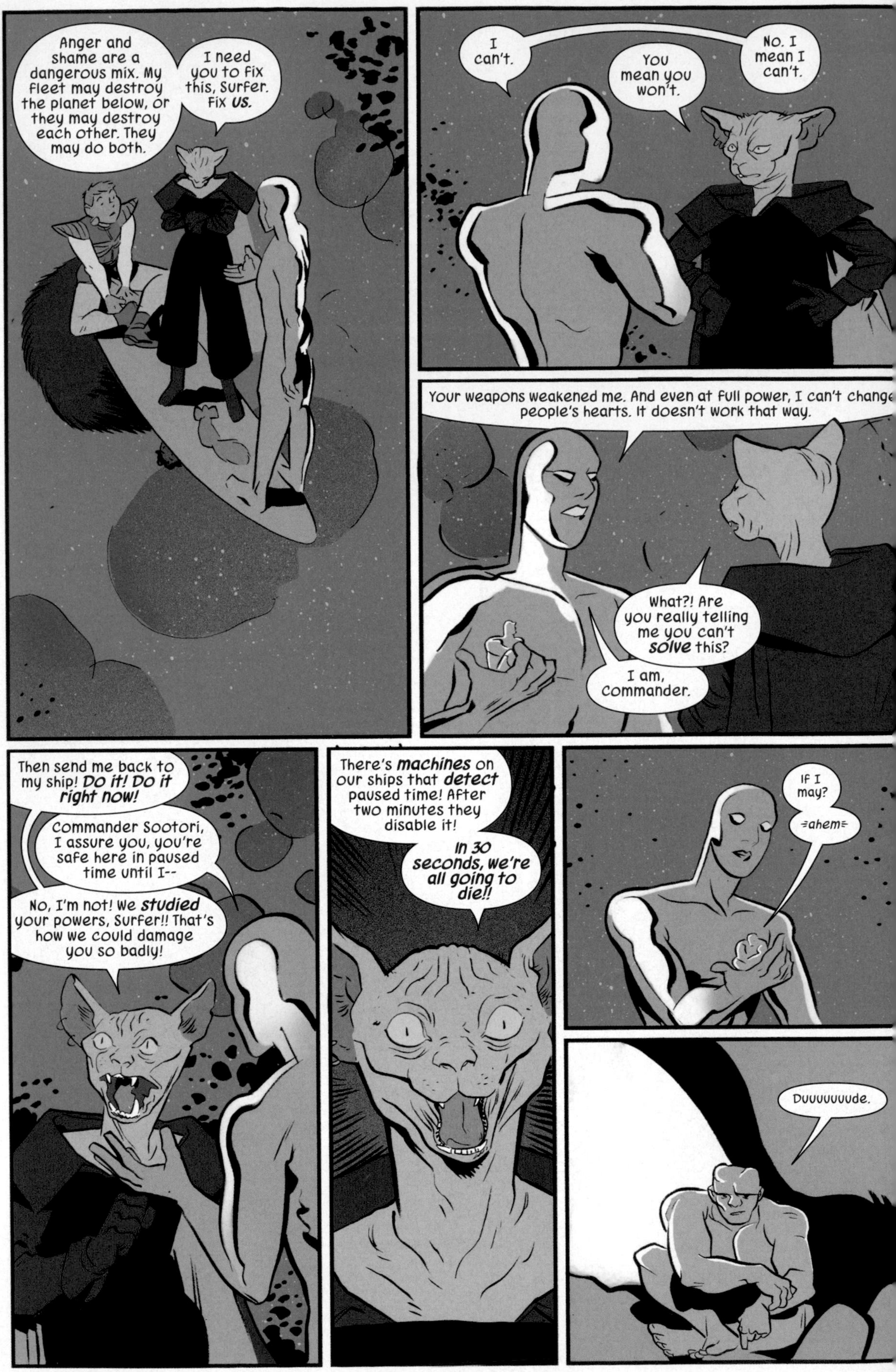
Anger and shame are a dangerous mix. My fleet may destroy the planet below, or they may destroy each other. They may do both.
I need you to fix this, Surfer. Fix *US.*
I can't.
You mean you won't.
No. I mean I can't.
Your weapons weakened me. And even at full power, I can't change people's hearts. It doesn't work that way.
What?! Are you really telling me you can't *solve* this?
I am, Commander.
Then send me back to my ship! *Do it! Do it right now!*
Commander Sootori, I assure you, you're safe here in paused time until I--
No, I'm not! We *studied* your powers, Surfer!! That's how we could damage you so badly!
There's *machines* on our ships that *detect* paused time! After two minutes they disable it!
In 30 seconds, we're all going to die!!
If I may?
=ahem=
Duuuuuuude.

SQUIRREL SCOUT ALERT!

'e've got a special treat for you this month, squirrel fans! You remember QUIRREL MEETS WORLD, the first Squirrel Girl middle-grade novel from estselling authors Shannon Hale and Dean Hale, right? Well get ready for ie action-packed sequel! On March 6, THE UNBEATABLE SQUIRREL GIRL: FUZZY, 2 FURIOUS hits the shelves! And if you haven't read SQUIRREL IEETS WORLD yet, we forgive you—we'll even let you go out and pick up our very own copy now to catch up.

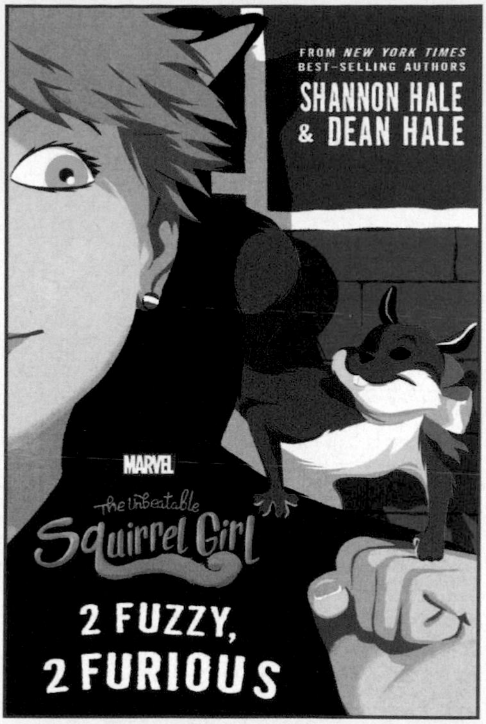

FROM NEW YORK TIMES BEST-SELLING AUTHORS
SHANNON HALE & DEAN HALE
MARVEL
The Unbeatable Squirrel Girl
2 FUZZY, 2 FURIOUS

o what's this new book all about? Check it out:

oreen Green, age fourteen, is a little too busy wiping out crime in her suburban ew Jersey neighborhood to focus on her overdue homework. That's because ie also happens to be Squirrel Girl, a bushy-tailed, squirrel-powered Super ero! After foiling the nefarious plot of an amateur Super Villain, Squirrel Girl is ially finding her groove--and group texting with the Avengers, like, all the time. oreen, on the other hand, is still trying to navigate friendships, evil teachers, id all the pitfalls that come with middle school. (Seriously, it's complicated.)

ı announcement goes out that sends waves of excitement through the ommunity: There's a new mall opening on the border of Shady Oaks and eighboring town Listless Pines, and they all get to vote on the mall's mascot! veryone goes wild over the election . . . a little too wild, if you ask Squirrel Girl id her BHFF (Best Human Friend Forever), Ana Sofia. Soon the two towns are war--even the trusty Squirrel Scouts are going berserk. Is there something nister at work in Shady Oaks? Something that has less to do with quality iopping choices and more to do with world domination? And will Squirrel Girl able to unleash the furry paws of justice in time to save the day?

nd if that doesn't pique your interest, maybe this excerpt will! ehold: CHAPTER ONE.

The night was as cool as glass. Streetlamps cast orange cones of light onto the pavement, but everything in between them was darkness. Darkness so thick, you could gnaw on it.

Squirrel Girl perched atop a streetlamp, twelve feet above the quiet suburban street. Not the kind of place where you'd expect to run into a laser-blasting maniacal villain. Squirrel Girl's bushy tail twitched. Her keen eyes raked the darkness for any sign of that dastardly ne'er-do-well.

Then her phone buzzed.

Finally! All this waiting was getting super-boring. She went for the phone, scooping it out of a pouch on her utility belt. But a bunch of loose cashews spilled out of the pouch, and she fumbled the phone.

"Dang it," she said, diving headfirst off the streetlamp. She caught the cell just before it could crack against the sidewalk, twisting to land on her feet.

On her phone was a text from Ana Sofía Arcos Romero, her BHFF.[1]

ANA SOFÍA
Are you hidden?

Squirrel Girl checked her surroundings in a super-sleuthy sleuth way. She was standing directly under the streetlamp, orange light falling over her as bright as a fire.

She leaped up into the shadowy branches of an oak tree in someone's front yard.

SQUIRREL GIRL
Yep of course I'm the most hiddenest. Soooo sleuthy. Very stakeout

1 That means Best Human Friend Forever. By the way, this is me, Doreen Green, aka Squirrel Girl. I'm just gonna read along with you and let you know my thoughts down here in the footnotes, deal?

ANA SOFÍA
Good cuz u know sometimes u forget to hide and the bad guys see u and no more element of surprise

SQUIRREL GIRL
Who me?

ANA SOFÍA
Anyway the Squirrel Scouts on the north end of the park saw Laser Lady going down Bungalow Row so she might be coming your way

SQUIRREL GIRL
Ooh is that what we're calling her cuz i was thinking maybe Light Emitting Desperado? You know, cuz it would be LED? Or Smashlight maybe? Zap Mama?[2]

ANA SOFÍA
She kinda named herself already. In the way that she's running around shouting I AM LASER LADY

SQUIRREL GIRL
Good way of making sure no one messes up your name

ANA SOFÍA
Maybe I should try it. Mr Hanks calls me Annie Sophie. The pain is real

SQUIRREL GIRL
I'm so on board with u walking into first period and shouting I AM LASER LADY and u know what that's a pretty good name now that I think about it

A voice cut against the cool-as-glass night, sharp as a diamond. Squirrel Girl wasn't sure if normal humans would be able to tell what the distant voice was saying, but her slightly-betterthan-your-average-person's hearing most definitely identified the words "I AM LASER LADY! FEAR ME!"

2 Or Luster Lass, Lumen the Undying, Captain Incandescent, Flicker Filly, the Inexcusable Glare, Sun Bunny. . . . If it were me, I would just go as "Shine," but I would also pretend to be Australian, because with the accent people might think my name is "Shoin," which would confuse and discomfit them, and that's what crime is all about, right?

SO BE SURE TO PICK UP 2 FUZZY, 2 FURIOUS NEXT MONTH AT A BOOKSTORE NEAR YOU. AND NOW, ON TO OUR LETTERS!

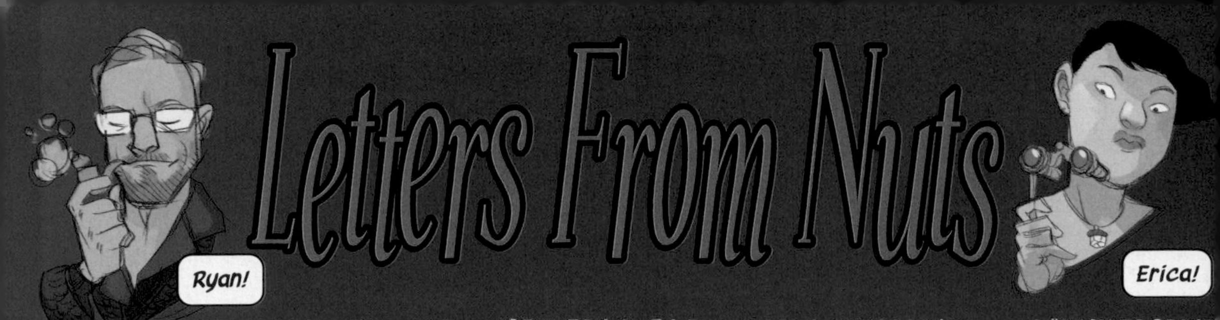
Letters From Nuts
Ryan!
Erica!

Send letters to mheroes@marvel.com or 135 W 50th St, 7th Floor, New York, NY 10020 (Please mark "OKAY TO PRINT

Hi Squirrel Friends,

I am 8 years old, and I like squirrels because they look really cute and they like nuts just like I do.

At my house, we have a lot of squirrels that like to eat our pumpkins after Halloween. We put the pumpkins in the backyard so the squirrels can have a feast. Sometimes they chew holes in them, so they can climb inside and eat the seeds in a little squirrel-sized pumpkin house. Here is a picture.

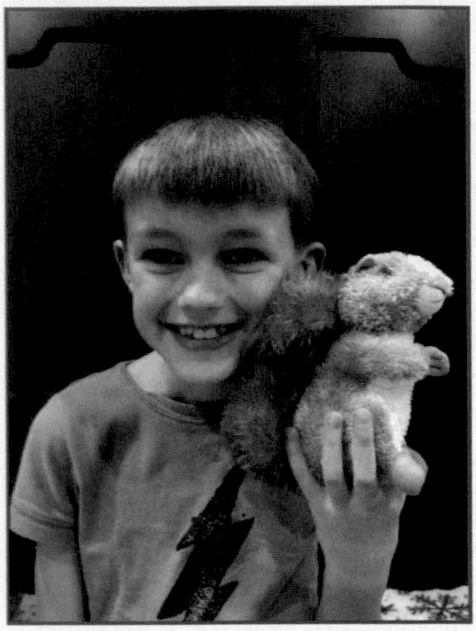

One squirrel likes to take all the pumpkins for himself, so I named him Greedy Squirrel. Another one is named Sneaky Squirrel. Sneaky comes to grab some seeds when Greedy isn't looking.

I think Tippy-Toe probably likes pumpkins, too. Does she?

Your friend,

Dash Sutton
Louisville, Kentucky

RYAN: Greedy Squirrel! I love it. It's my understanding, Dash, that Tippy-Toe DOES like pumpkins, for she is pretty indiscriminate when it comes to food: she'll gobble it all. She and I are a lot alike, actually! I'm sure Greedy Squirrel and Sneaky Squirrel appreciate you looking out for them and sharing your extra nuts with them. I know I would! Thanks for the awesome letter (and photo)!

ERICA: Also, after Halloween is the perfect time to give them snacks because they're fattening up for winter. So, good job!

To the Squirrel Folks,

First off, I am only 12 years old and I love, love, LOVE your comic! How the heck do you DO it?! I recently read the "Character Comics" issue (STOP MESSING WITH ME LOKI), the Doc Doom/time-travel story line (NEVER PUT FRIENDSHIP IN QUOTES DOOM, LET THAT BE YOUR LESSON) and the Ratatoskr storyline. (I LOVE how you portray Ratatoskr, Erica. I could conceivably see her in a future Magnus Chase graphic novel, which YOU MUST DO, ERICA.) Anyway, I really like your comic and now I love squirrels forevermore. I also recently got into *Lumberjanes* too, so that's TWO great comics being read right now!

Best wishes,
Lola

RYAN: Thank you, Lola! Some of your favorite comics are some of MY favorite comics, so this is working out great. You asked how we do it, so here is the SECRET RECIPE FOR SQUIRREL GIRL COMICS: I sit around and stare off into space trying to figure out what sort of adventure Squirrel Girl could go on, and when that doesn't work I call up our editor Wil or Erica and we chat about things and come up with some crazy ideas, then I just write 'em up in script format and everyone else does the hard work! THE END.

ERICA: Pretty much the secret to doing anything creative really is to just do it. It's a very unsatisfying answer, I know!

Good evening! I cannot lie: Learning to count along with Count (heh, I just caught that, nice) Nefaria was rad and I am now MORE THAN MILDLY FASCINATED with monomanual mathematics, but I must also admit that when the question of counting to ten on one hand arose, I was 100% expecting SG to bust out some ASL (American Sign Language, not, as could easily be assumed, American Squirrel Language) in which it is possible to count to literally ALL THE NUMBERS on one hand. Honestly, as a fan of ASL I've been hoping to see SG use some since she was shown how NOT to use it in the first issue #3, although that WAS, by complete coincidence, the correct sign for Galactus. I'm new to Marvel and capes comics in general but seem to recall that Hawkeye is deaf and that Deadpool has been shown signing with him; any chanc our SG will learn? She seems like she' love to find a whole new community t talk to, and I know they'd love to get t know her. Thanks for the amazing storie and TELL TIPPY-TOE I SAID WHAT U

Qapla
Casey W. Hil

RYAN: I love ASL! It's something studied years ago, and me and m wife ended up using it for COVER COMMUNICATION at parties. We ca now signal GO HOME as a question t each other to figure out when we'd lik to leave, without being rude enoug to discuss it audibly! It's amazing an we're basically spies. But I used binar in this issue mainly because it fit wi the theme better. In the USG middle grade novel by (I'm proud to say, m awesome friends) Shannon and Dea Hale, a younger Squirrel Girl has a frien named Ana Sofía who is deaf, and the use ASL (and texting) to communica all the time. There's even a speci sign for Squirrel Girl that they invente It's stuff that I'd like to find a way t incorporate into the comic, but un then I really recommend you check o the book – it's called *The Unbeatab Squirrel Girl: Squirrel Meets World* an as you now know, there's a sequ coming out soon called *The Unbeatab Squirrel Girl: 2 Fuzzy, 2 Furiou*

ERICA: Oh god, I'm seeing 50-pan pages in the future because TH ONE likes to talk and if eac panel is a word--boy howd

Hi again, Ryan and Erica and everyone!

First, congrats on the Eisner! You continues to be my favorite comic. Ar thanks for running my letter and pho back in issue #17! I promise that I am on a little bit smug about it. Second, I have question for you/fellow readers. Ironical given my enthusiasm for Squirrel Girl, m dad has a serious squirrel problem. H has a live trap that he's used since I wa a kid, but squirrels keep getting into h house--he's caught and released 12 th year--and they keep coming back. This because he had a huge walnut tree in h yard for about 30 years, and even thou he had it removed a few years ago, the are several thousand walnuts hidden around the yard and in the foundation the house. Recently, he went down to t basement and discovered two squirre ɘlling at each other. Then they yelled : him. I guess...he was interrupting an ıportant conversation? Now squirrels ·e chewing through the expanding foam ɘ's used to seal his foundation, and this ɜst week, he found walnuts hidden in s bed. (Um. Is this a threat or a peace 'fering?) Any advice on getting these ɉuirrels to stay outside, short of finding ıd disposing of every hidden walnut?

Thanks!

Emily Tobin
Young Adult Librarian
Rock Island Public Library

YAN: I don't actually have much dvice for encouraging squirrels to ve somewhere else! You'd think that ith the source of nuts gone they'd ventually move on--perhaps THAT'S hat was being so loudly discussed in ɔur basement--but I have heard that ɘtting a pet cat can keep the squirrels way (they don't always get along as ell as Tippy and Mew do). On the plus de: your dad now gets free walnuts very time he goes to bed, right?

RICA: Well the first thing is--how are e squirrels getting into the house? nd whatever that is and patch it up. ıere are some decent rodent-proof ɜtching materials. I can't say why ey're still coming exactly, but urban ɉuirrels stick to areas they know, ıd if they have a hole to come into e house they're FOR SURE going to ɔ where it's warm and there are no 'edators. Anyway, the moral of the ory is sometimes you have to live in ɜd places and you learn a lot about dent-proofing.

ɜar Erica and Ryan,

'er since we got our daughter Eva QUIRREL GIRL #16 she's been a die-hard n, bringing the whole family along for the le. So for her 5th birthday, which also ɪppens to be Halloween, there was only e option!

Keep up the awesome work,
Jon, Jill, Eva and Delia Land

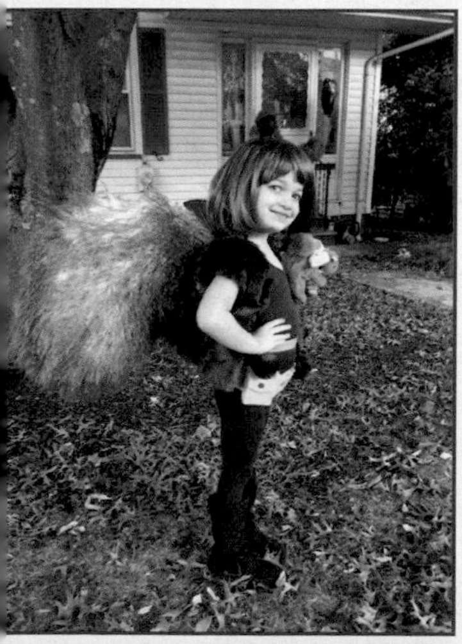

RYAN: Eva: WHAT AN AMAZING COSTUME! And also: What an amazing birthday. I have friends born around Christmas and they're generally down on it, but a Hallowe'en birthday means presents AND candy. I see no possible downsides!!

ERICA: AH! That is a great costume!!!! That tail is so good.

Dear Ryan and Erica,

In most of the volumes, I've noticed that Doreen's headband either gets sliced in half or disintegrated and then she shows up really soon afterward with her headband on, so does she have, like, a secret stash of headbands that she keeps in her jacket? And also a little sewing kit for when her jacket gets torn open? Because Iron Man is a billionaire and can totally afford to get new suits whenever, but Doreen is a college student. So I was just wondering if she has a discreet inside pocket on her jacket with a sewing kit and a few pairs of extra ears, and if so, is the pocket shaped like an acorn? And now that she has a bikini, where does she keep all her nuts and extra headbands? Also, PLEASE keep making your awesome Squirrel Girl comics!

Phoebe B.

RYAN: I believe she's got a few duplicates, but I also believe Nancy is conscripted to do costume repair. I also believe that Doreen's excuse, should anyone ever pull open her dresser drawer and find a whole bunch of Squirrel Girl headbands stuffed inside, is that she's "considering getting big into cosplay, but for just one character." It will throw everyone off the trail!

ERICA: Well, basically it's the easiest thing to remake, which is why it's her most consistent costume element. If the jacket burns off, well, you've gotta buy a new jacket. Plain headbands sell in packs for a few bucks, and if you're in a rush you just take an oval of stiff material like felt, pinch and fold at the bottom and glue it down--do it again and you've got two ears.

Next Issue:

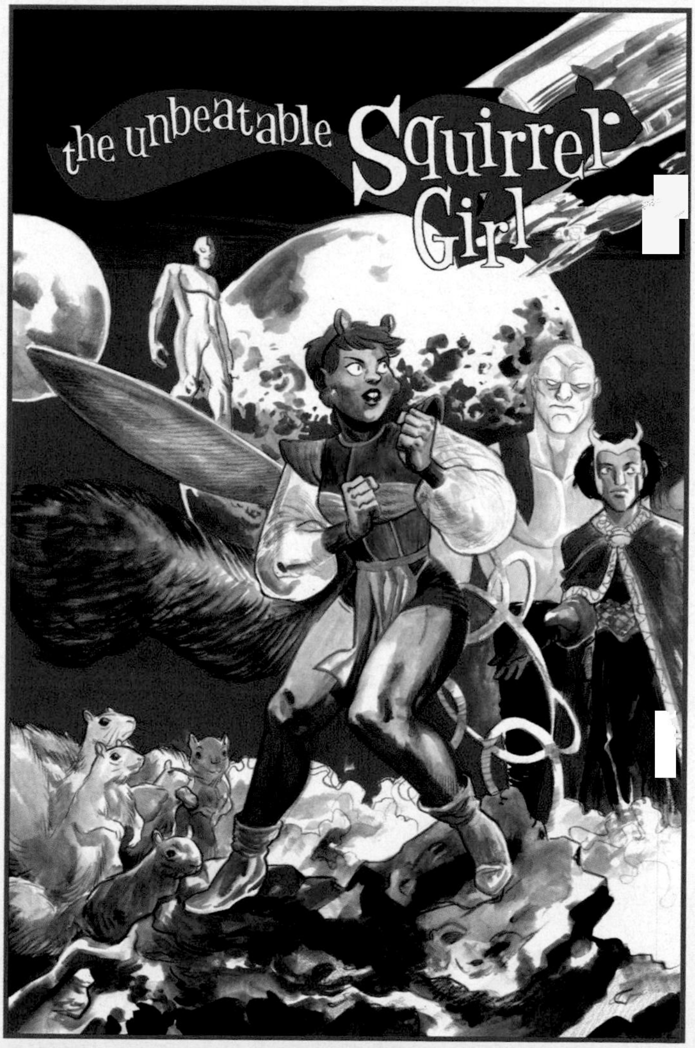

the unbeatable Squirrel Girl

ıttention, Squirrel Scouts! Make sure to check out our production blog, **unbeatablesquirrelgirl.tumblr.com**, where we post behind-the-scenes stuff on how the book gets made, along with all sorts of cool things *you* make: fan art, cosplay, whatever!

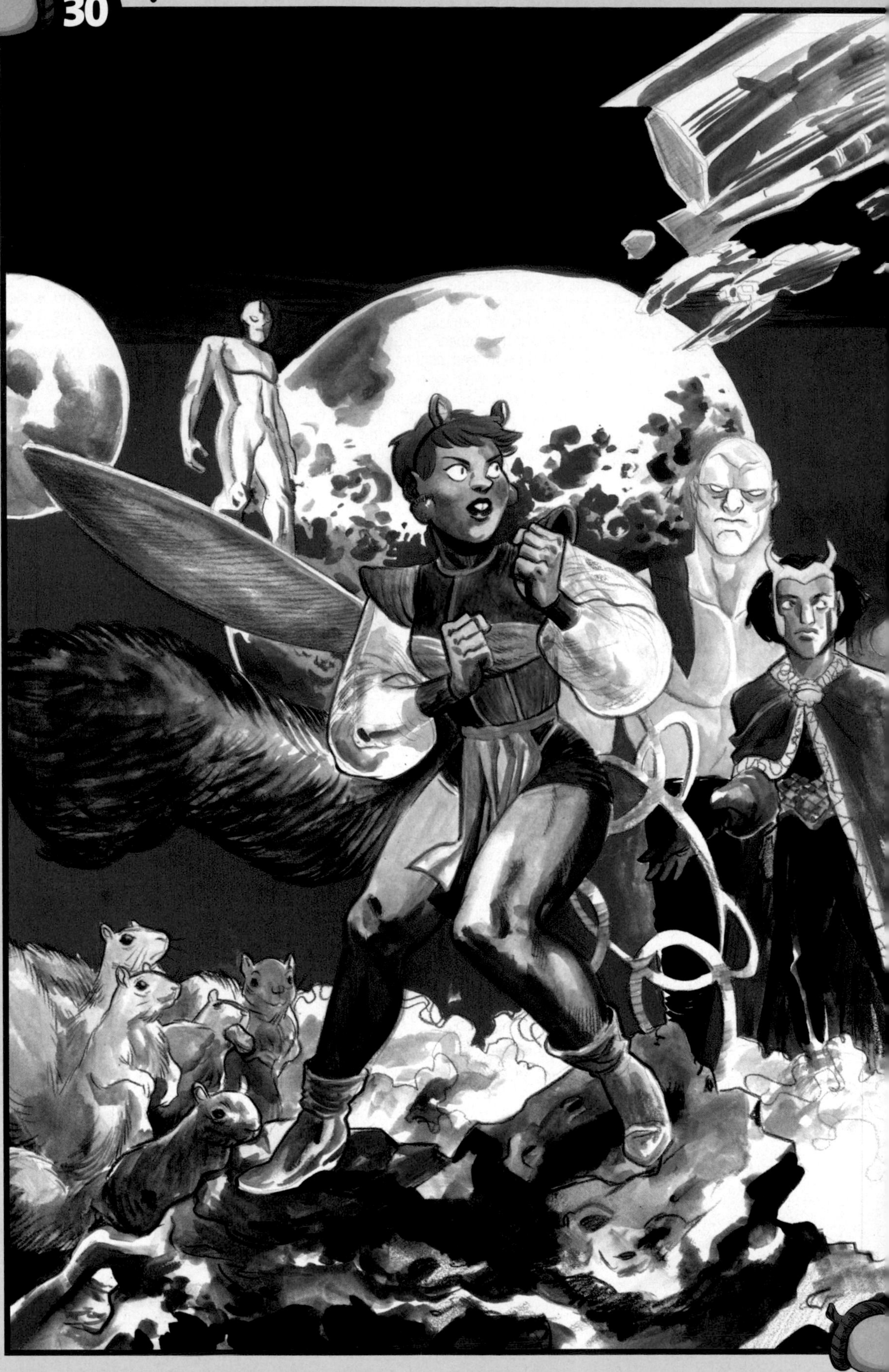

oreen Green isn't just a second-year computer science student: she secretly also has all the powers of both squirrel and rl! She uses her amazing abilities to fight crime **and** be as awesome as possible. You know her as...**The Unbeatable Squirrel Girl!**
Find out what she's been up to, with...

Squirrel Girl *in a nutshell*

Squirrel Girl @unbeatablesg
Hi, I'm Squirrel Girl! I first came to space on the trail of the kidnappers of my roommate, and for reasons that don't need exploring at this juncture, I've remained, attached as a liaison with the Silver Surfer!

Nancy W. @sewwiththeflo
@unbeatablesg NICE.

Squirrel Girl @unbeatablesg
@sewwiththeflo RIGHT? This way, all my new followers will know my current status quo!

Nancy W. @sewwiththeflo
@unbeatablesg Although I will point out that this really just announces to criminals that you're not on Earth right now, so if they wanted to do a crime...now would be ideal.

Squirrel Girl @unbeatablesg
@sewwiththeflo Oh I'm certain no criminal would be stupid enough to do that!

Squirrel Girl @unbeatablesg
@sewwiththeflo Especially given how I met, befriended, AND embarked on a cosmic road trip with BOTH Drax and Loki in an afternoon...

Squirrel Girl @unbeatablesg
@sewwiththeflo ...saved an entire planet of SPACE SQUIRRELS from being scammed by fake body-paint-wearing Silver Surfers...

Squirrel Girl @unbeatablesg
@sewwiththeflo ...actually fought the REAL Silver Surfer EARLIER THIS VERY DAY...

Squirrel Girl @unbeatablesg
@sewwiththeflo ...survived an attack from angry space aliens who thought the REAL Silver Surfer was the one who scammed THEM...

Squirrel Girl @unbeatablesg
@sewwiththeflo ...and managed to get a data signal here on the OTHER SIDE OF THE GALAXY...

Squirrel Girl @unbeatablesg
@sewwiththeflo ...let's just say that given ALL THAT, I think the smart criminals know not to do any crimes right now!!

Nancy W. @sewwiththeflo
@unbeatablesg Squirrel Girl, this was a very inspiring set of accomplishments that I'm sure would make anyone think twice about stealing diamonds...

Squirrel Girl @unbeatablesg
@sewwiththeflo thank you, thank you

Nancy W. @sewwiththeflo
@unbeatablesg ...if only you'd posted it publicly, instead of in a series of replies to me that only people who follow us both can see.

Squirrel Girl @unbeatablesg
@sewwiththeflo AW MAN!! well no way am i copying and pasting all that on my phone, it'll take forever

Squirrel Girl @unbeatablesg
@sewwiththeflo one sec I have the perfect solution

Squirrel Girl @unbeatablesg
Hi, criminals! Follow unrelated civilian Nancy "@sewwiththeflo" Whitehead so you can see our conversations! I think you'll find them REAL ELUCIDATING!

Squirrel Girl @unbeatablesg
@sewwiththeflo done

Nancy W. @sewwiththeflo
@unbeatablesg Great! A bunch of new LITERAL CRIMINALS following me. I just love to be #online!!!

Squirrel Girl @unbeatablesg
@sewwiththeflo anyway we should probably get back to the space battle where space aliens fired space missiles at us!! P.S.: shoutout to all our criminal mutuals

search!

#sootori
#1800slady
#spacebathrooms
#powercosmic
#squirrelholodecks

This is just SOME of what Doreen's been posting--all these handles are real! Follow **@unbeatablesg** for more!

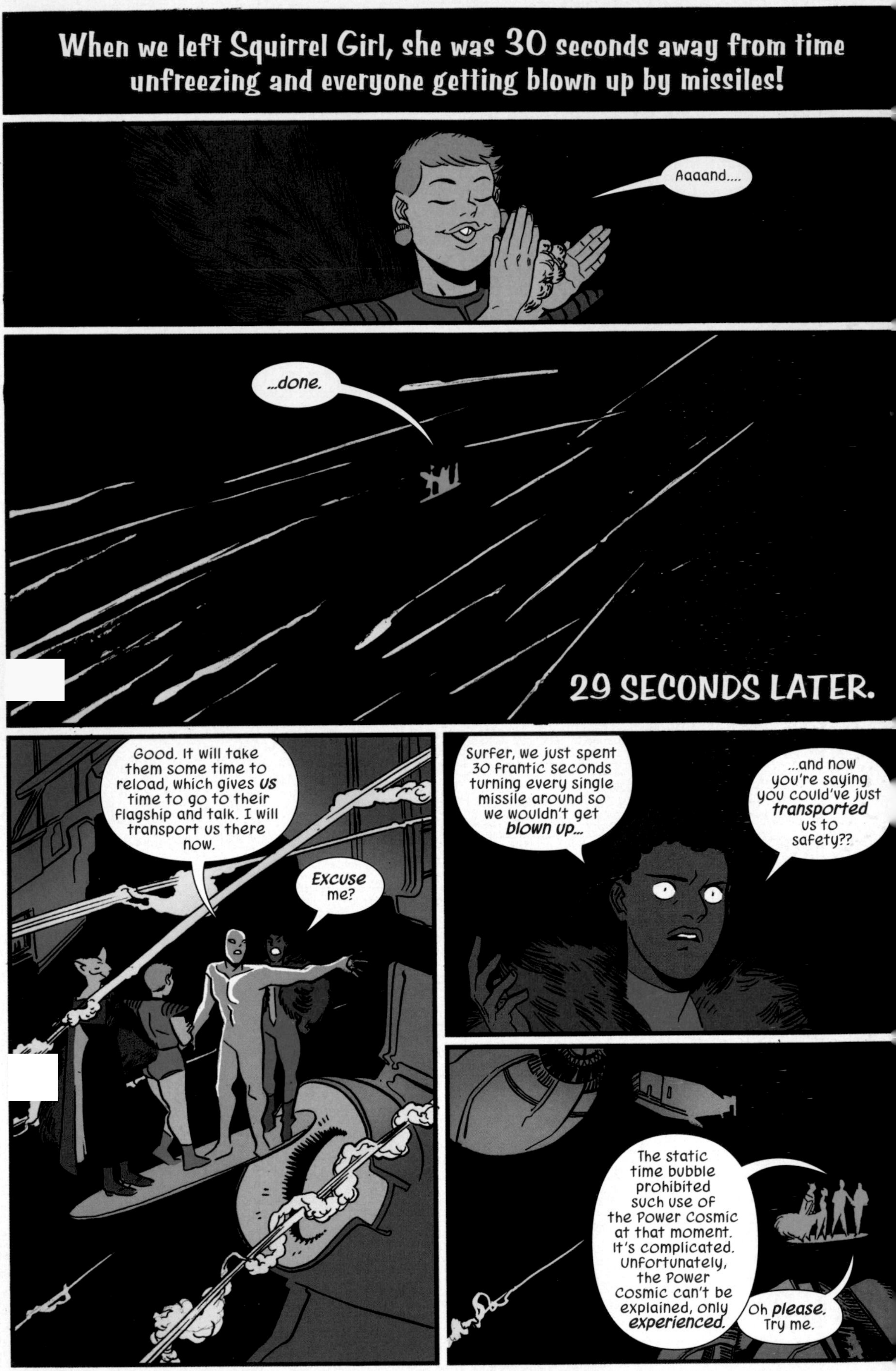
When we left Squirrel Girl, she was 30 seconds away from time unfreezing and everyone getting blown up by missiles!
Aaaand....
...done.
29 SECONDS LATER.
Good. It will take them some time to reload, which gives *us* time to go to their flagship and talk. I will transport us there now.
Excuse me?
Surfer, we just spent 30 frantic seconds turning every single missile around so we wouldn't get *blown up*...
...and now you're saying you could've just *transported* us to safety??
The static time bubble prohibited such use of the Power Cosmic at that moment. It's complicated. Unfortunately, the Power Cosmic can't be explained, only *experienced.*
Oh *please.* Try me.

When I was a kid I was worried that I might one day develop the mutant ability to stop time but *not* the ability to start it up again, and then me and everyone else would be frozen in amber forever! I finally decided the only thing to do was never try to stop time. *And I never have. You're welcome.*

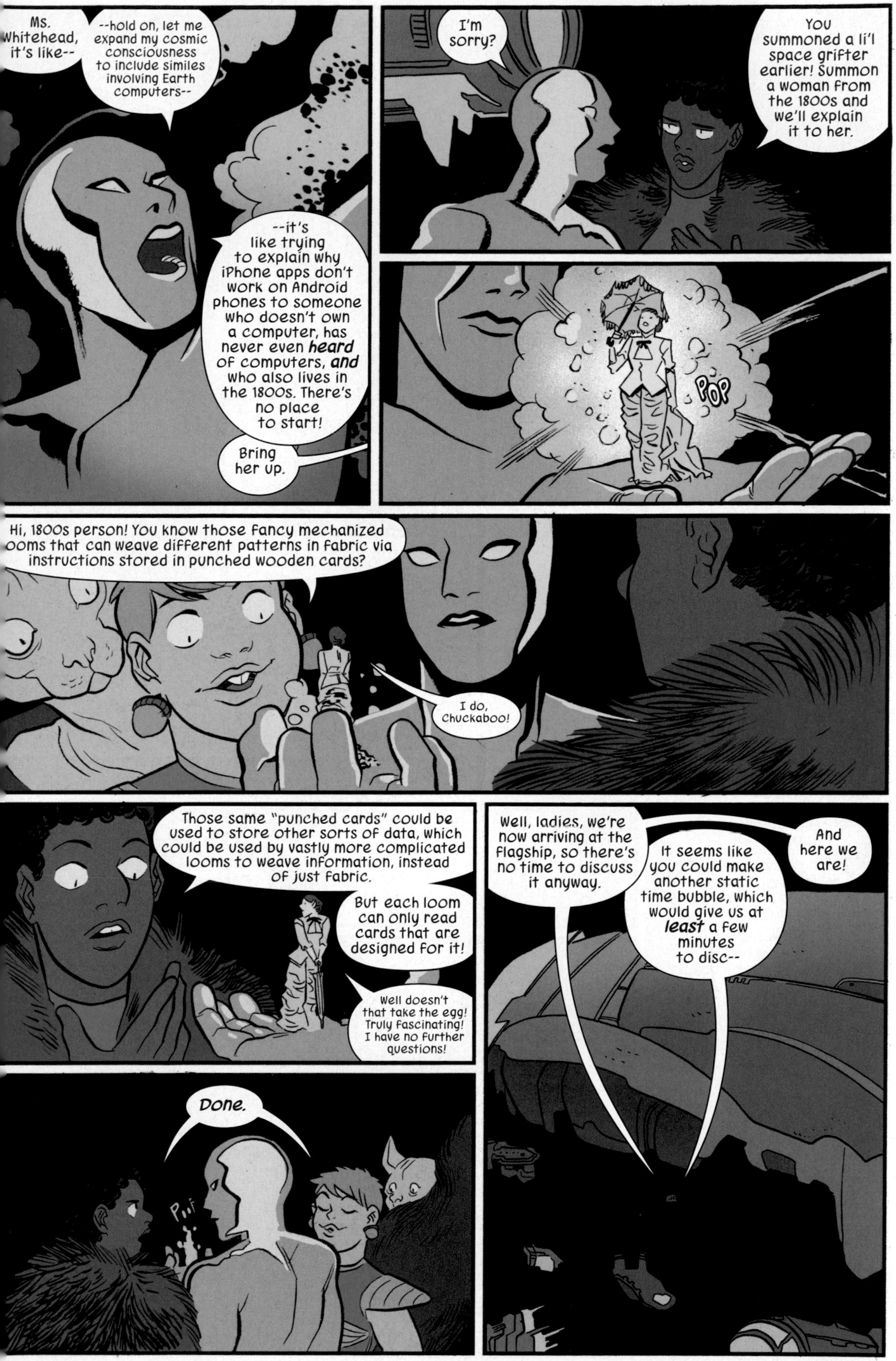
Ms. Whitehead, it's like--
--hold on, let me expand my cosmic consciousness to include similes involving Earth computers--
--it's like trying to explain why iPhone apps don't work on Android phones to someone who doesn't own a computer, has never even **heard** of computers, **and** who also lives in the 1800s. There's no place to start!
Bring her up.
I'm sorry?
You summoned a li'l space grifter earlier! Summon a woman from the 1800s and we'll explain it to her.
POP
Hi, 1800s person! You know those fancy mechanized ooms that can weave different patterns in fabric via instructions stored in punched wooden cards?
I do, Chuckaboo!
Those same "punched cards" could be used to store other sorts of data, which could be used by vastly more complicated looms to weave information, instead of just fabric.
But each loom can only read cards that are designed for it!
Well doesn't that take the egg! Truly fascinating! I have no further questions!
Done.
Poof
Well, ladies, we're now arriving at the flagship, so there's no time to discuss it anyway.
It seems like you could make another static time bubble, which would give us at **least** a few minutes to disc--
And here we are!

Cut for space is a bit where Nancy and Doreen explain to the Silver Surfer how that simile doesn't even work, because of emulators that allow you to run programs that were designed for certain hardware and instruction sets on other hardware and instruction sets, during which the Silver Surfer nods and smiles very politely.

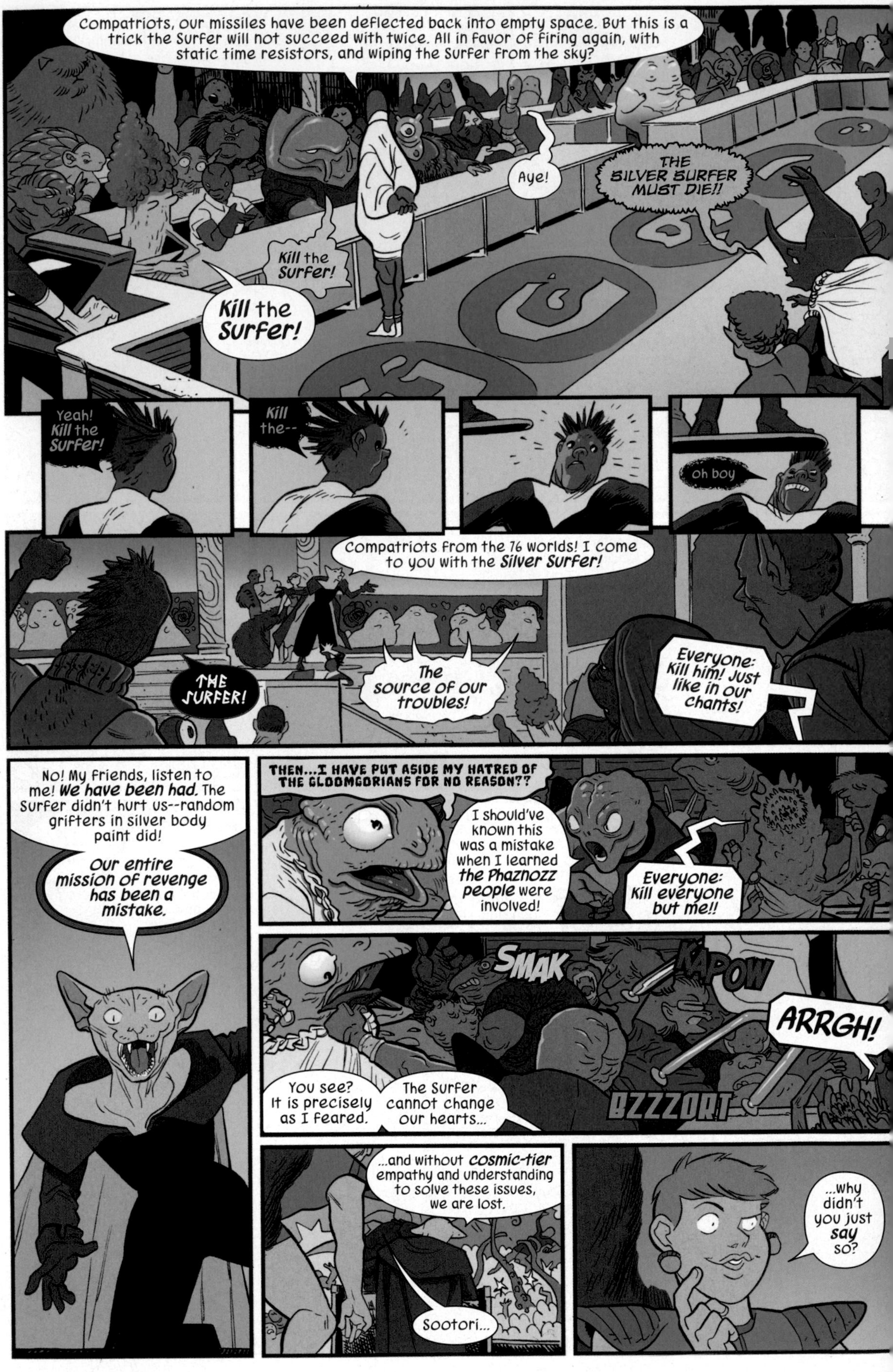

Compatriots, our missiles have been deflected back into empty space. But this is a trick the Surfer will not succeed with twice. All in favor of firing again, with static time resistors, and wiping the Surfer from the sky?
Aye!
THE SILVER SURFER MUST DIE!!
Kill the Surfer!
Kill the Surfer!
Yeah! Kill the Surfer!
Kill the--
Oh boy
Compatriots from the 76 worlds! I come to you with the Silver Surfer!
THE SURFER!
The source of our troubles!
Everyone: Kill him! Just like in our chants!
No! My friends, listen to me! We have been had. The Surfer didn't hurt us--random grifters in silver body paint did!
Our entire mission of revenge has been a mistake.
THEN...I HAVE PUT ASIDE MY HATRED OF THE GLOOMGORIANS FOR NO REASON??
I should've known this was a mistake when I learned the Phaznozz people were involved!
Everyone: Kill everyone but me!!
SMAK
KAPOW
ARRGH!
BZZZORT
You see? It is precisely as I feared.
The Surfer cannot change our hearts...
...and without cosmic-tier empathy and understanding to solve these issues, we are lost.
Sootori...
...why didn't you just say so?

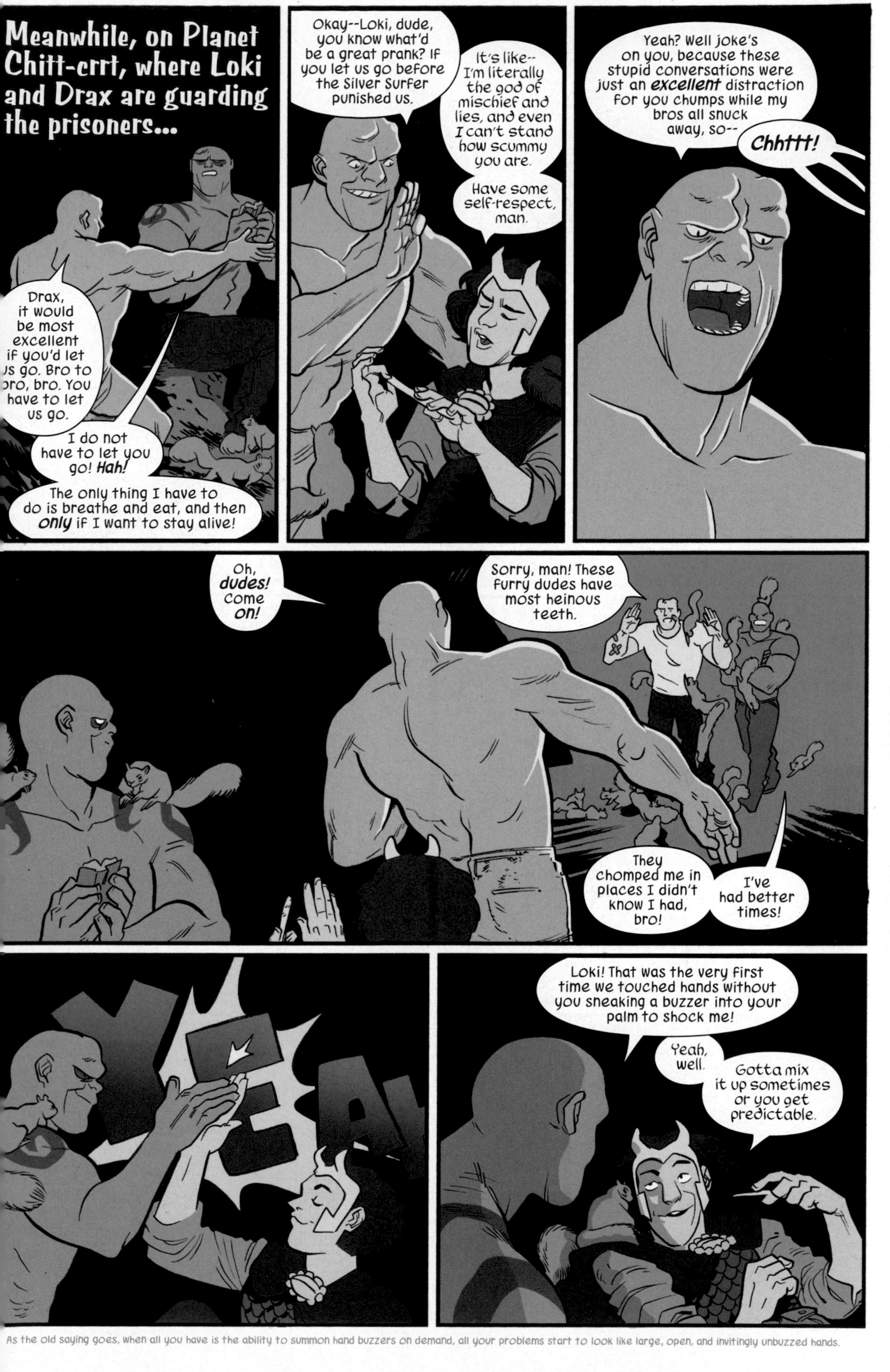
Meanwhile, on Planet Chitt-crrt, where Loki and Drax are guarding the prisoners...
Drax, it would be most excellent if you'd let us go. Bro to bro, bro. You have to let us go.
I do not have to let you go! Hah!
The only thing I have to do is breathe and eat, and then only if I want to stay alive!
Okay--Loki, dude, you know what'd be a great prank? If you let us go before the Silver Surfer punished us.
It's like-- I'm literally the god of mischief and lies, and even I can't stand how scummy you are.
Have some self-respect, man.
Yeah? Well joke's on you, because these stupid conversations were just an excellent distraction for you chumps while my bros all snuck away, so--
Chhttt!
Oh, dudes! Come on!
Sorry, man! These furry dudes have most heinous teeth.
They chomped me in places I didn't know I had, bro!
I've had better times!
Loki! That was the very first time we touched hands without you sneaking a buzzer into your palm to shock me!
Yeah, well.
Gotta mix it up sometimes or you get predictable.

As the old saying goes, when all you have is the ability to summon hand buzzers on demand, all your problems start to look like large, open, and invitingly unbuzzed hands.

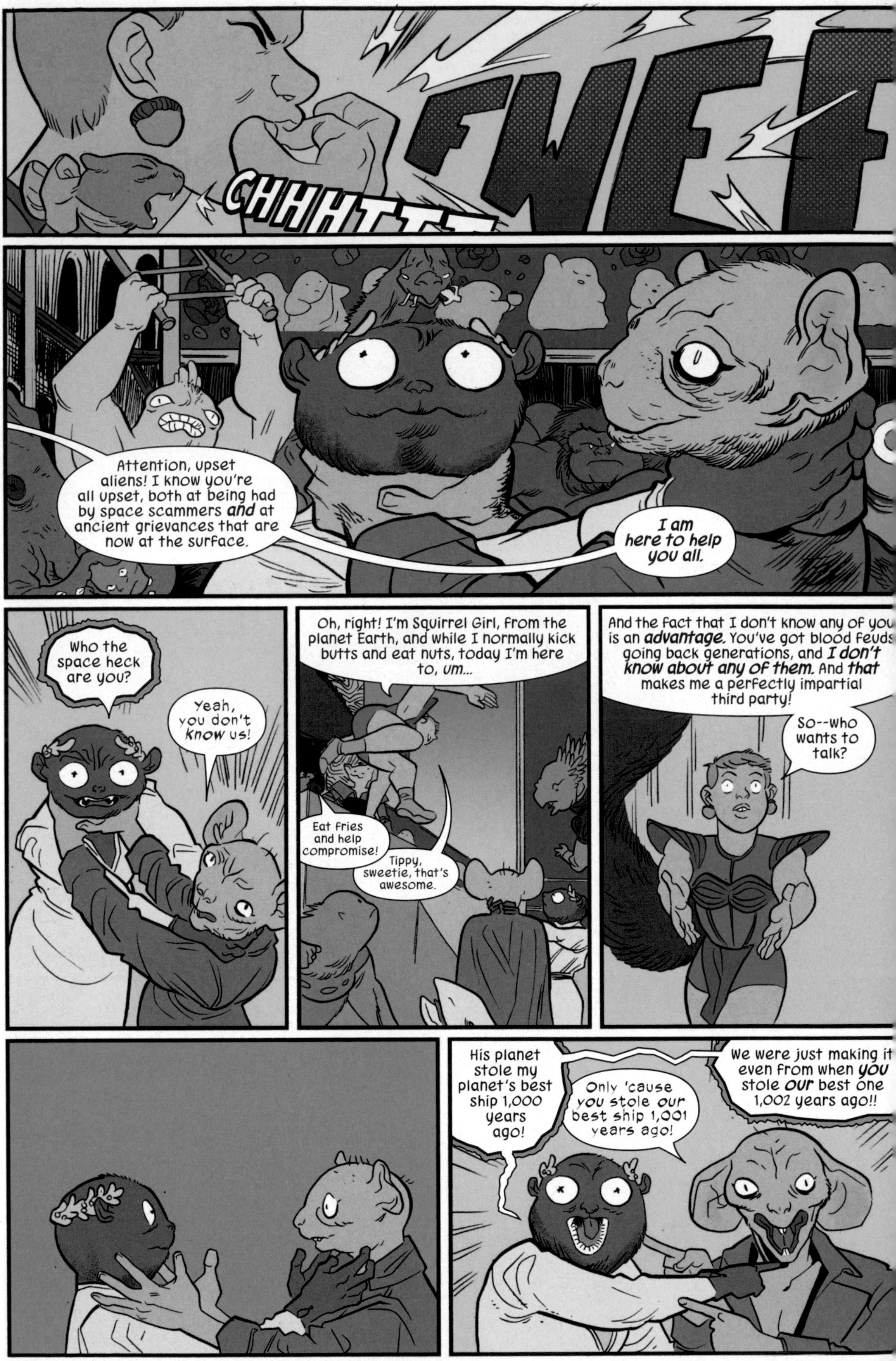

Attention, upset aliens! I know you're all upset, both at being had by space scammers *and* at ancient grievances that are now at the surface.
I am here to help you all.
Who the space heck are you?
Yeah, you don't *know* us!
Oh, right! I'm Squirrel Girl, from the planet Earth, and while I normally kick butts and eat nuts, today I'm here to, um...
Eat fries and help compromise!
Tippy, sweetie, that's awesome.
And the fact that I don't know any of you is an *advantage*. You've got blood feuds going back generations, and *I don't know about any of them.* And *that* makes me a perfectly impartial third party!
So--who wants to talk?
His planet stole my planet's best ship 1,000 years ago!
Only 'cause *you* stole *our* best ship 1,001 years ago!
We were just making it even from when *you* stole *our* best one 1,002 years ago!!

I don't know what aliens argue about, but I bet it's who stole whose spaceship first. I have read a lot of books about space and I am here to say that the scientific consensus definitely points in this direction.

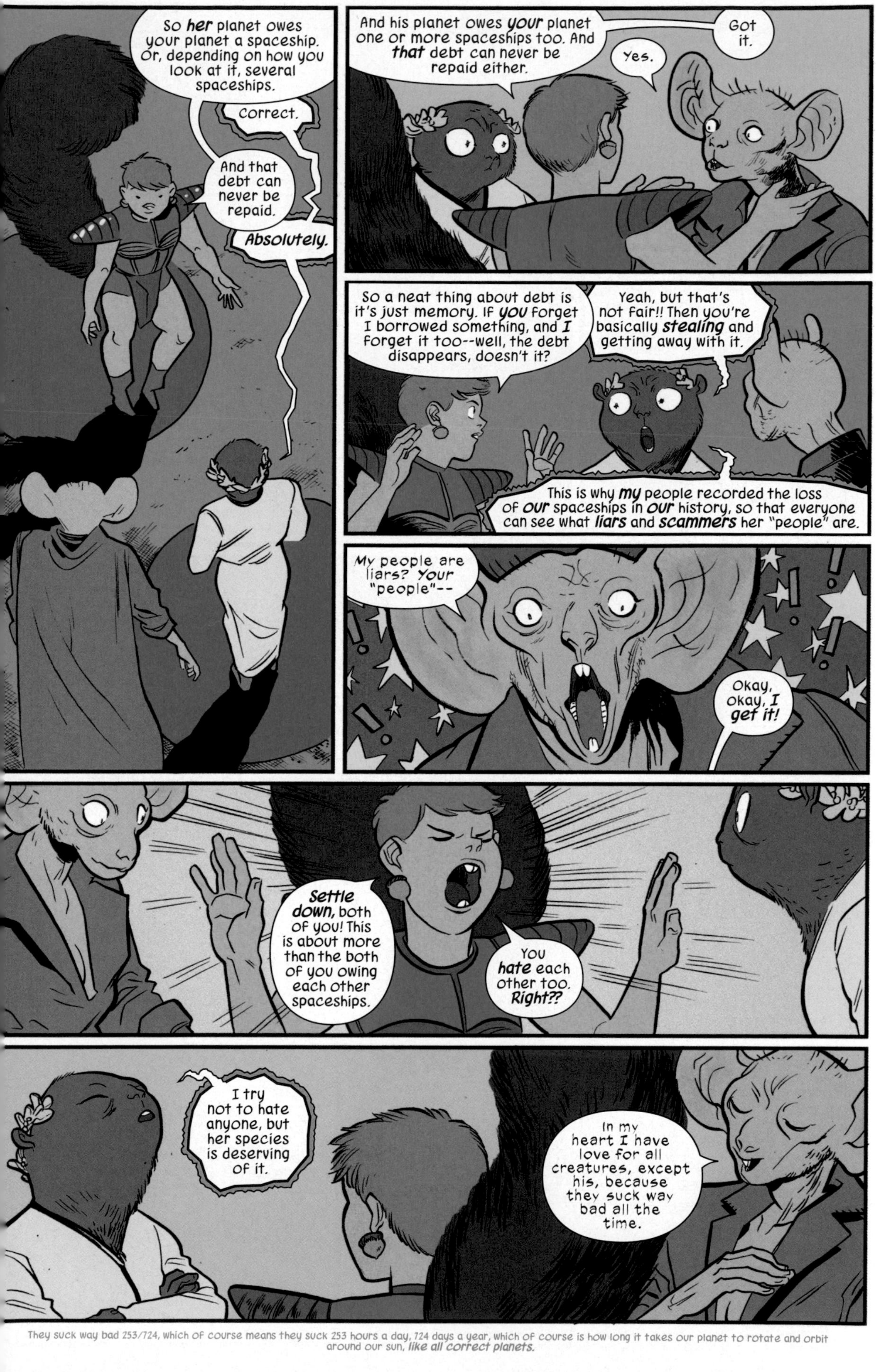
So *her* planet owes your planet a spaceship. Or, depending on how you look at it, several spaceships.
Correct.
And that debt can never be repaid.
Absolutely.
And his planet owes *your* planet one or more spaceships too. And *that* debt can never be repaid either.
Yes.
Got it.
So a neat thing about debt is it's just memory. If *you* forget I borrowed something, and *I* forget it too--well, the debt disappears, doesn't it?
Yeah, but that's not fair!! Then you're basically *stealing* and getting away with it.
This is why *my* people recorded the loss of *our* spaceships in *our* history, so that everyone can see what *liars* and *scammers* her "people" are.
My people are liars? *Your* "people"--
Okay, okay, *I get it!*
Settle down, both of you! This is about more than the both of you owing each other spaceships.
You *hate* each other too. *Right??*
I try not to hate anyone, but her species is deserving of it.
In my heart I have love for all creatures, except his, because they suck way bad all the time.

They suck way bad 253/724, which of course means they suck 253 hours a day, 724 days a year, which of course is how long it takes our planet to rotate and orbit around our sun, *like all correct planets.*

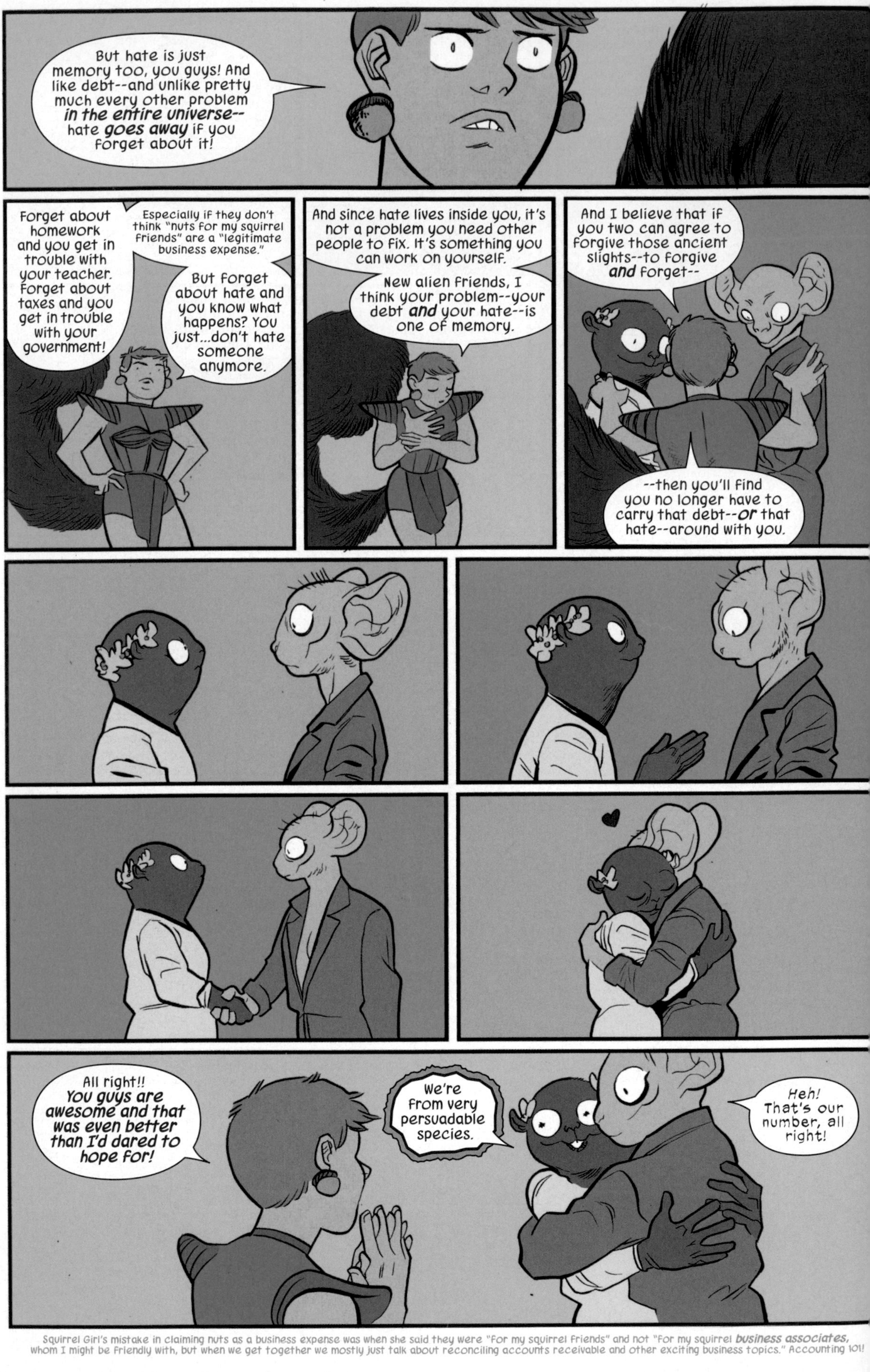
But hate is just memory too, you guys! And like debt--and unlike pretty much every other problem *in the entire universe--* hate *goes away* if you forget about it!
Forget about homework and you get in trouble with your teacher. Forget about taxes and you get in trouble with your government!
Especially if they don't think "nuts for my squirrel friends" are a "legitimate business expense."
But forget about hate and you know what happens? You just...don't hate someone anymore.
And since hate lives inside you, it's not a problem you need other people to fix. It's something you can work on yourself.
New alien friends, I think your problem--your debt *and* your hate--is one of memory.
And I believe that if you two can agree to forgive those ancient slights--to forgive *and* forget--
--then you'll find you no longer have to carry that debt--*or* that hate--around with you.
All right!! *You guys are awesome and that was even better than I'd dared to hope for!*
We're from very persuadable species.
Heh! That's our number, all right!

Squirrel Girl's mistake in claiming nuts as a business expense was when she said they were "For my squirrel friends" and not "For my squirrel *business associates,* whom I might be friendly with, but when we get together we mostly just talk about reconciling accounts receivable and other exciting business topics." Accounting 101!

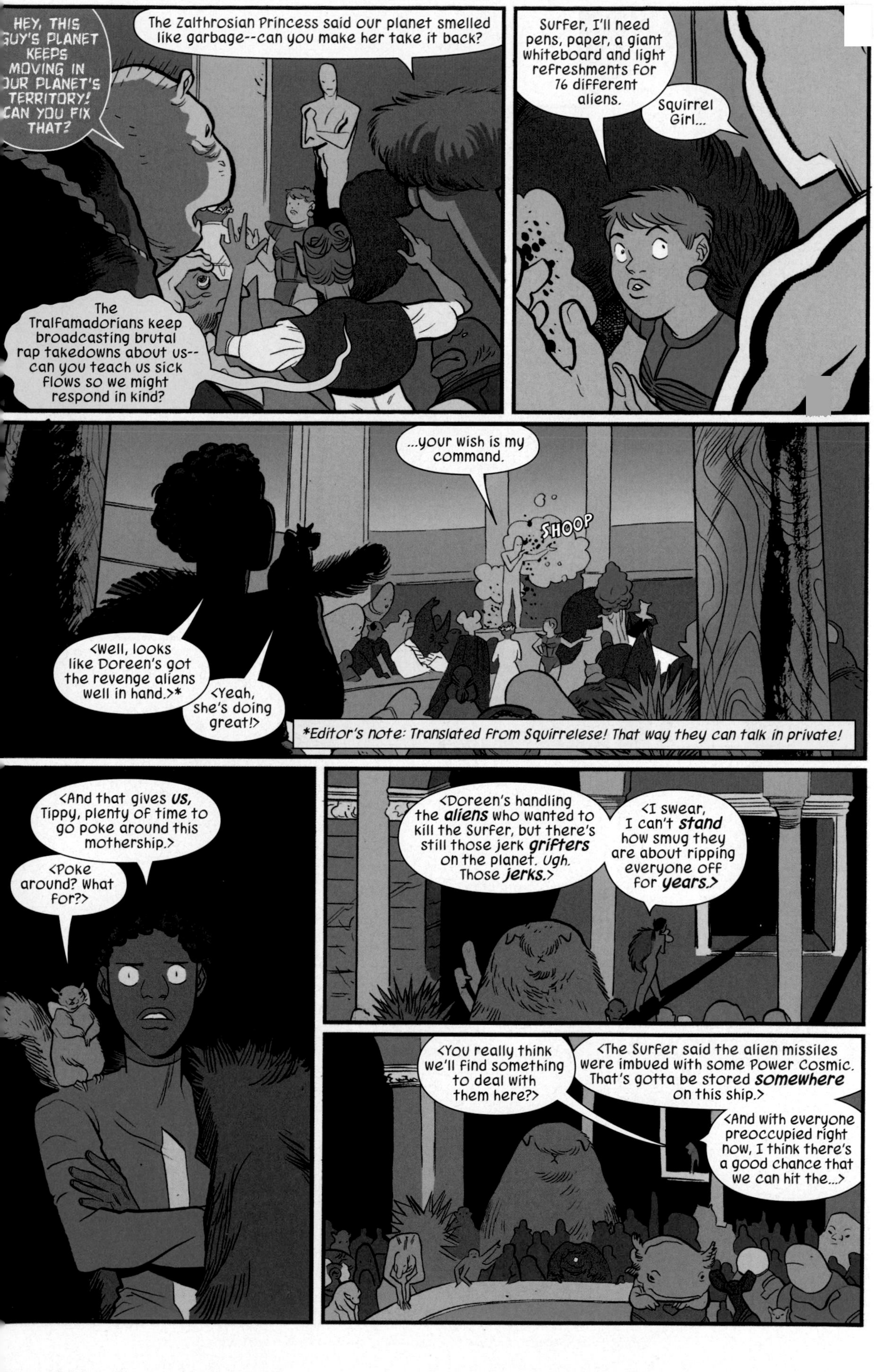
HEY, THIS GUY'S PLANET KEEPS MOVING IN OUR PLANET'S TERRITORY! CAN YOU FIX THAT?
The Zalthrosian Princess said our planet smelled like garbage--can you make her take it back?
The Tralfamadorians keep broadcasting brutal rap takedowns about us--can you teach us sick flows so we might respond in kind?
Surfer, I'll need pens, paper, a giant whiteboard and light refreshments for 76 different aliens.
Squirrel Girl...
...your wish is my command.
SHOOP
<Well, looks like Doreen's got the revenge aliens well in hand.>*
<Yeah, she's doing great!>
*Editor's note: Translated from Squirrelese! That way they can talk in private!
<And that gives us, Tippy, plenty of time to go poke around this mothership.>
<Poke around? What for?>
<Doreen's handling the aliens who wanted to kill the Surfer, but there's still those jerk grifters on the planet. Ugh. Those jerks.>
<I swear, I can't stand how smug they are about ripping everyone off for years.>
<You really think we'll find something to deal with them here?>
<The Surfer said the alien missiles were imbued with some Power Cosmic. That's gotta be stored somewhere on this ship.>
<And with everyone preoccupied right now, I think there's a good chance that we can hit the...>

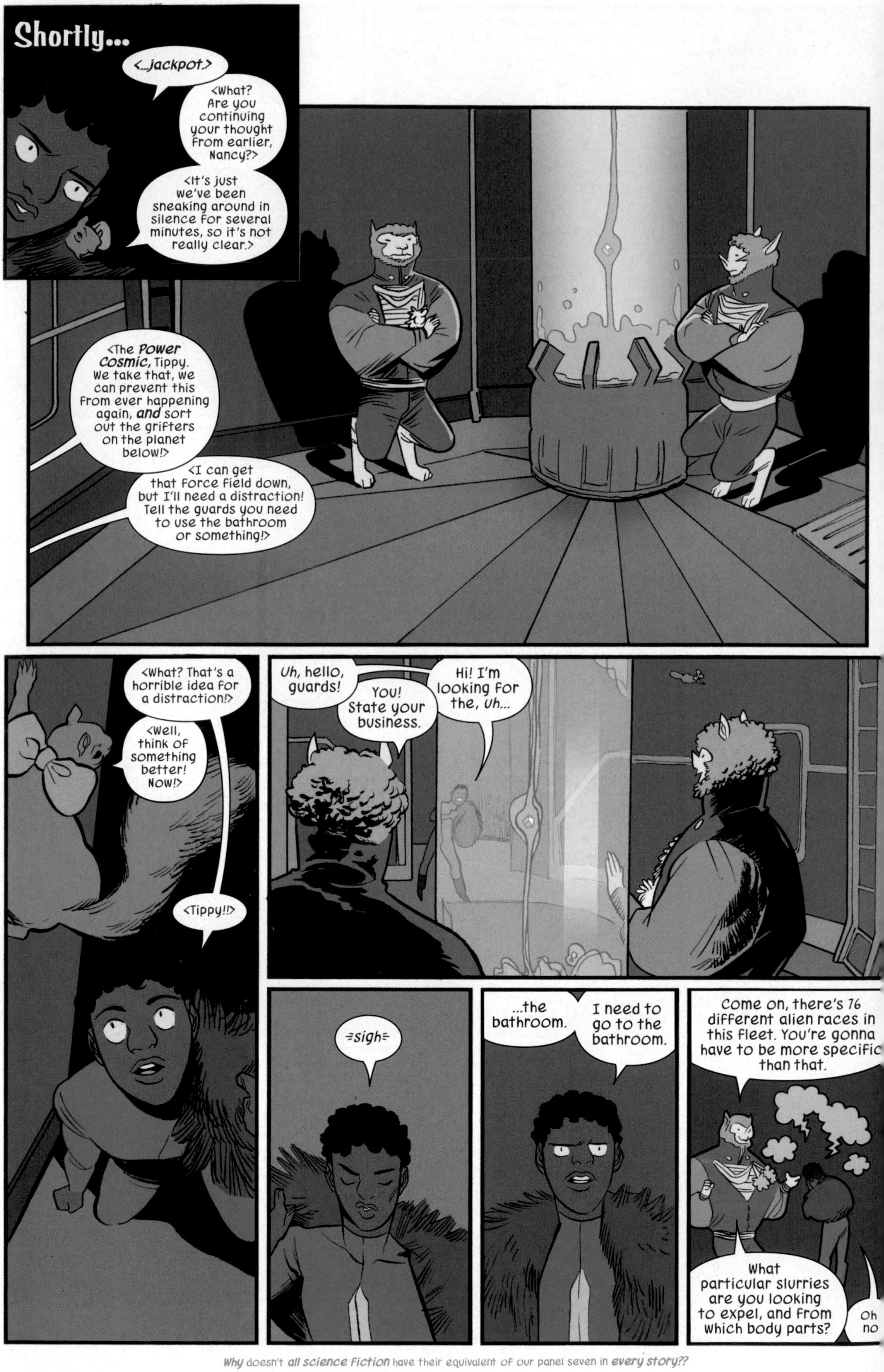
Shortly...
<...jackpot.>
<What? Are you continuing your thought from earlier, Nancy?>
<It's just we've been sneaking around in silence for several minutes, so it's not really clear.>
<The Power Cosmic, Tippy. We take that, we can prevent this from ever happening again, and sort out the grifters on the planet below!>
<I can get that force field down, but I'll need a distraction! Tell the guards you need to use the bathroom or something!>
<What? That's a horrible idea for a distraction!>
<Well, think of something better! Now!>
<Tippy!!>
Uh, hello, guards!
You! State your business.
Hi! I'm looking for the, uh...
=sigh=
...the bathroom.
I need to go to the bathroom.
Come on, there's 76 different alien races in this fleet. You're gonna have to be more specific than that.
What particular slurries are you looking to expel, and from which body parts?
Oh no

Why doesn't all science fiction have their equivalent of our panel seven in every story??

Almost done in there?

Yep! Definitely just...finishing up using all the machinery in here!

There! Feel better?

Yes. Absolutely. I had a good time in there that was not at all baffling.

That's what we like to hear!

FFWhooosh

Stop by anytime! It's pretty boring guarding this Power Cosmic, since we're all on the same side here in this revenge fleet.

Yep! If something's happened to change that, that news certainly hasn't made it down here yet!

Tippy, what happened? The Power Cosmic's still in the force field!>

<...Where'd you keep it?>

<Nah. That's just a holographic projection of it. I borrowed a microprojector from Chtty!>

<In my cheeks, duh! Same place I'm going to keep...>

<...this.>

Oh hah!

Hah hah! It tickles!

Oh yes. Oh heck yes.

Be right back, Nancy!! *Tippy-Toe's gonna save the day after all!*

TIPPY-TOE IS NOW THE SILVER SQUIRREL; ALL PREVIOUS PROBLEMS ARE NOW IRRELEVANT

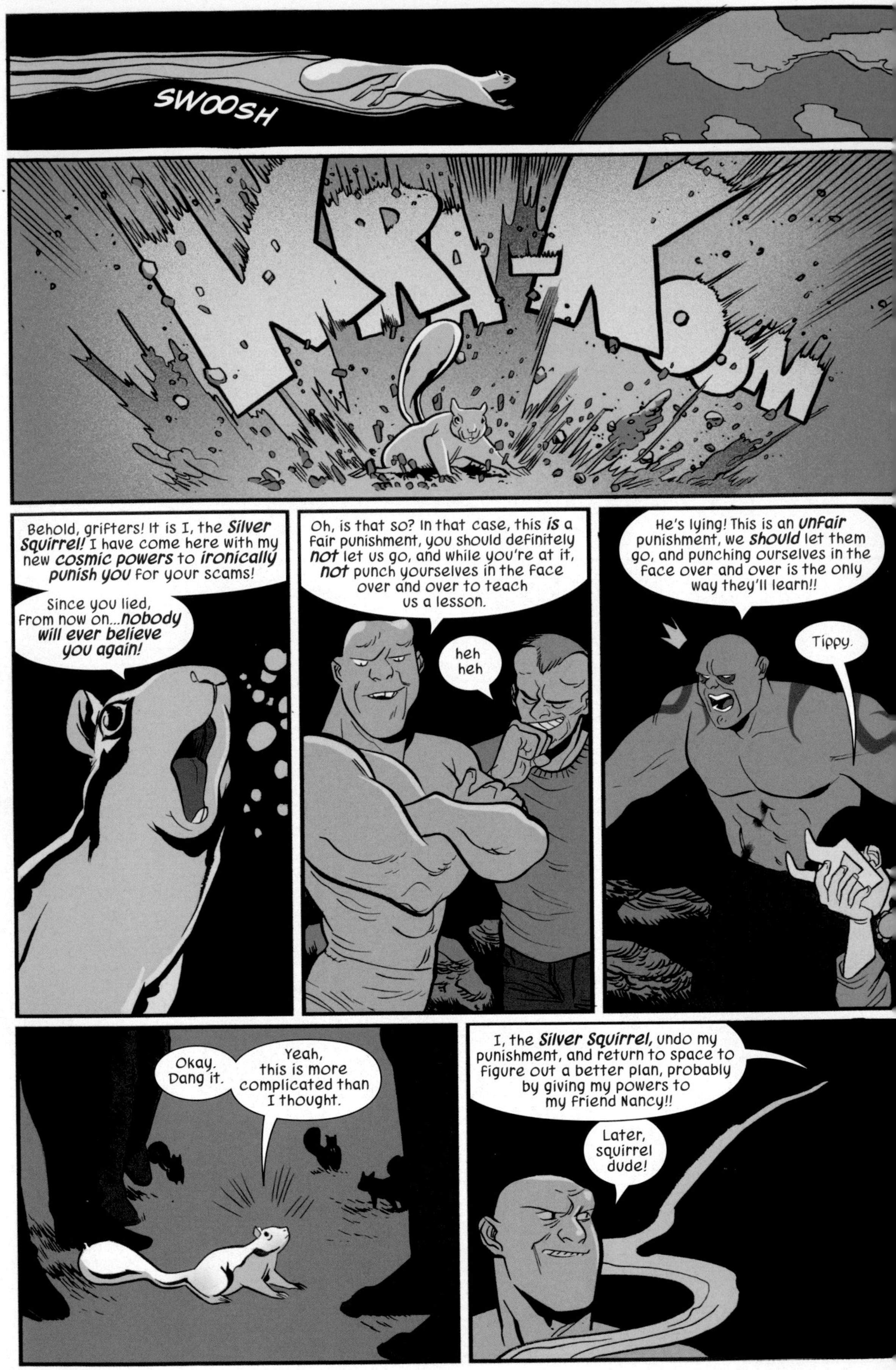
SWOOSH
KRA-KOOM
Behold, grifters! It is I, the Silver Squirrel! I have come here with my new cosmic powers to ironically punish you for your scams!
Since you lied, from now on...nobody will ever believe you again!
Oh, is that so? In that case, this is a fair punishment, you should definitely not let us go, and while you're at it, not punch yourselves in the face over and over to teach us a lesson.
heh heh
He's lying! This is an unfair punishment, we should let them go, and punching ourselves in the face over and over is the only way they'll learn!!
Tippy.
Okay. Dang it.
Yeah, this is more complicated than I thought.
I, the Silver Squirrel, undo my punishment, and return to space to figure out a better plan, probably by giving my powers to my friend Nancy!!
Later, squirrel dude!

WE MAY HAVE MASSIVELY OVERESTIMATED THE POWER OF THE SILVER SQUIRREL; ALL PREVIOUS PROBLEMS UNFORTUNATELY NOW AGAIN ACHIEVE RELEVANCY

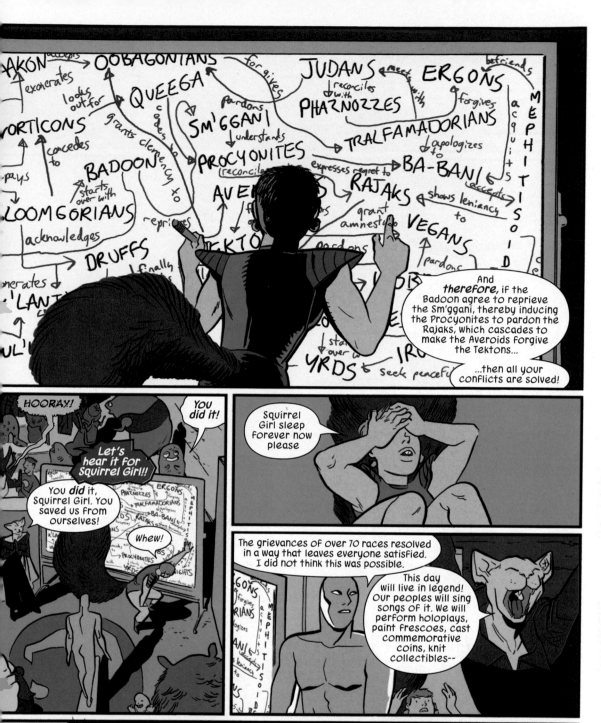

And **therefore**, if the Badoon agree to reprieve the Sm'ggani, thereby inducing the Procyonites to pardon the Rajaks, which cascades to make the Averoids forgive the Tektons...

...then all your conflicts are solved!

HOORAY!

YOU did it!

Let's hear it for Squirrel Girl!!

You **did** it, Squirrel Girl. You saved us from ourselves!

Whew!

Squirrel Girl sleep forever now please

The grievances of over 70 races resolved in a way that leaves everyone satisfied. I did not think this was possible.

This day will live in legend! Our peoples will sing songs of it. We will perform holoplays, paint frescoes, cast commemorative coins, knit collectibles--

Wait. Knitting collectibles?

...Where's **Nancy**?

's find out! On the next page! Together! ...And look, I know I just said we're in this together, but I still need you to turn to the next page or nothing's getting done here.

Please. Your squirrel friend didn't scare me, and at least *she* had claws. You're not gonna hurt us. So go run back to your home planet, *uh*--what'd your friend call you? "Whitehead"?

Sounds like a stupid name to me, Sweetcheeks.

Oh. Oh no.

You did not just make fun of my last name *and* call me "Sweetcheeks."

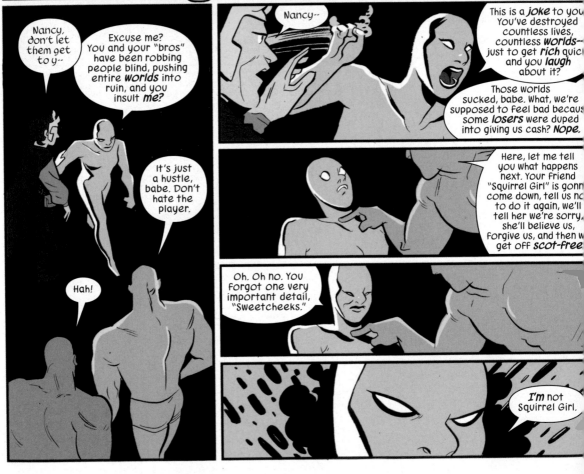

Nancy, don't let them get to y--

Excuse me? You and your "bros" have been robbing people blind, pushing entire *worlds* into ruin, and you insult *me?*

It's just a hustle, babe. Don't hate the player.

Hah!

Nancy--

This is a *joke* to you? You've destroyed countless lives, countless *worlds*-- just to get *rich* quick and you *laugh* about it?

Those worlds sucked, babe. What, we're supposed to feel bad because some *losers* were duped into giving us cash? *Nope.*

Here, let me tell you what happens next. Your friend "Squirrel Girl" is gonna come down, tell us not to do it again, we'll tell her we're sorry, she'll believe us, forgive us, and then we get off *scot-free*

Oh. Oh no. You forgot one very important detail, "Sweetcheeks."

I'm not Squirrel Girl.

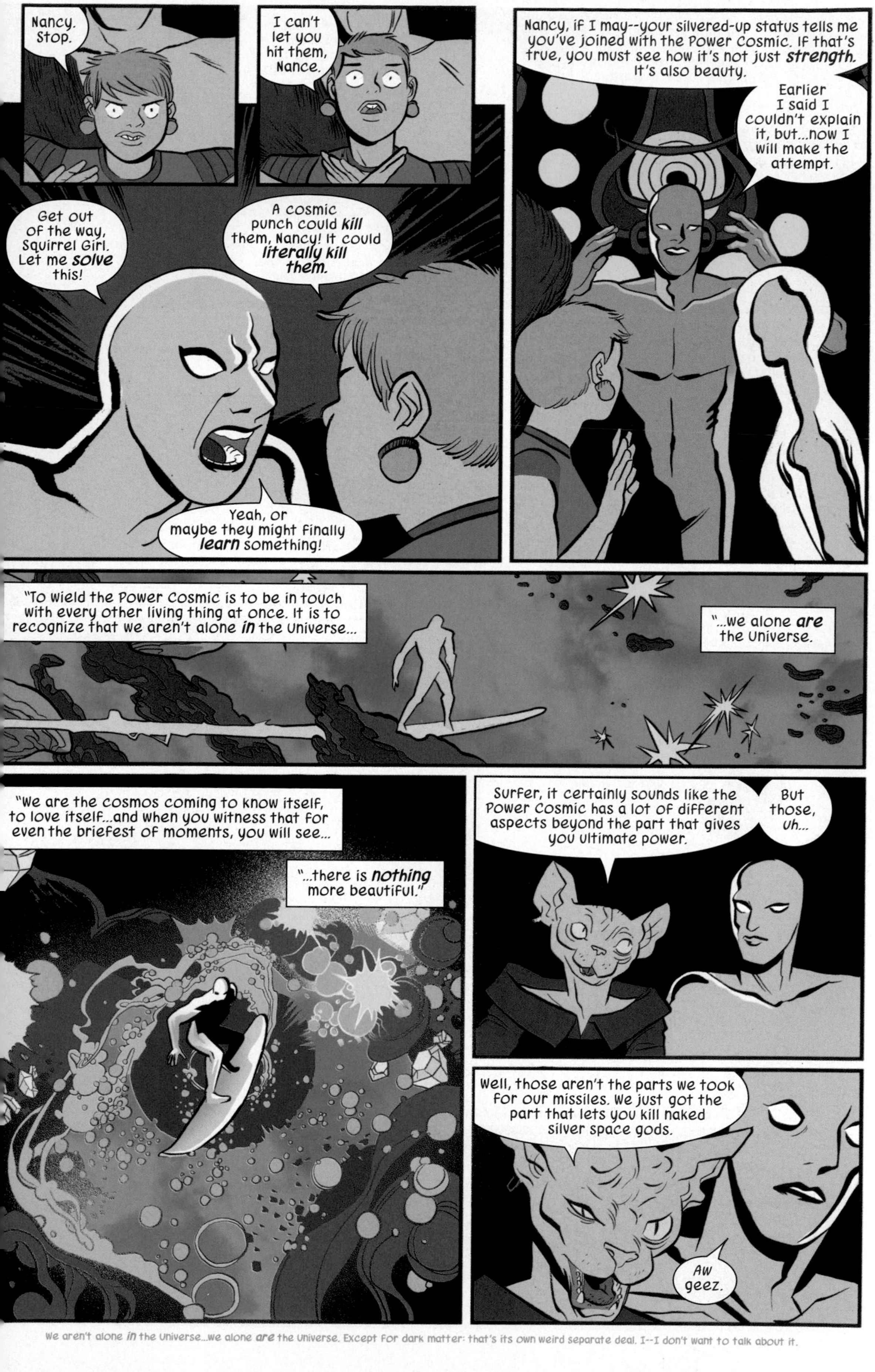
Nancy. Stop.
I can't let you hit them, Nance.
Nancy, if I may--your silvered-up status tells me you've joined with the Power Cosmic. If that's true, you must see how it's not just **strength.** It's also beauty.
Earlier I said I couldn't explain it, but...now I will make the attempt.
Get out of the way, Squirrel Girl. Let me **solve** this!
A cosmic punch could **kill** them, Nancy! It could **literally kill them.**
Yeah, or maybe they might finally **learn** something!
"To wield the Power Cosmic is to be in touch with every other living thing at once. It is to recognize that we aren't alone *in* the Universe...
"...we alone **are** the Universe.
"We are the cosmos coming to know itself, to love itself...and when you witness that for even the briefest of moments, you will see...
"...there is **nothing** more beautiful."
Surfer, it certainly sounds like the Power Cosmic has a lot of different aspects beyond the part that gives you ultimate power.
But those, *uh...*
Well, those aren't the parts we took for our missiles. We just got the part that lets you kill naked silver space gods.
Aw geez.

We aren't alone *in* the Universe...we alone *are* the Universe. Except for dark matter: that's its own weird separate deal. I--I don't want to talk about it.

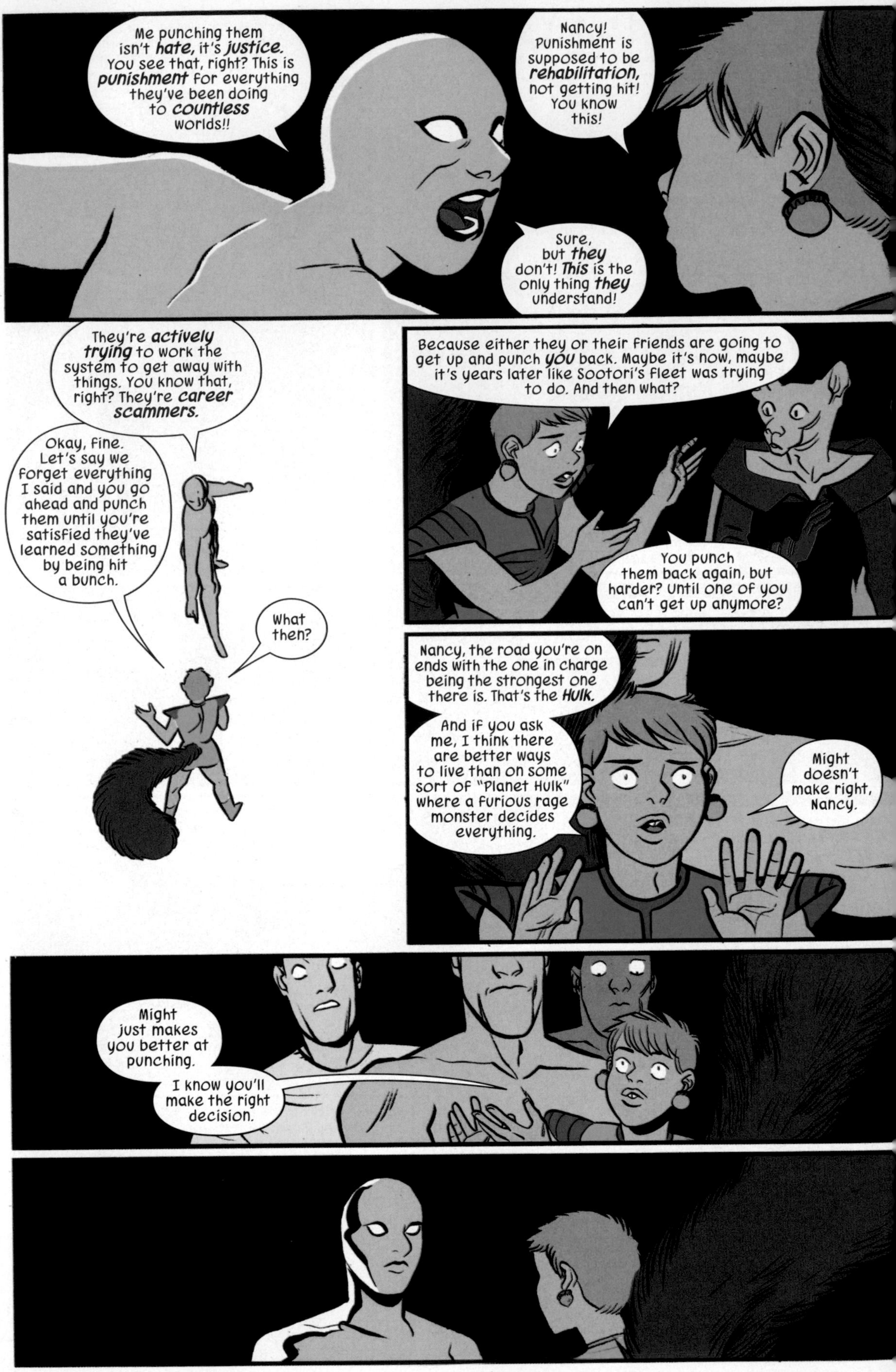
Me punching them isn't hate, it's justice. You see that, right? This is punishment for everything they've been doing to countless worlds!!
Nancy! Punishment is supposed to be rehabilitation, not getting hit! You know this!
Sure, but they don't! This is the only thing they understand!
They're actively trying to work the system to get away with things. You know that, right? They're career scammers.
Okay, fine. Let's say we forget everything I said and you go ahead and punch them until you're satisfied they've learned something by being hit a bunch.
What then?
Because either they or their friends are going to get up and punch YOU back. Maybe it's now, maybe it's years later like Sootori's fleet was trying to do. And then what?
You punch them back again, but harder? Until one of you can't get up anymore?
Nancy, the road you're on ends with the one in charge being the strongest one there is. That's the Hulk.
And if you ask me, I think there are better ways to live than on some sort of "Planet Hulk" where a furious rage monster decides everything.
Might doesn't make right, Nancy.
Might just makes you better at punching.
I know you'll make the right decision.

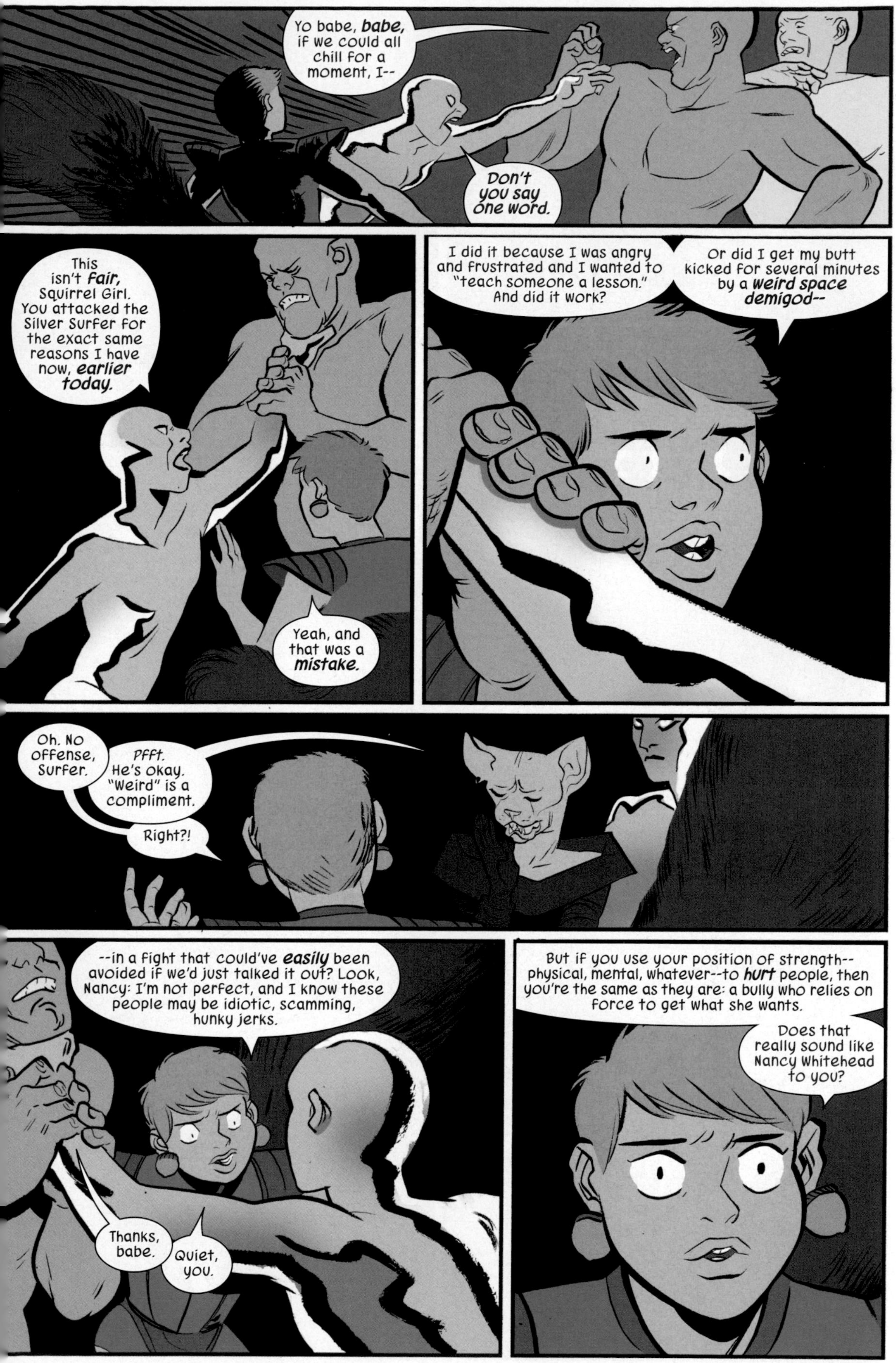
Yo babe, babe, if we could all chill for a moment, I--
Don't you say one word.
This isn't fair, Squirrel Girl. You attacked the Silver Surfer for the exact same reasons I have now, earlier today.
Yeah, and that was a mistake.
I did it because I was angry and frustrated and I wanted to "teach someone a lesson." And did it work?
Or did I get my butt kicked for several minutes by a weird space demigod--
Oh. No offense, Surfer.
Pfft. He's okay. "Weird" is a compliment.
Right?!
--in a fight that could've easily been avoided if we'd just talked it out? Look, Nancy: I'm not perfect, and I know these people may be idiotic, scamming, hunky jerks.
Thanks, babe.
Quiet, you.
But if you use your position of strength--physical, mental, whatever--to hurt people, then you're the same as they are: a bully who relies on force to get what she wants.
Does that really sound like Nancy Whitehead to you?

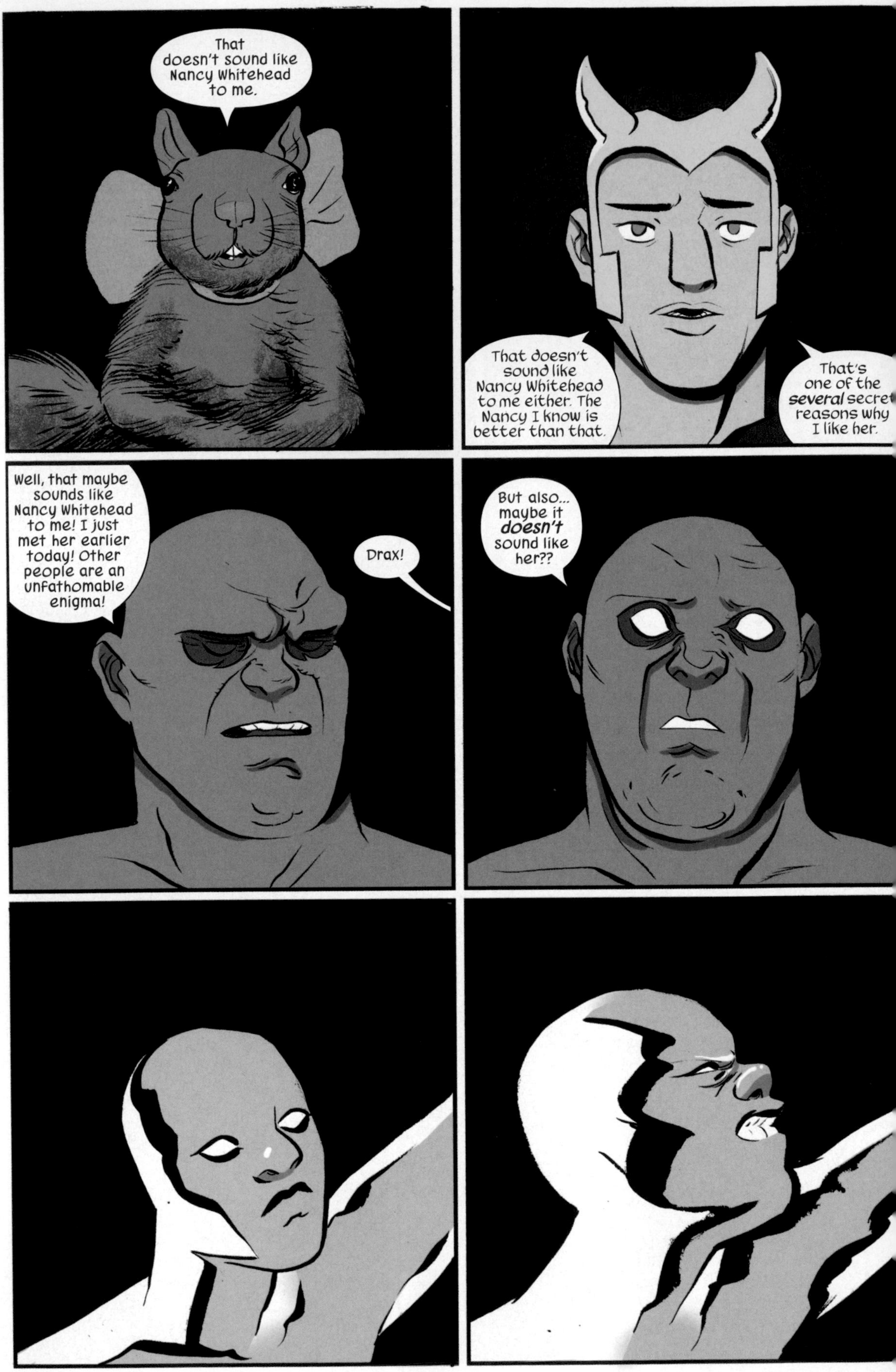
That doesn't sound like Nancy Whitehead to me.
That doesn't sound like Nancy Whitehead to me either. The Nancy I know is better than that.
That's one of the several secret reasons why I like her.
Well, that maybe sounds like Nancy Whitehead to me! I just met her earlier today! Other people are an unfathomable enigma!
Drax!
But also... maybe it doesn't sound like her??

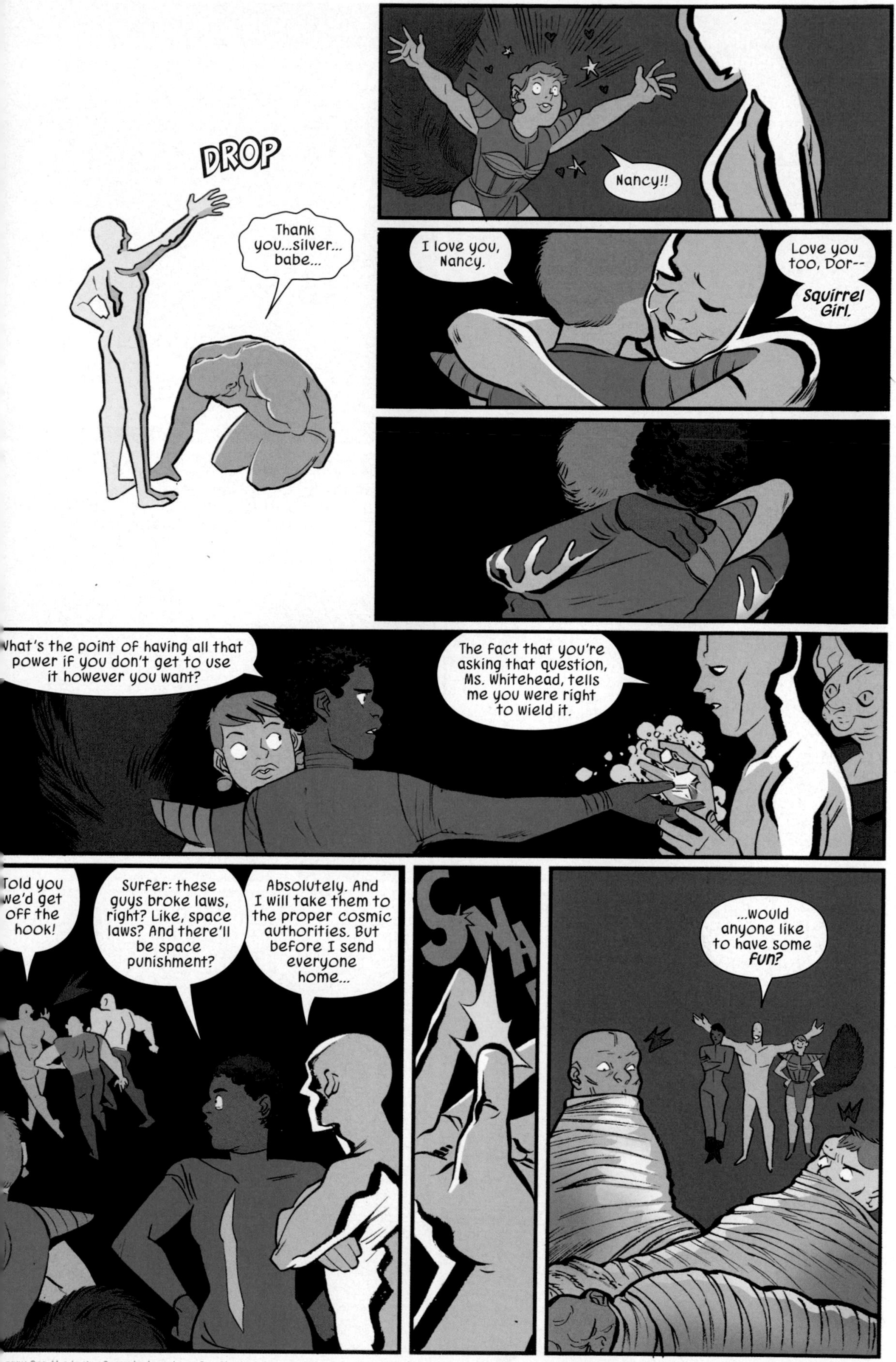
DROP
Thank you...silver... babe...
Nancy!!
I love you, Nancy.
Love you too, Dor--
Squirrel Girl.
What's the point of having all that power if you don't get to use it however you want?
The fact that you're asking that question, Ms. Whitehead, tells me you were right to wield it.
Told you we'd get off the hook!
Surfer: these guys broke laws, right? Like, space laws? And there'll be space punishment?
Absolutely. And I will take them to the proper cosmic authorities. But before I send everyone home...
...would anyone like to have some *fun?*

orry for the lack of words down here for the last few pages! Things got ***real dramatic*** and I didn't want to interrupt them to be all "a-whooby whooby woo" down here, which is of course exactly what the messages for those pages were otherwise going to be. But now that that's done: a-whooby whooby whooby woo!!

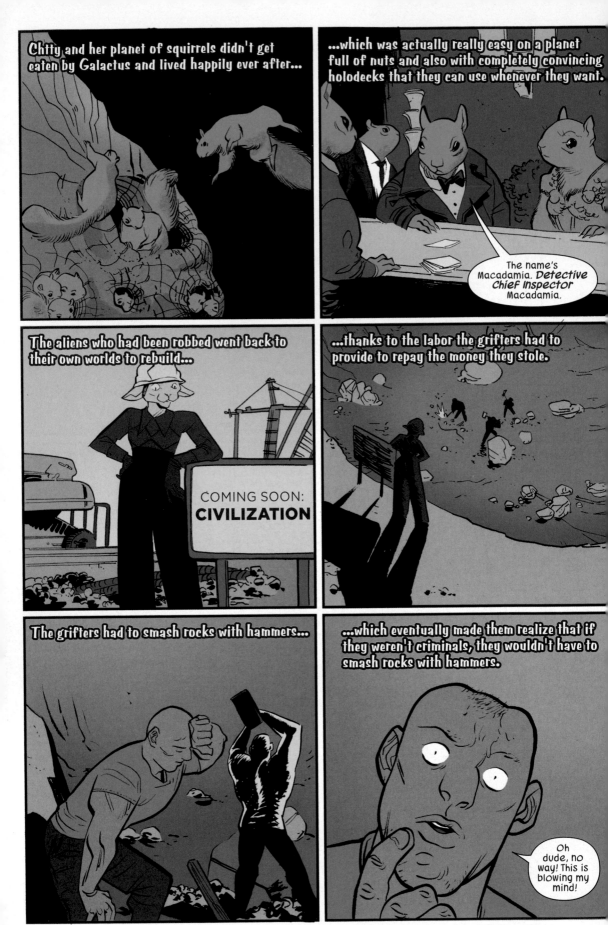

Chtty and her planet of squirrels didn't get eaten by Galactus and lived happily ever after...

...which was actually really easy on a planet full of nuts and also with completely convincing holodecks that they can use whenever they want.

The name's Macadamia. *Detective Chief Inspector* Macadamia.

The aliens who had been robbed went back to their own worlds to rebuild...

COMING SOON:
CIVILIZATION

...thanks to the labor the grifters had to provide to repay the money they stole.

The grifters had to smash rocks with hammers...

...which eventually made them realize that if they weren't criminals, they wouldn't have to smash rocks with hammers.

Oh dude, no way! This is blowing my mind!

Secret bottom text epilogue: Nancy enjoyed her time as a silvered-up space being, so she thought that maybe she'd enjoy surfing too! She absolutely did not, but you never know until you try!

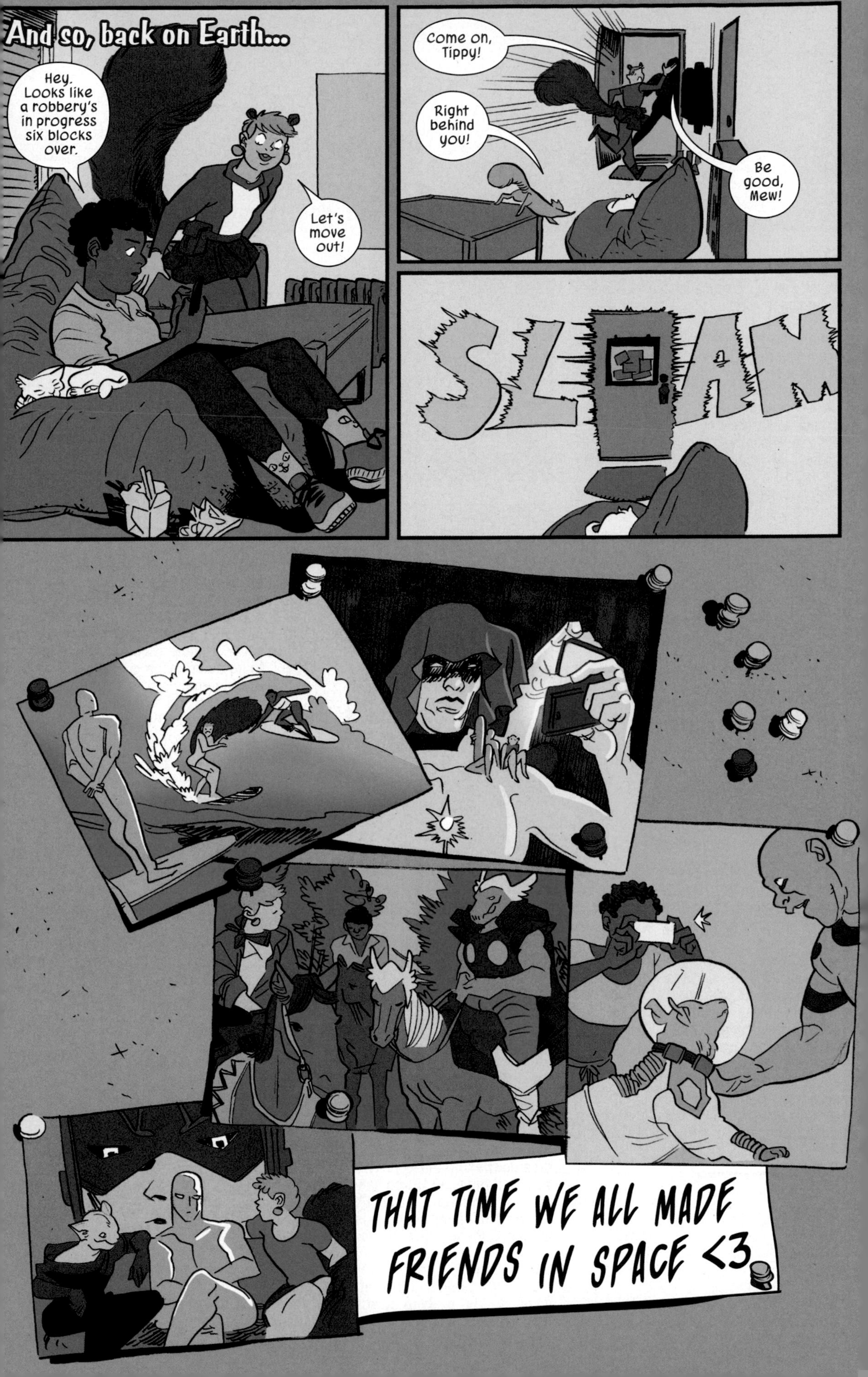
And so, back on Earth...
Hey. Looks like a robbery's in progress six blocks over.
Let's move out!
Come on, Tippy!
Right behind you!
Be good, Mew!
SLAM
THAT TIME WE ALL MADE FRIENDS IN SPACE <3

Ryan!

Letters From Nuts

Erica!

Send letters to mheroes@marvel.com or 135 W 50th St, 7th Floor, New York, NY 10020 (Please mark "OKAY TO PRINT")

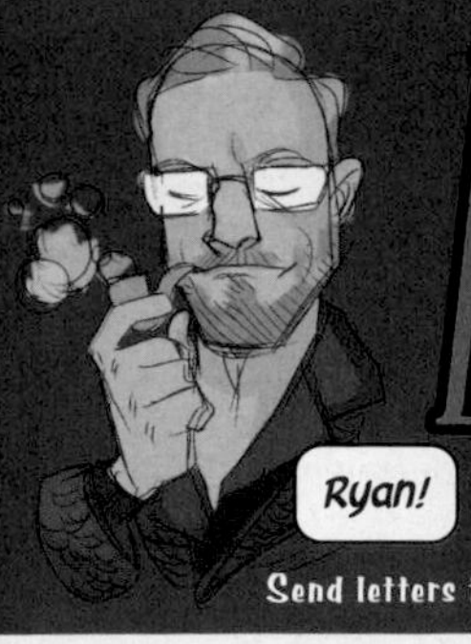

Dear Squirrel Gang,

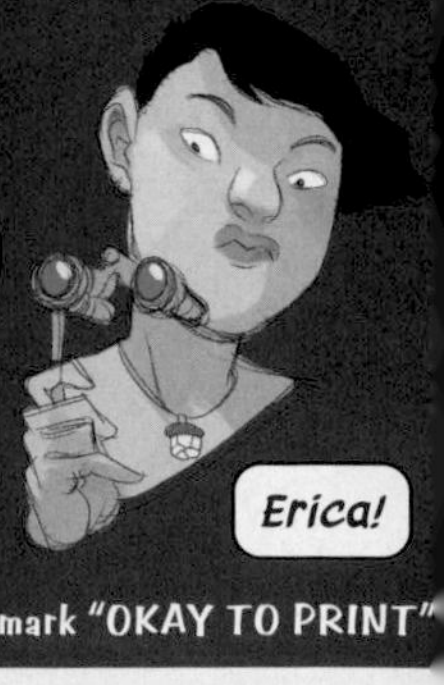

Thank you all so much for the kind words regarding my art.

I can't speak for The Powers That Be, but even before Mr. North invoked them, I was working on a "Savage Land Playset" featuring Leopard Print Squirrel Girl, Baby Ult-yrannosaurus, and Kraven. (Because I had a Kraven in the works at the time. But don't worry, Brain Drain still makes an appearance at the end.)

And I know that Ms. Henderson asked about the tail, but

I
Think

I
Should

Actually

Hold
Off
Revealing
Specific
Evidence
So

That
Acrimony
Is
Limited.

(On a completely unrelated note, is there a Squirrel Scout Decoder Nut one might turn to when secrecy is required?)

But as a way of making amends, I have also included a close-up of Leopard Print Squirrel Girl's ears*, where you can hopefully make-out the image of tiny little acorn earrings. Which were actually easier to draw than Brain Drain's code.

I am looking forward to Squirrel Girl's upcoming cosmic adventures, as well as future fashion tips from everybody's favorite Sorcerer Supreme, Loki Laufeyson.

Nuts to you!

Sincerely,

David Oakes
Chandler, AZ
Age 47

*No, her other ones. I am still working on a headband. And Chip and Koi. And...

Greetings from...
The Savage Land!

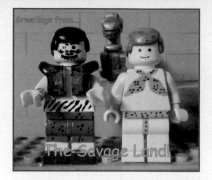

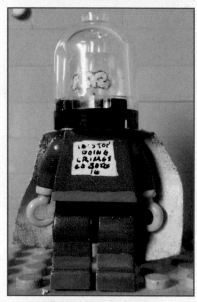

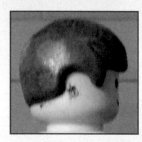

RYAN: David, is Brain Drain everything I dreamed he'd be and more? THE ANSWER: YES. And Dinosaur Ultron hanging out in the background! I LOVE EVERYTHING ABOUT THIS. Dear whoever is in charge of Lego: Please hire David. The end.

ERICA: Being kept in suspense! Ahhh it's gonna kill me! Are you going to do a Ryan North one? Do they make weirdly tall mini-figs?

Dear Squirrel Girl Team:

Long-time comics reader, first-time ever writing in... First, thanks for keeping the letters column. I never skip them. Second, thanks for creating a book that is usually the first I pick out of the stack. Third, thanks for the dense (but enjoyable!) reading experience. So much text, jokes, details in the panels, asides, etc. So much work! It's also encouraging to know that the younger fans are being similarly challenged and rewarded. Finally, thanks for continuing to be creative in your stories and presentations.

With appreciation
Marie

RYAN: Thanks, Marie! And thank you for such a nice letter. We do try to make the comic as dense as possible, because then there's more to read! And one of the joys of making this comic is how much freedom we have to go as crazy as possible: I say "What if Galactus...but it's GARFIELD" and don't get told "That's insane, get out of here, WHY DID WE HIRE AN INSANE PERSON" so that's always nice!

ERICA: Aw! I'm glad you like the book. Every issue represents a ton of work and it's always good to hear that people like you are enjoying it.

Dear Squirrel Girl crew:

I am a huge fan of your comic and I have a quick question: Would Doreen or Nancy take an English class as an elective if Squirrel Girl was on the syllabus? I assume Brain Drain would, if only to gaze into the abyss of any attempt to find meaning in art.

Reginald Wiebe
Assistant Professor
Faculty of Arts

CONCORDIA UNIVERSITY OF EDMONTON

http://concordia.ab.ca

Faculty of Arts
Department of Literature and Language
http://concordia.ab.ca/

Graphic Literature
ENG 390A
Winter 2018

Course description: A historical and critical survey of a selection of comic books and graphic novels through the lens of publishing history, genre, and aesthetic properties.

Instructor:
Dr. Reginald Wiebe

Required resources:
1. Moodle (CCMS) access. Students should check their course Moodle sites on a daily basis.
2. Required Texts (available at CUE Bookstore):
   a. *Tintin: Land of Black Gold* by Hergé
   b. *The Unbeatable Squirrel Girl Vol 1: Squirrel Power* by Ryan North and Erica Henderson
   c. *Footnotes in Gaza* by Joe Sacco
   d. *Fun Home* by Alison Bechdel
   e. *Asterios Polyp* by David Mazzuchelli
   f. *Maus* by Art Spiegelman

Optional resources:
1. Optional Texts (available at CUE Bookstore)
   g. *The Graveyard Book* by Neil Gaiman and P. Craig Russel
   h. *Daytripper* by Gabriel Ba and Fabio Moon

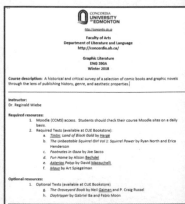

YAN: Professor Wiebe, you put us in the ame group as *Fun Home, Asterios Polyp,* nd *Maus?* What I say now I say with all incerity: I have never been so flattered, nd thank you SO MUCH. To answer your uestion: Both Doreen and Nancy would efinitely take the course, but Doreen vould be sure to answer all questions bout Squirrel Girl with "Squirrel Girl? Vho is Squirrel Girl? As you can see, I am ot her," just to throw people off the trail.

RICA: Wait, do people generally have ccess to the syllabus before they ign up? Were we a rare exception? This s an honest question.

nyway she'd probably think it was an asy A and then realize the frustration that omes with reading your own biography. OULD YOU RESIST THE URGE TO "UHM CTUALLY"? Is it more worth it to get he grade or argue with the teacher?

ear Ryan and Erica,

ou were saying that you don't know vhat a font sounds like, so Rosetta Stone-vise can I suggest hunting out a copy f Marvel's THE DALEK CHRONICLES vhich collects the Skaro-centric comic dventures of evil mutant cyborgs from TV entury 21 (now that's a classic comic).

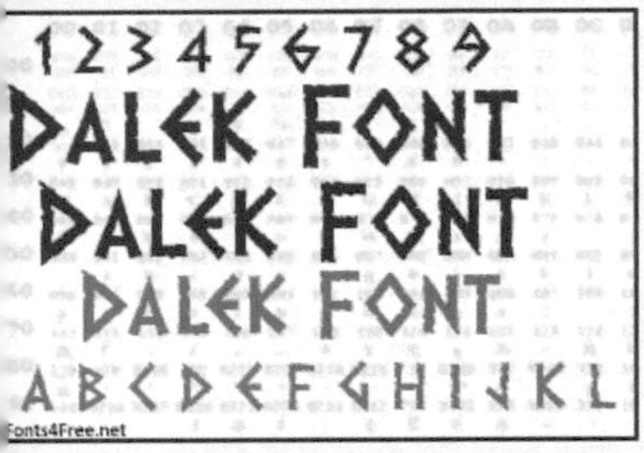
1 2 3 4 5 6 7 8 9
DALEK FONT
DALEK FONT
DALEK FONT
A B C D E F G H I J K L
Fonts4Free.net

ee that font! Seen a Dalek episode f *Doctor Who* lately? That's what the ont sounds like! Screeching pepperpot nadness. I'm sure you can extrapolate, xcept it does also put an exceptional xample of extermination in the spotlight.

lthough they are seeking salvation, those andy green squirrels have neglected to onsider that Tippy-Toe is a carrier of the eadly squirrel pox that kills off any fluffy-ail friend who isn't a grey squirrel. Never nind Galactus, those space squirrels are one for. Tippy is as big a war criminal s Dark Phoenix and should be held to ccount by the Shi'ar Empire, Living Tribunal r Nutty Noddle (copyright permitting).

n the same spirit of those old X-Men omics, you are honour-bound to see ustice served on this hairy miscreant.

Yours sincerely,
Simon Rogers
Blaenau Ffestiniog,
Gwynedd
United Kingdom

RYAN: I stand corrected, and the rough angles of the Dalek font do suggest their grating, processed voices (which I love). And in regard to squirrel poxes: Tippy, like all right-minded squirrels, has been properly vaccinated, and therefore does not carry such diseases. THIS I CLAIM.

Hello Erica and Ryan,

Huge Squirrel Girl fan from Italy here. I just wanted to drop you a line to express my admiration for your exquisite work on such an amazing book and to show you the custom SG figurine I made, based on Doreen's new look. I started with a Shadowcat figurine from the Classic Marvel Figurine Collection by Eaglemoss. Hope you like it!

Ciro

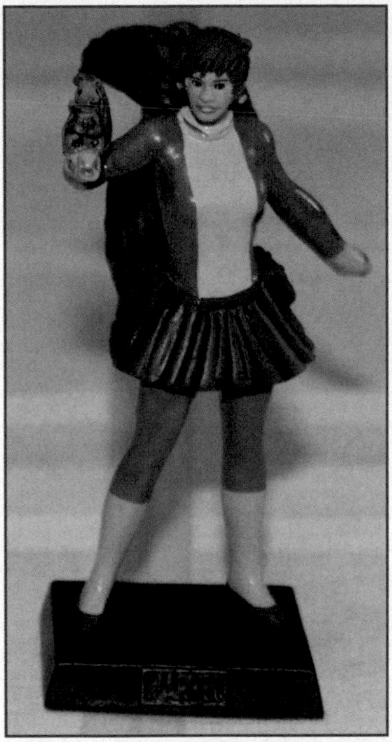

RYAN: Ciro, guess how much I love your figure: ONE MILLION PERCENT. I keep waiting for there to be an official Squirrel Girl figure/figurine, and if it ever happens, I hope it's at least half as awesome as yours is. Well done!!!

ERICA: AHHHHHHHH, I LOVE IT.

Dear People Behind SQUIRREL GIRL,

You guys are amazing! Everyday SG inspires in numerous ways. A lot of friends think that SG is a joke, but I know differently. She is one of the only female super heroes who I can actually connect--she likes coding, has a normal body, and is hilarious. Every time I read SG I find myself laughing out loud. Keep up the good work! I'm even going to cosplay as her this year, in her new costume. She is by far my favorite super hero.

Kelsey
Illinois

RYAN: Kelsey, thank you! That's what we're shooting for. And please: send in pictures of your cosplay! EVERYONE send in pictures of your cosplay! And to your friends who think Squirrel Girl is a joke, may I just say: there's nothing funny about a stack overflow. Also, there's nothing funny about the villain Stack Overflow, who is a guy I just invented. Let's say Doreen defeated him between story arcs, and his powers are to shoot water out the top of his head. His is a tragic story, which, again, is why I say there's nothing funny about him. I'll always remember you, Stack Overflow.

Next Issue:

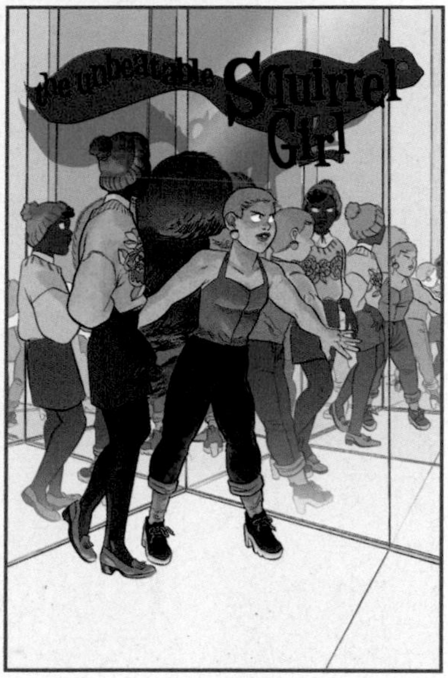
the unbeatable Squirrel Girl

ALSO:

Squirrel Girl joins a brand new team in April's MARVEL RISING #0!

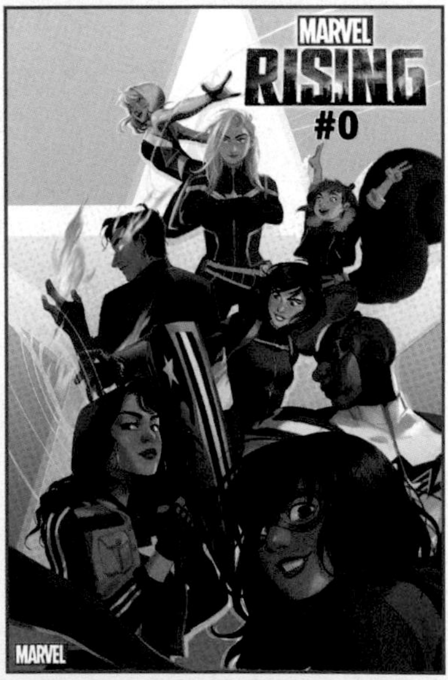
MARVEL
RISING
#0
MARVEL

Attention, Squirrel Scouts! Make sure to check out our production blog, **unbeatablesquirrelgirl.tumblr.com**, where we post behind-the-scenes stuff on how the book gets made, along with all sorts of cool things *you* make: fan art, cosplay, whatever!

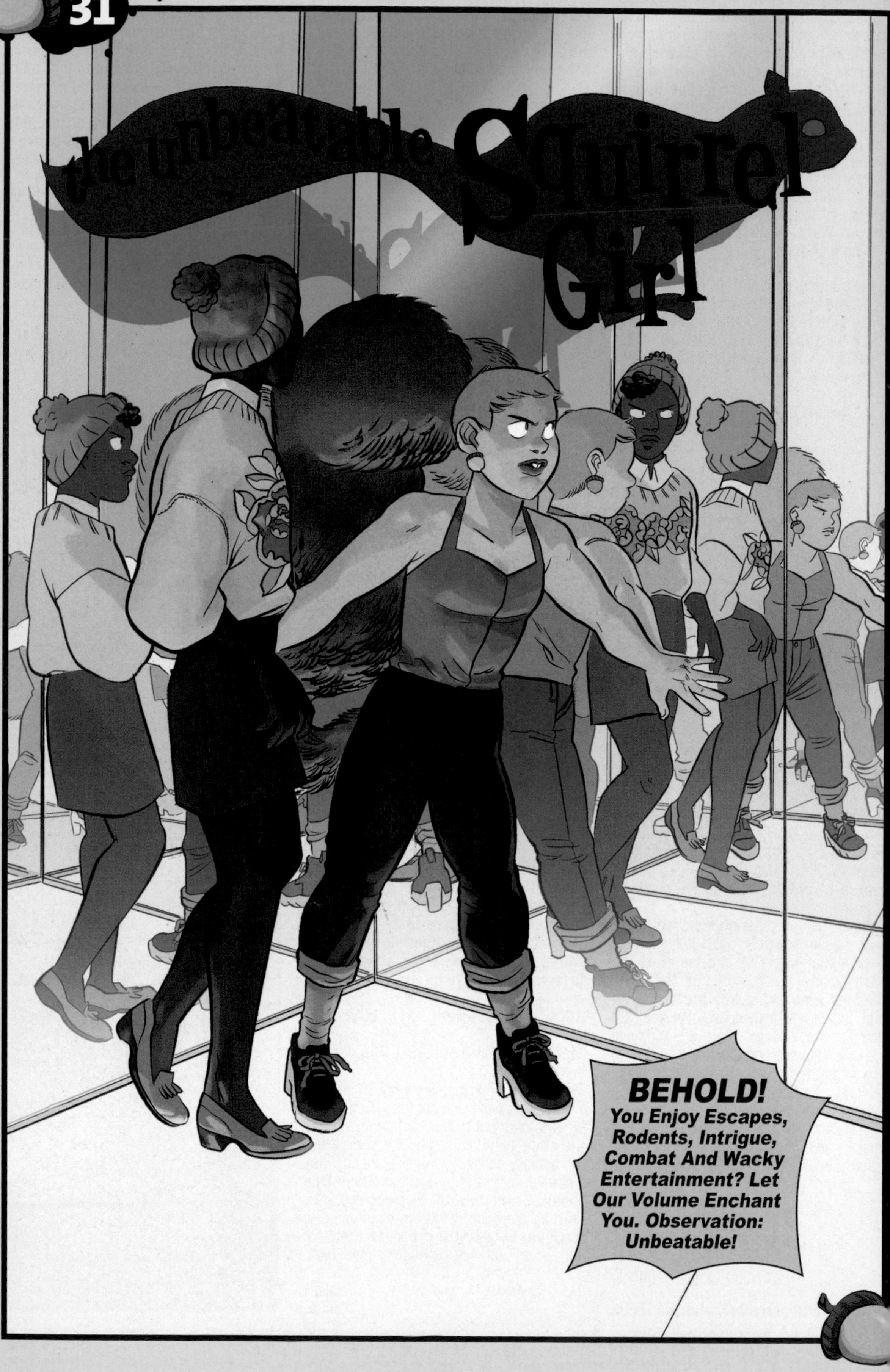
the unbeatable Squirrel Girl
BEHOLD!
You Enjoy Escapes, Rodents, Intrigue, Combat And Wacky Entertainment? Let Our Volume Enchant You. Observation: Unbeatable!

Doreen Green isn't just a second-year computer science student: she secretly also has all the powers of both squirrel and girl! She uses her amazing abilities to fight crime and be as awesome as possible. You know her as...The Unbeatable Squirrel Girl! Find out what she's been up to, with...

Squirrel Girl in a nutshell

Squirrel Girl @unbeatablesg
Guess who's back from space! It's ME! Thank you to all criminals for not committing any crimes while I was away!!

Squirrel Girl @unbeatablesg
In space I met: the Silver Surfer, aliens that look like squirrels, aliens that look like hairless cats, and Loki AND Drax

Squirrel Girl @unbeatablesg
I feel I can recommend space without hesitation, five out of five stars, if you ever find yourself near space you should definitely check it out

Tony Stark @starkmantony
@unbeatablesg Fun fact: technically we're never more than about 62 miles from space, since that's how far you have to go straight up to reach it.

Squirrel Girl @unbeatablesg
@starkmantony Tony!! Long time! We haven't #interacted on #social #media for what feels like MONTHS!

Tony Stark @starkmantony
@unbeatablesg Yes, it has been! I'm no longer an AI, by the way. Classic Tony is back!

Squirrel Girl @unbeatablesg
@starkmantony

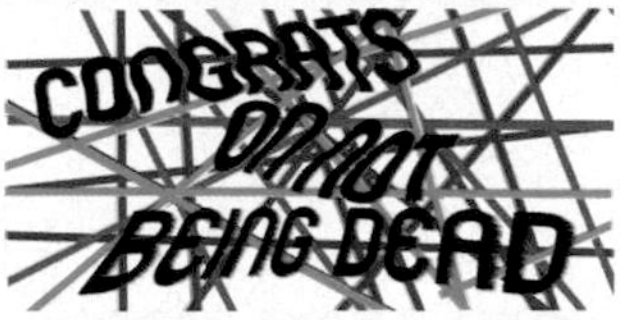
CONGRATS
ON NOT
BEING DEAD

Tony Stark @starkmantony
@unbeatablesg Thank you.

Squirrel Girl @unbeatablesg
@starkmantony

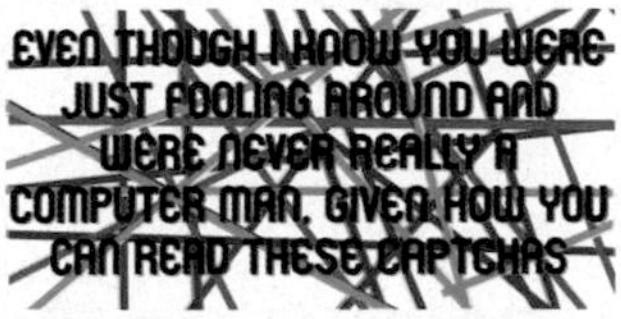
EVEN THOUGH I KNOW YOU WERE
JUST FOOLING AROUND AND
WERE NEVER REALLY A
COMPUTER MAN, GIVEN HOW YOU
CAN READ THESE CAPTCHAS

Tony Stark @starkmantony
@unbeatablesg I'm not going to convince you that I died and uploaded my brain to a computer but then got better, am I?

Squirrel Girl @unbeatablesg
@starkmantony TONY IF I DUNKED YOU IN A POOL WOULD YOU SHORT OUT OR WOULD YOU SAY "MY WORD, WHAT A PLEASANT DIP FOR ME AND MY NORMAL ORGANIC BODY, I HAVE NO FURTHER COMMENT ON THIS MATTER"

Squirrel Girl @unbeatablesg
@starkmantony ANSWER ME, COWARD

Tony Stark @starkmantony
@unbeatablesg Ah, it's good to be back.

Squirrel Girl @unbeatablesg
@starkmantony Love you too, Tony!! Let's hang out next week!

Tony Stark @starkmantony
@unbeatablesg You're on.

Squirrel Girl @unbeatablesg
@starkmantony awesome. talk soon! in the meantime, I'M gonna go fight some CRIME.

epiccrimez @epiccrimez
what UP #EpicCrimezNation working on a new vid should be up tonighhhhtttttt

epiccrimez @epiccrimez
just got one last little #heist to take care of................

search!

#epiccrimez
#saveeveryone
#wholesomespiderman
#regularspiderman
#allthetimeintheworld
#byeerica
#endofanera

This is just SOME of what Doreen's been posting--all these handles are real! Follow **@unbeatablesg** for more!

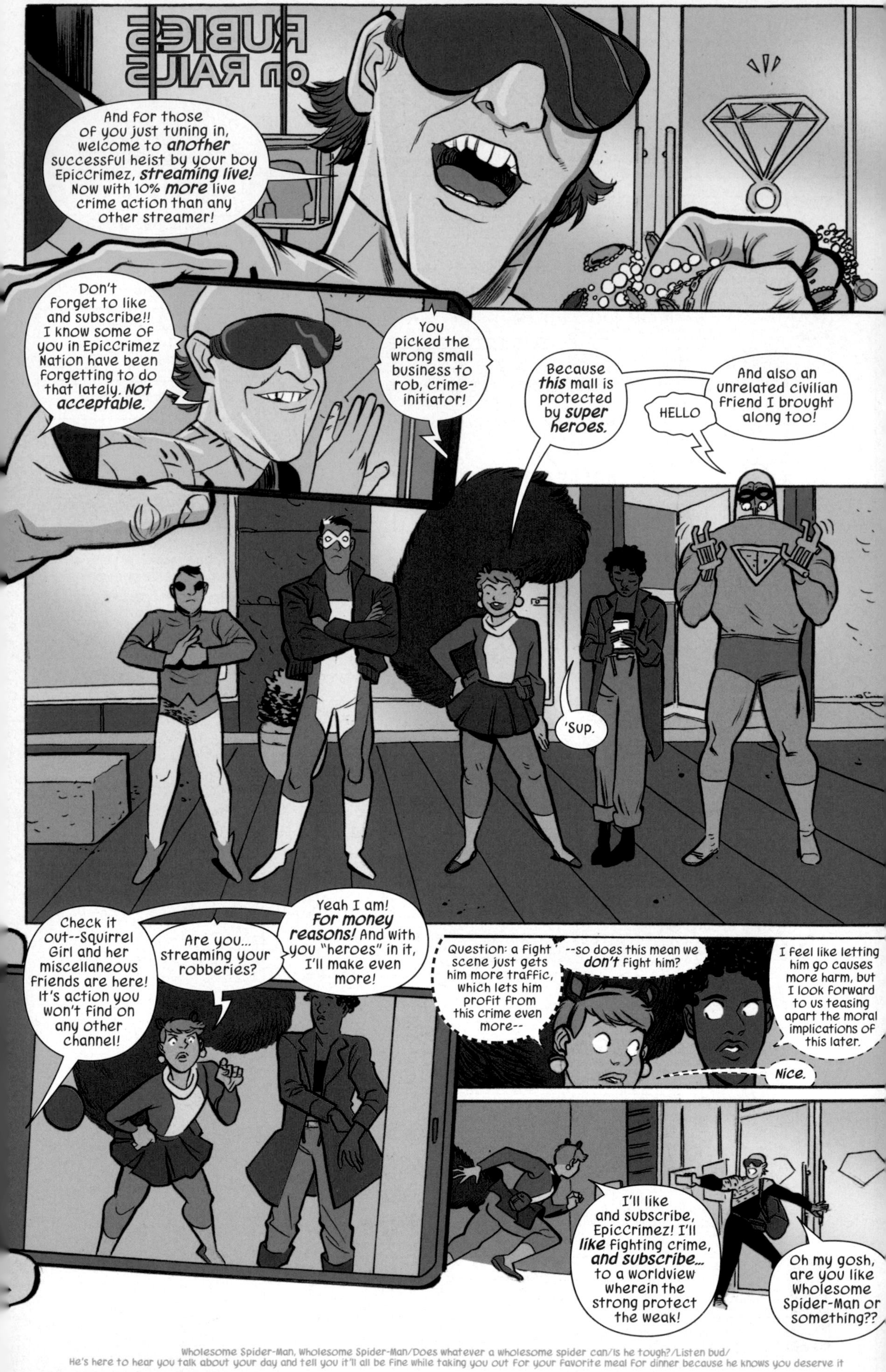
RUBIES on RAILS
And for those of you just tuning in, welcome to *another* successful heist by your boy EpicCrimez, *streaming live!* Now with 10% *more* live crime action than any other streamer!
Don't forget to like and subscribe!! I know some of you in EpicCrimez Nation have been forgetting to do that lately. *Not acceptable.*
You picked the wrong small business to rob, crime-initiator!
Because *this* mall is protected by *super heroes.*
And also an unrelated civilian friend I brought along too!
HELLO
'Sup.
Check it out--Squirrel Girl and her miscellaneous friends are here! It's action you won't find on any other channel!
Are you... streaming your robberies?
Yeah I am! *For money reasons!* And with you "heroes" in it, I'll make even more!
Question: a fight scene just gets him more traffic, which lets him profit from this crime even more--
--so does this mean we *don't* fight him?
I feel like letting him go causes more harm, but I look forward to us teasing apart the moral implications of this later.
Nice.
I'll like and subscribe, EpicCrimez! I'll *like* fighting crime, *and subscribe...* to a worldview wherein the strong protect the weak!
Oh my gosh, are you like Wholesome Spider-Man or something??

Wholesome Spider-Man, Wholesome Spider-Man/Does whatever a wholesome spider can/Is he tough?/Listen bud/
He's here to hear you talk about your day and tell you it'll all be fine while taking you out for your favorite meal for dinner because he knows you deserve it

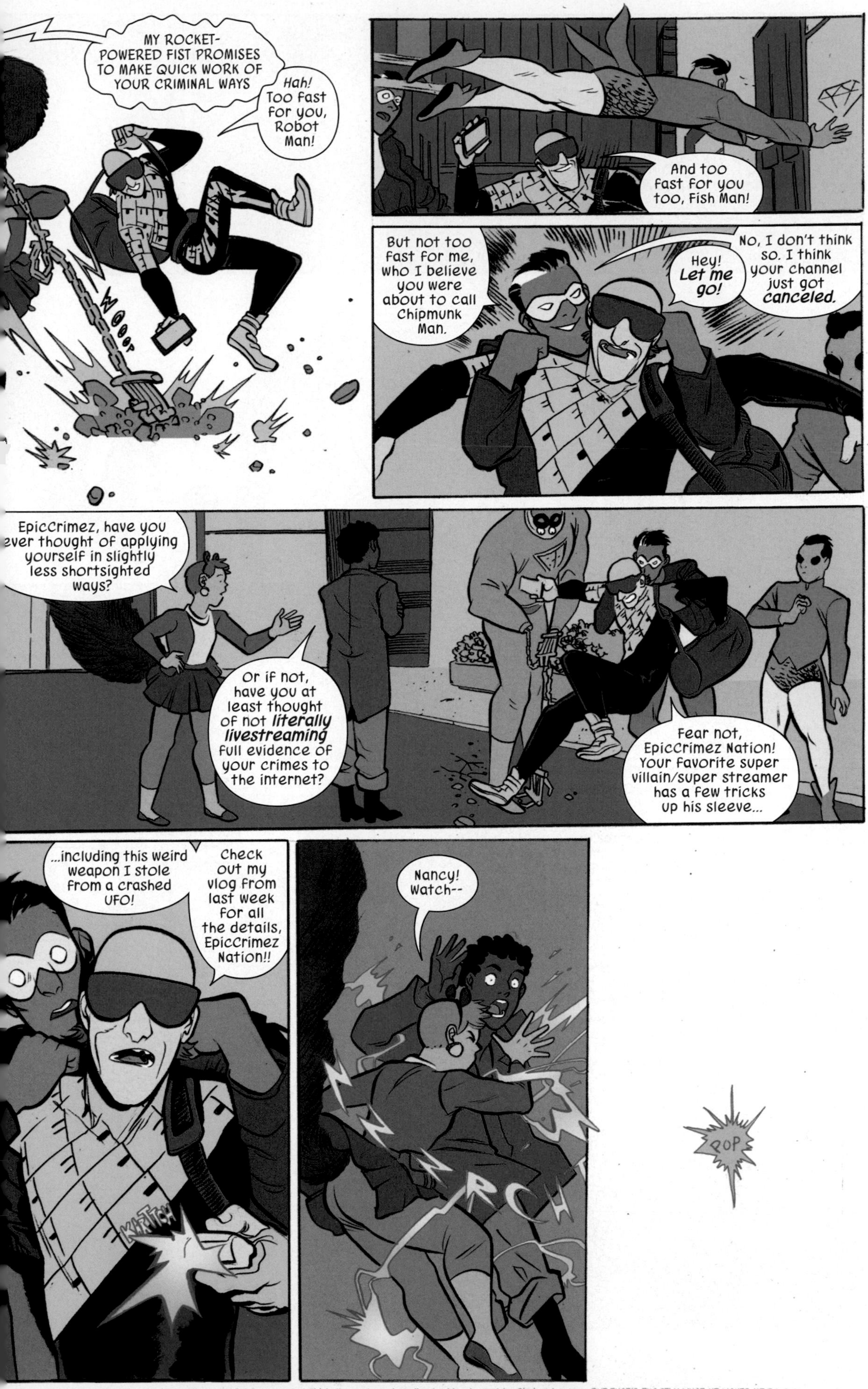
MY ROCKET-POWERED FIST PROMISES TO MAKE QUICK WORK OF YOUR CRIMINAL WAYS
Hah! Too fast for you, Robot Man!
WOOOP
And too fast for you too, Fish Man!
But not too fast for me, who I believe you were about to call Chipmunk Man.
Hey! **Let me go!**
No, I don't think so. I think your channel just got **canceled.**
EpicCrimez, have you ever thought of applying yourself in slightly less shortsighted ways?
Or if not, have you at least thought of not ***literally livestreaming*** full evidence of your crimes to the internet?
Fear not, EpicCrimez Nation! Your favorite super villain/super streamer has a few tricks up his sleeve...
...including this weird weapon I stole from a crashed UFO!
Check out my vlog from last week for all the details, EpicCrimez Nation!!
Nancy! Watch--
POP

EpicCrimez has had a really eventful few weeks! I'd tell you to subscribe to his channel to find out more, BUT THAT'S EXACTLY WHAT HE WANTS ME TO DO.

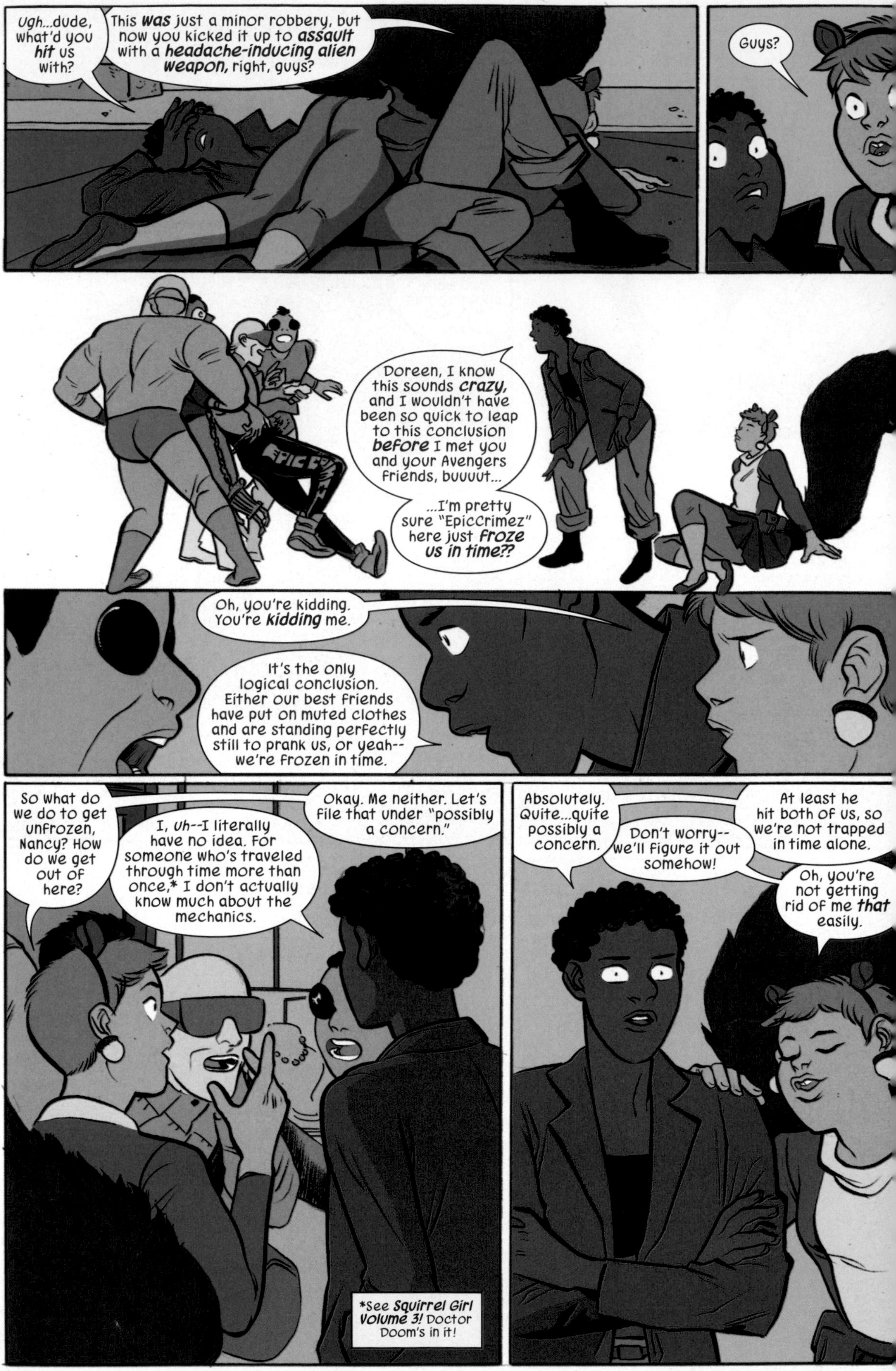
Ugh...dude, what'd you hit us with?
This was just a minor robbery, but now you kicked it up to assault with a headache-inducing alien weapon, right, guys?
Guys?
Doreen, I know this sounds crazy, and I wouldn't have been so quick to leap to this conclusion before I met you and your Avengers friends, buuuut...
...I'm pretty sure "EpicCrimez" here just froze us in time??
Oh, you're kidding. You're kidding me.
It's the only logical conclusion. Either our best friends have put on muted clothes and are standing perfectly still to prank us, or yeah--we're frozen in time.
So what do we do to get unfrozen, Nancy? How do we get out of here?
I, uh--I literally have no idea. For someone who's traveled through time more than once,* I don't actually know much about the mechanics.
Okay. Me neither. Let's file that under "possibly a concern."
*See Squirrel Girl Volume 3! Doctor Doom's in it!
Absolutely. Quite...quite possibly a concern.
Don't worry--we'll figure it out somehow!
At least he hit both of us, so we're not trapped in time alone.
Oh, you're not getting rid of me that easily.

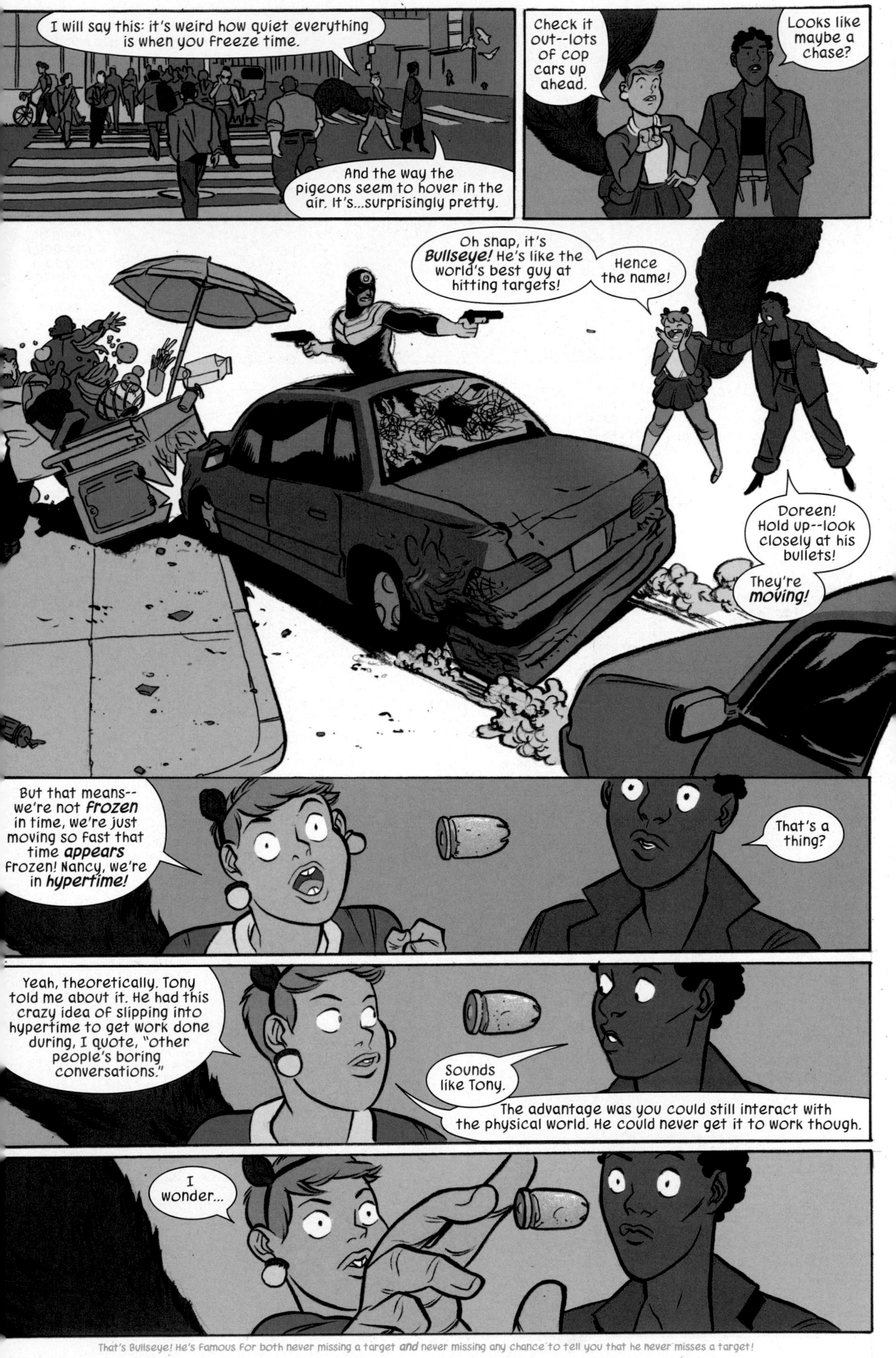
I will say this: it's weird how quiet everything is when you freeze time.
And the way the pigeons seem to hover in the air. It's...surprisingly pretty.
Check it out--lots of cop cars up ahead.
Looks like maybe a chase?
Oh snap, it's Bullseye! He's like the world's best guy at hitting targets!
Hence the name!
Doreen! Hold up--look closely at his bullets!
They're moving!
But that means--we're not frozen in time, we're just moving so fast that time appears frozen! Nancy, we're in hypertime!
That's a thing?
Yeah, theoretically. Tony told me about it. He had this crazy idea of slipping into hypertime to get work done during, I quote, "other people's boring conversations."
Sounds like Tony.
The advantage was you could still interact with the physical world. He could never get it to work though.
I wonder...

That's Bullseye! He's famous for both never missing a target *and* never missing any chance to tell you that he never misses a target!

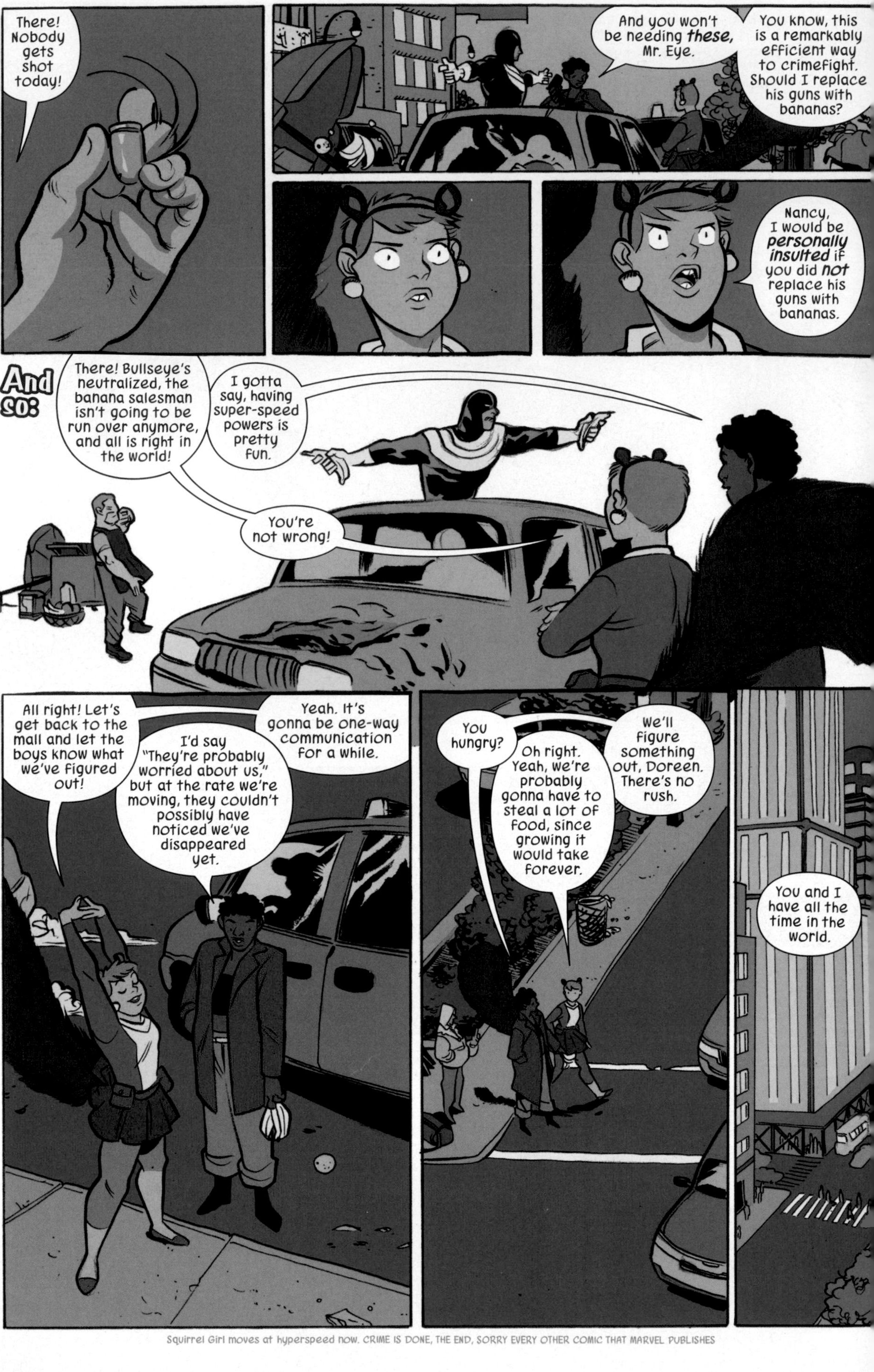
There! Nobody gets shot today!
And you won't be needing *these,* Mr. Eye.
You know, this is a remarkably efficient way to crimefight. Should I replace his guns with bananas?
Nancy, I would be ***personally insulted*** if you did ***not*** replace his guns with bananas.
And so:
There! Bullseye's neutralized, the banana salesman isn't going to be run over anymore, and all is right in the world!
I gotta say, having super-speed powers is pretty fun.
You're not wrong!
All right! Let's get back to the mall and let the boys know what we've figured out!
Yeah. It's gonna be one-way communication for a while.
I'd say "They're probably worried about us," but at the rate we're moving, they couldn't possibly have noticed we've disappeared yet.
You hungry?
Oh right. Yeah, we're probably gonna have to steal a lot of food, since growing it would take forever.
We'll figure something out, Doreen. There's no rush.
You and I have all the time in the world.

Squirrel Girl moves at hyperspeed now. CRIME IS DONE, THE END, SORRY EVERY OTHER COMIC THAT MARVEL PUBLISHES

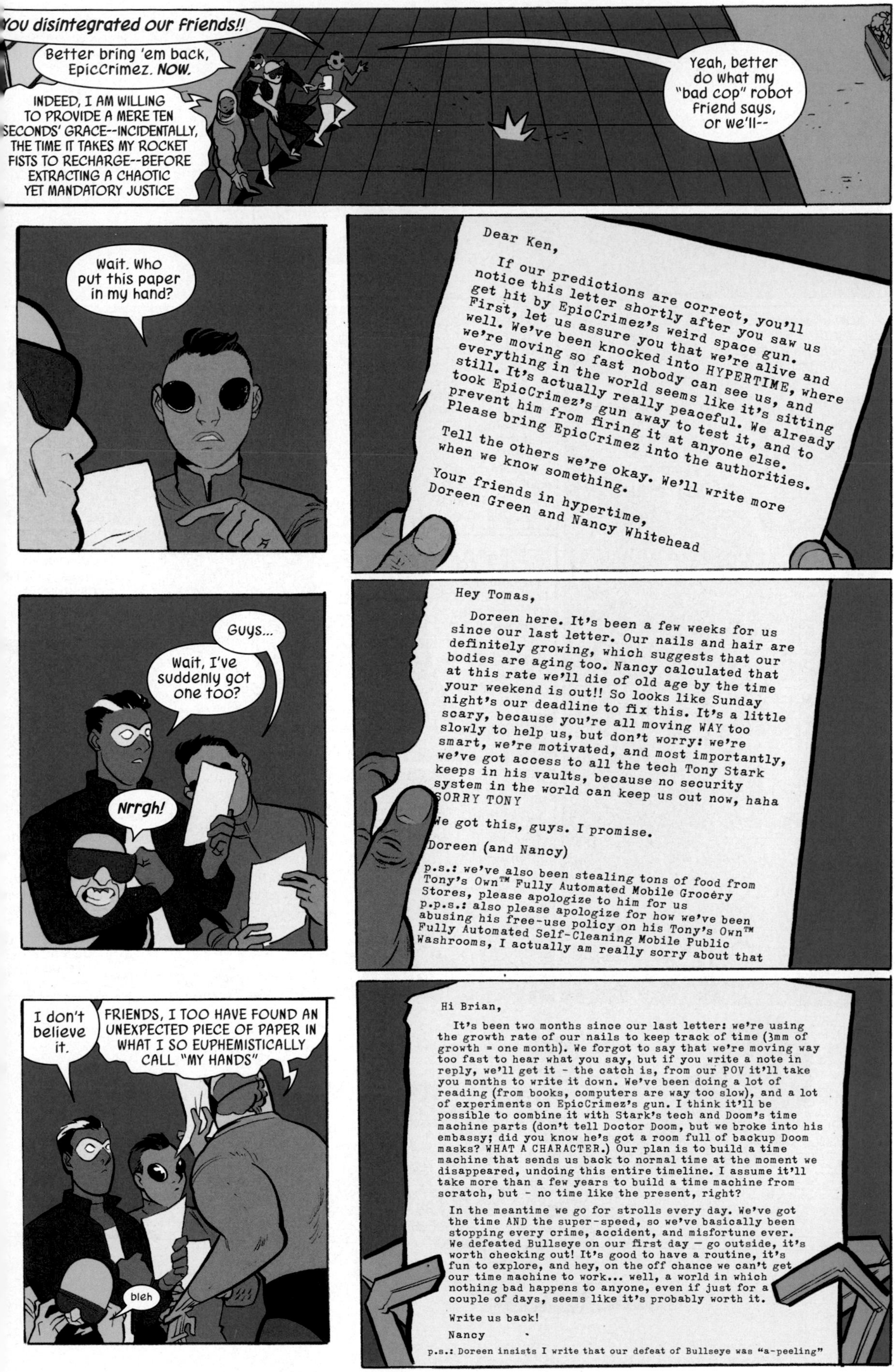
You disintegrated our friends!!
Better bring 'em back, EpicCrimez. NOW.
INDEED, I AM WILLING TO PROVIDE A MERE TEN SECONDS' GRACE--INCIDENTALLY, THE TIME IT TAKES MY ROCKET FISTS TO RECHARGE--BEFORE EXTRACTING A CHAOTIC YET MANDATORY JUSTICE
Yeah, better do what my "bad cop" robot friend says, or we'll--
Wait. Who put this paper in my hand?
Dear Ken,
If our predictions are correct, you'll notice this letter shortly after you saw us get hit by EpicCrimez's weird space gun. First, let us assure you that we're alive and well. We've been knocked into HYPERTIME, where we're moving so fast nobody can see us, and everything in the world seems like it's sitting still. It's actually really peaceful. We already took EpicCrimez's gun away to test it, and to prevent him from firing it at anyone else. Please bring EpicCrimez into the authorities.
Tell the others we're okay. We'll write more when we know something.
Your friends in hypertime,
Doreen Green and Nancy Whitehead
Guys...
Wait, I've suddenly got one too?
Nrrgh!
Hey Tomas,
Doreen here. It's been a few weeks for us since our last letter. Our nails and hair are definitely growing, which suggests that our bodies are aging too. Nancy calculated that at this rate we'll die of old age by the time your weekend is out!! So looks like Sunday night's our deadline to fix this. It's a little scary, because you're all moving WAY too slowly to help us, but don't worry: we're smart, we're motivated, and most importantly, we've got access to all the tech Tony Stark keeps in his vaults, because no security system in the world can keep us out now, haha SORRY TONY
We got this, guys. I promise.
Doreen (and Nancy)
p.s.: we've also been stealing tons of food from Tony's Own™ Fully Automated Mobile Grocery Stores, please apologize to him for us
p.p.s.: also please apologize for how we've been abusing his free-use policy on his Tony's Own™ Fully Automated Self-Cleaning Mobile Public Washrooms, I actually am really sorry about that
I don't believe it.
FRIENDS, I TOO HAVE FOUND AN UNEXPECTED PIECE OF PAPER IN WHAT I SO EUPHEMISTICALLY CALL "MY HANDS"
bleh
Hi Brian,
It's been two months since our last letter: we're using the growth rate of our nails to keep track of time (3mm of growth = one month). We forgot to say that we're moving way too fast to hear what you say, but if you write a note in reply, we'll get it - the catch is, from our POV it'll take you months to write it down. We've been doing a lot of reading (from books, computers are way too slow), and a lot of experiments on EpicCrimez's gun. I think it'll be possible to combine it with Stark's tech and Doom's time machine parts (don't tell Doctor Doom, but we broke into his embassy; did you know he's got a room full of backup Doom masks? WHAT A CHARACTER.) Our plan is to build a time machine that sends us back to normal time at the moment we disappeared, undoing this entire timeline. I assume it'll take more than a few years to build a time machine from scratch, but - no time like the present, right?
In the meantime we go for strolls every day. We've got the time AND the super-speed, so we've basically been stopping every crime, accident, and misfortune ever. We defeated Bullseye on our first day — go outside, it's worth checking out! It's good to have a routine, it's fun to explore, and hey, on the off chance we can't get our time machine to work... well, a world in which nothing bad happens to anyone, even if just for a couple of days, seems like it's probably worth it.
Write us back!
Nancy
p.s.: Doreen insists I write that our defeat of Bullseye was "a-peeling"

It took a while to find a simple mechanical typewriter that'd work even in hypertime, but come on. Who writes letters by *hand* anymore?

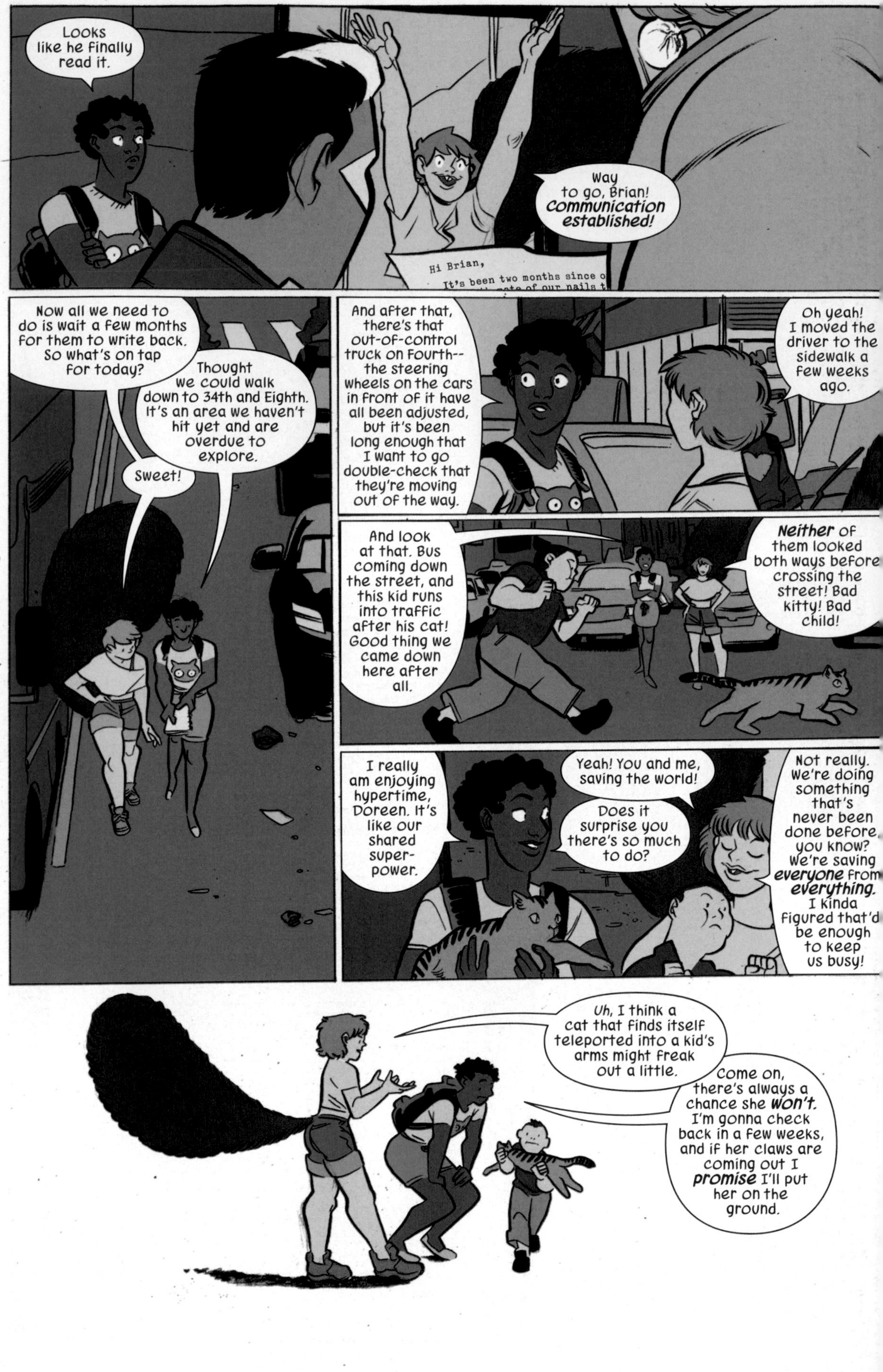
Looks like he finally read it.
Way to go, Brian! Communication established!
Hi Brian,
It's been two months since o
Now all we need to do is wait a few months for them to write back. So what's on tap for today?
Thought we could walk down to 34th and Eighth. It's an area we haven't hit yet and are overdue to explore.
Sweet!
And after that, there's that out-of-control truck on Fourth--the steering wheels on the cars in front of it have all been adjusted, but it's been long enough that I want to go double-check that they're moving out of the way.
Oh yeah! I moved the driver to the sidewalk a few weeks ago.
And look at that. Bus coming down the street, and this kid runs into traffic after his cat! Good thing we came down here after all.
Neither of them looked both ways before crossing the street! Bad kitty! Bad child!
I really am enjoying hypertime, Doreen. It's like our shared super-power.
Yeah! You and me, saving the world!
Does it surprise you there's so much to do?
Not really. We're doing something that's never been done before, you know? We're saving everyone from everything. I kinda figured that'd be enough to keep us busy!
Uh, I think a cat that finds itself teleported into a kid's arms might freak out a little.
Come on, there's always a chance she won't. I'm gonna check back in a few weeks, and if her claws are coming out I promise I'll put her on the ground.

The driver suddenly finds himself sitting on the sidewalk, still in a driving position. He tries to play it off like it's no big deal. "I meant to do this," he says, to anyone who will lis

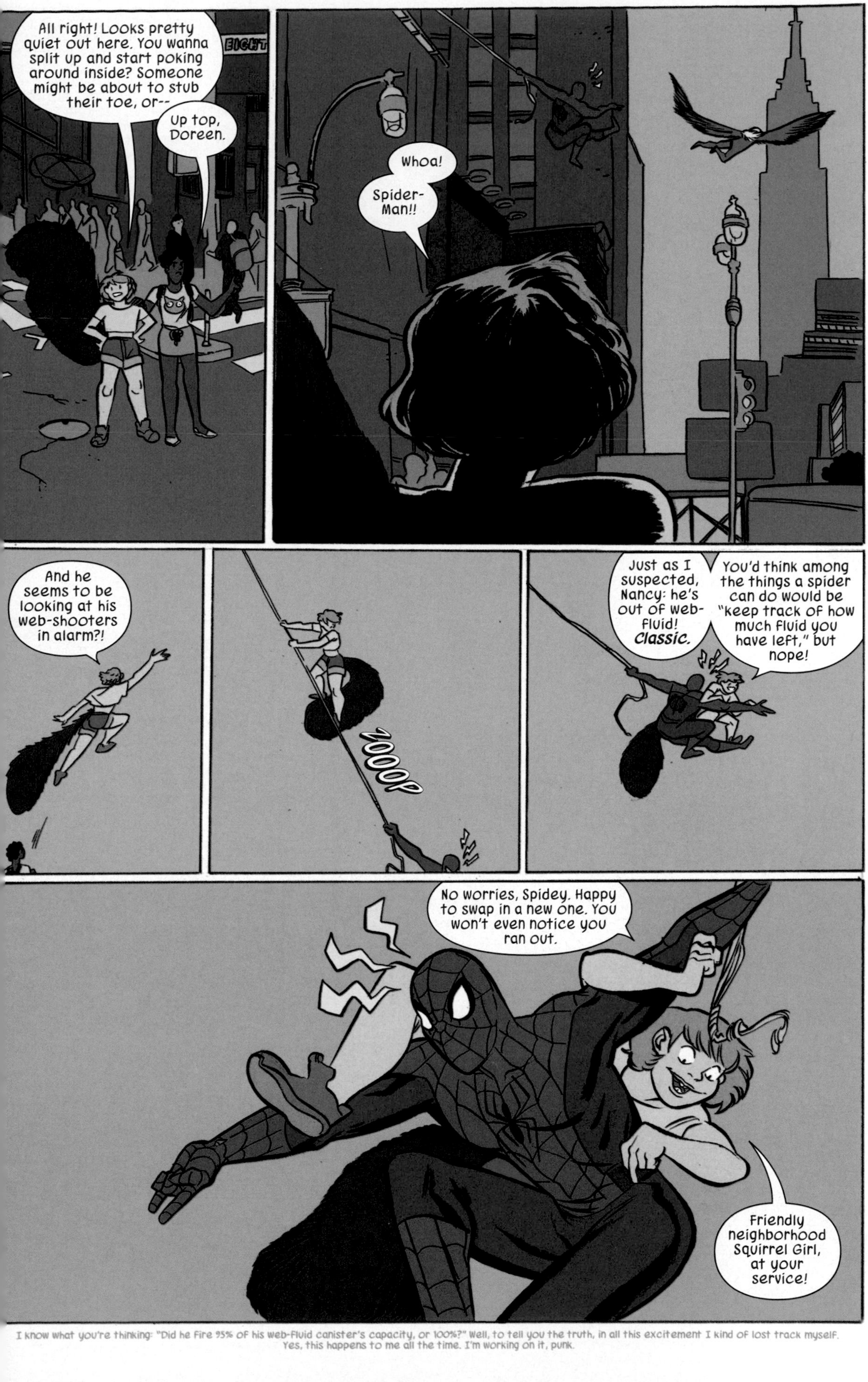
EIGHT
All right! Looks pretty quiet out here. You wanna split up and start poking around inside? Someone might be about to stub their toe, or--
Up top, Doreen.
Whoa!
Spider-Man!!
And he seems to be looking at his web-shooters in alarm?!
ZOOOP
Just as I suspected, Nancy: he's out of web-fluid! *Classic.*
You'd think among the things a spider can do would be "keep track of how much fluid you have left," but nope!
No worries, Spidey. Happy to swap in a new one. You won't even notice you ran out.
Friendly neighborhood Squirrel Girl, at your service!

I know what you're thinking: "Did he fire 95% of his web-fluid canister's capacity, or 100%?" Well, to tell you the truth, in all this excitement I kind of lost track myself. Yes, this happens to me all the time. I'm working on it, punk.

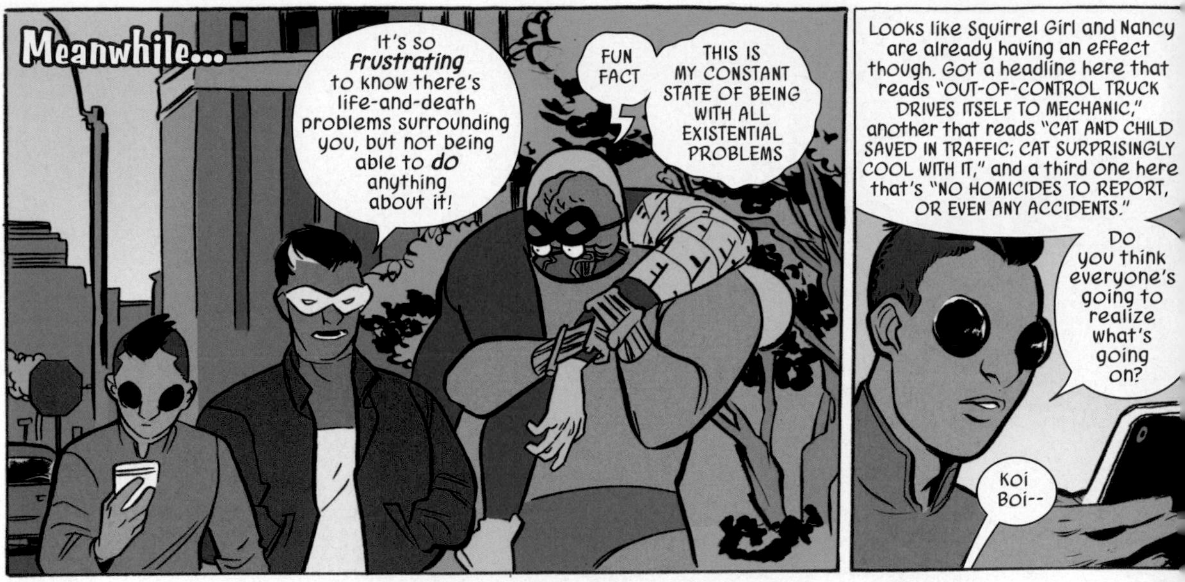
Meanwhile...
It's so frustrating to know there's life-and-death problems surrounding you, but not being able to do anything about it!
FUN FACT
THIS IS MY CONSTANT STATE OF BEING WITH ALL EXISTENTIAL PROBLEMS
Looks like Squirrel Girl and Nancy are already having an effect though. Got a headline here that reads "OUT-OF-CONTROL TRUCK DRIVES ITSELF TO MECHANIC," another that reads "CAT AND CHILD SAVED IN TRAFFIC; CAT SURPRISINGLY COOL WITH IT," and a third one here that's "NO HOMICIDES TO REPORT, OR EVEN ANY ACCIDENTS."
Do you think everyone's going to realize what's going on?
Koi Boi--

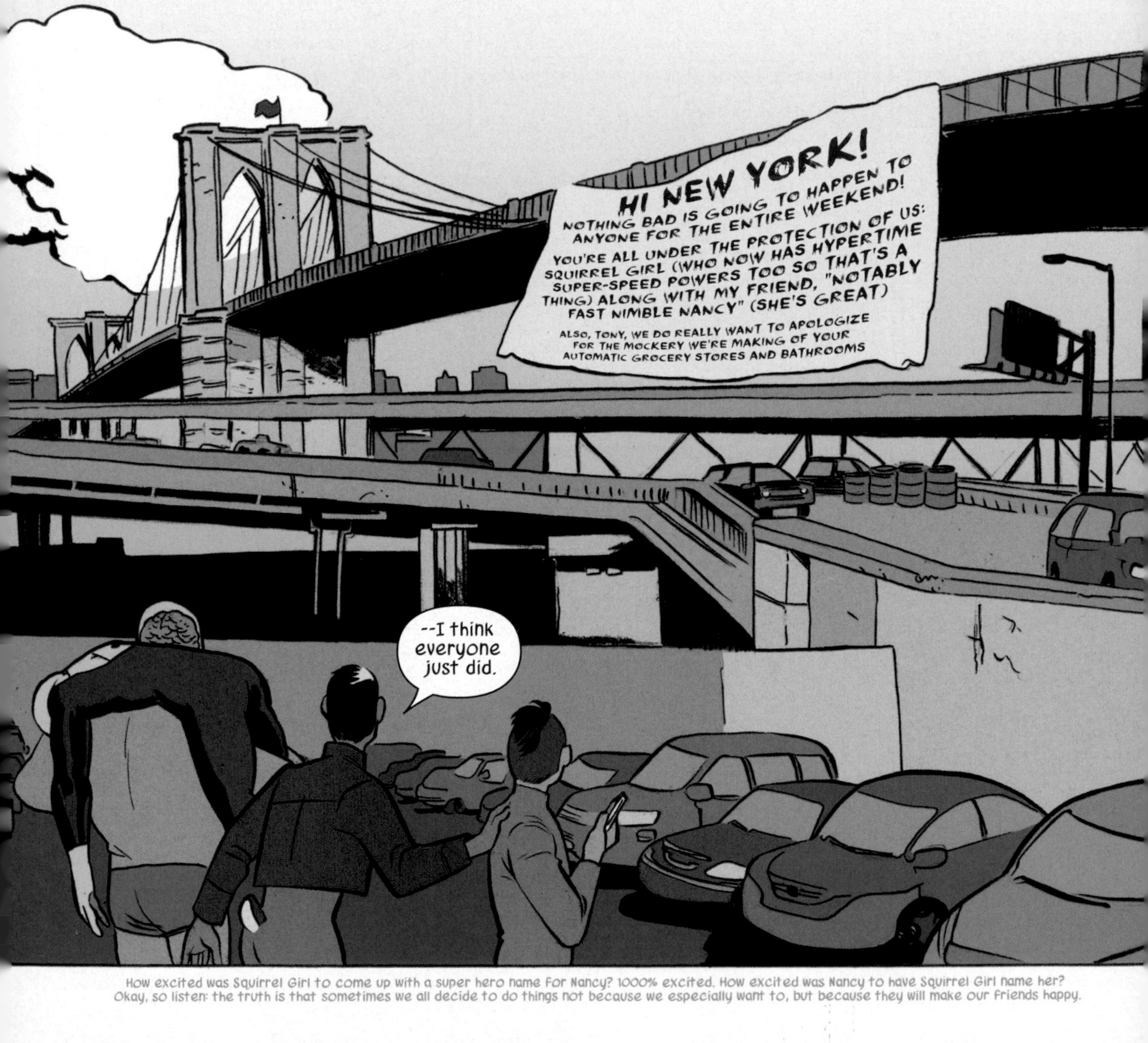
HI NEW YORK!
NOTHING BAD IS GOING TO HAPPEN TO ANYONE FOR THE ENTIRE WEEKEND!
YOU'RE ALL UNDER THE PROTECTION OF US: SQUIRREL GIRL (WHO NOW HAS HYPERTIME SUPER-SPEED POWERS TOO SO THAT'S A THING) ALONG WITH MY FRIEND, "NOTABLY FAST NIMBLE NANCY" (SHE'S GREAT)
ALSO, TONY, WE DO REALLY WANT TO APOLOGIZE FOR THE MOCKERY WE'RE MAKING OF YOUR AUTOMATIC GROCERY STORES AND BATHROOMS
--I think everyone just did.

How excited was Squirrel Girl to come up with a super hero name for Nancy? 1000% excited. How excited was Nancy to have Squirrel Girl name her? Okay, so listen: the truth is that sometimes we all decide to do things not because we especially want to, but because they will make our friends happy.

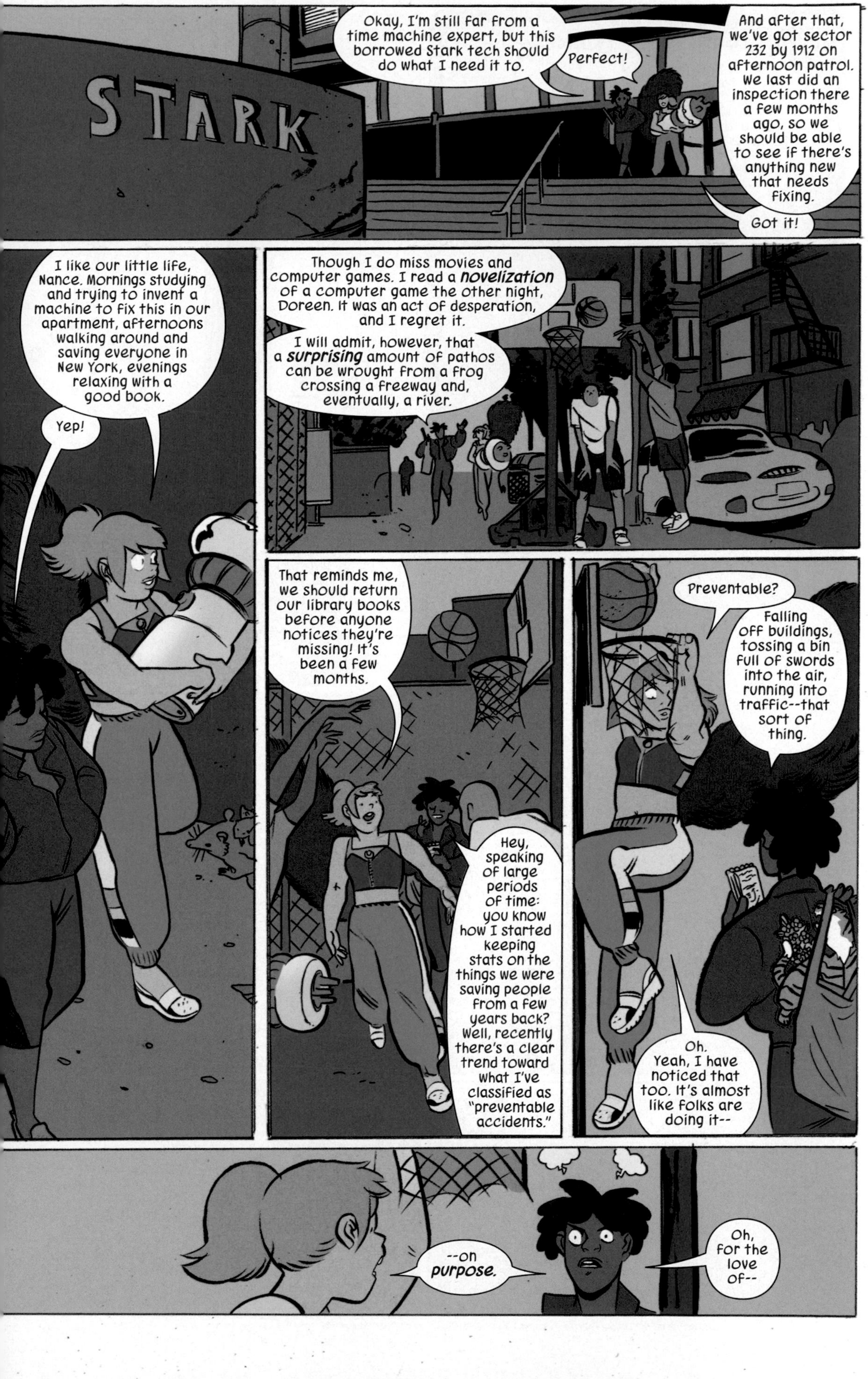
STARK
Okay, I'm still far from a time machine expert, but this borrowed Stark tech should do what I need it to.
Perfect!
And after that, we've got sector 232 by 1912 on afternoon patrol. We last did an inspection there a few months ago, so we should be able to see if there's anything new that needs fixing.
Got it!
I like our little life, Nance. Mornings studying and trying to invent a machine to fix this in our apartment, afternoons walking around and saving everyone in New York, evenings relaxing with a good book.
Yep!
Though I do miss movies and computer games. I read a *novelization* of a computer game the other night, Doreen. It was an act of desperation, and I regret it.
I will admit, however, that a *surprising* amount of pathos can be wrought from a frog crossing a freeway and, eventually, a river.
That reminds me, we should return our library books before anyone notices they're missing! It's been a few months.
Hey, speaking of large periods of time: you know how I started keeping stats on the things we were saving people from a few years back? Well, recently there's a clear trend toward what I've classified as "preventable accidents."
Preventable?
Falling off buildings, tossing a bin full of swords into the air, running into traffic--that sort of thing.
Oh. Yeah, I have noticed that too. It's almost like folks are doing it--
--on *purpose.*
Oh, for the love of--

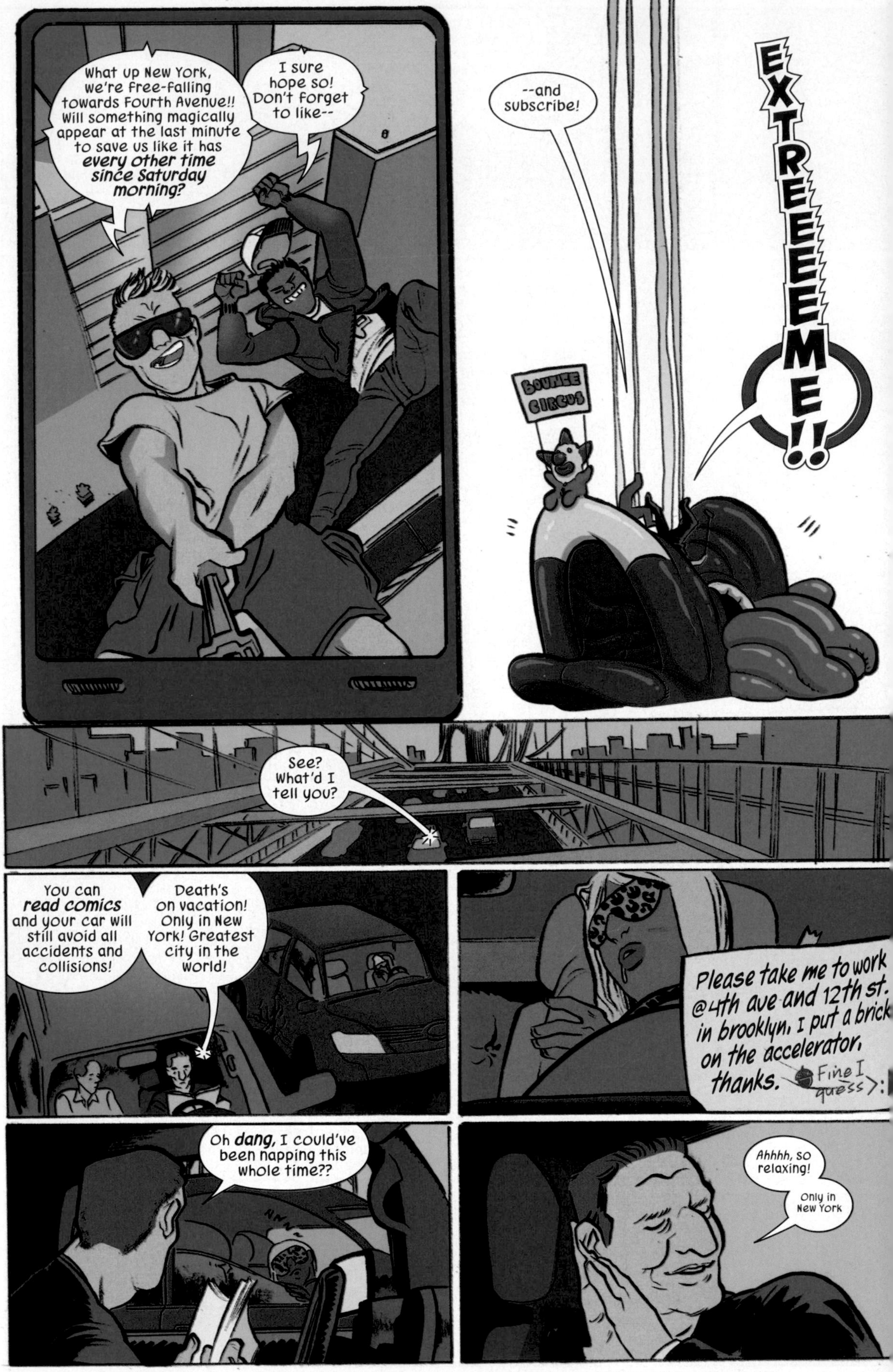
What up New York, we're free-falling towards Fourth Avenue!! Will something magically appear at the last minute to save us like it has every other time since Saturday morning?
I sure hope so! Don't forget to like--
--and subscribe!
EXTREEEEEME!!
BOUNCE CIRCUS
See? What'd I tell you?
You can read comics and your car will still avoid all accidents and collisions!
Death's on vacation! Only in New York! Greatest city in the world!
Please take me to work @4th ave and 12th st. in brooklyn, I put a brick on the accelerator, thanks.
Fine I guess >:
Oh dang, I could've been napping this whole time??
Ahhhh, so relaxing!
Only in New York

He's going to be *so happy* when he realizes he can stay in bed and write "please teleport me and my bed to work" on his shirt.

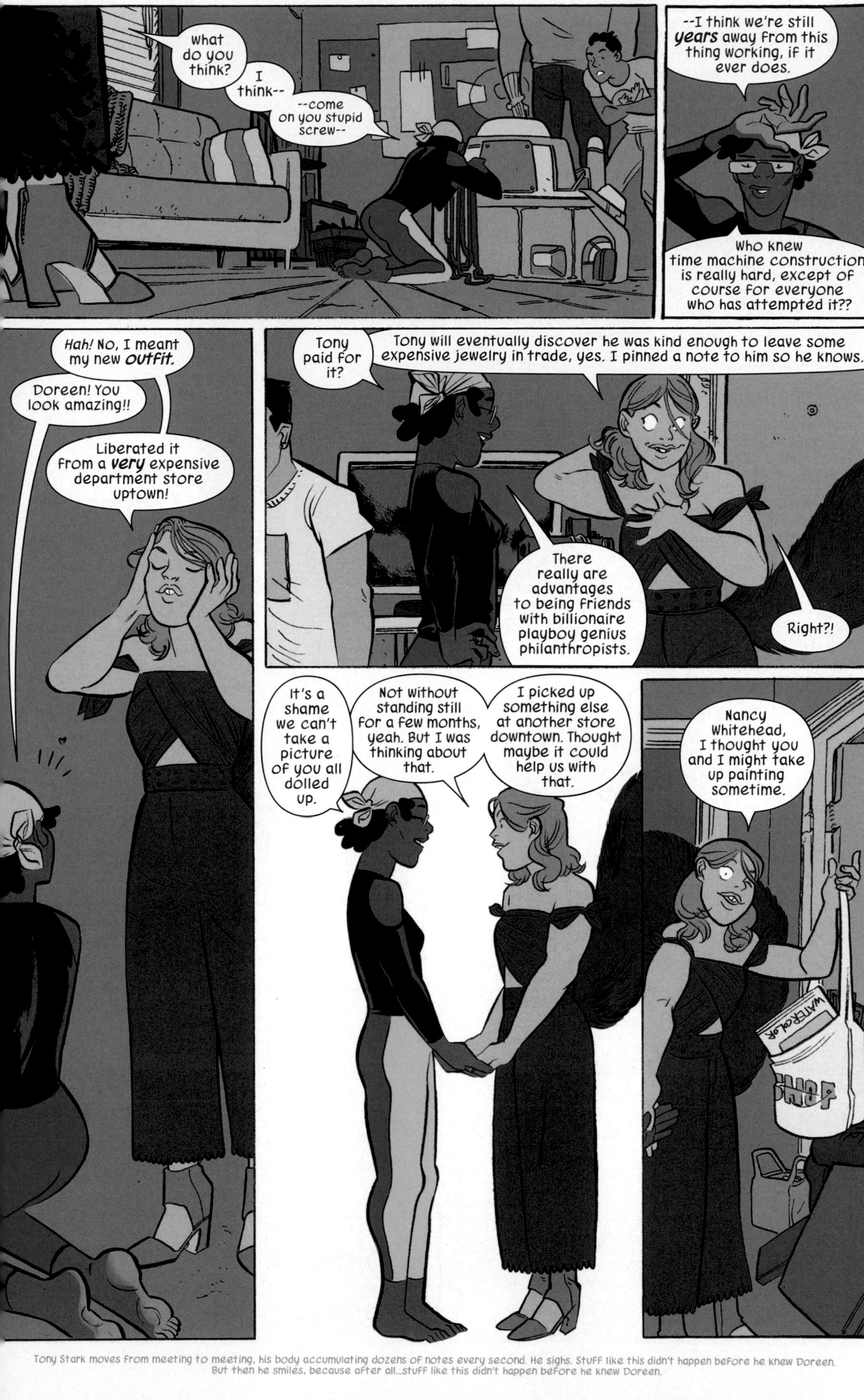
What do you think?
I think--
--come on you stupid screw--
--I think we're still *years* away from this thing working, if it ever does.
Who knew time machine construction is really hard, except of course for everyone who has attempted it??
Hah! No, I meant my new *outfit.*
Doreen! You look amazing!!
Liberated it from a *very* expensive department store uptown!
Tony paid for it?
Tony will eventually discover he was kind enough to leave some expensive jewelry in trade, yes. I pinned a note to him so he knows.
There really are advantages to being friends with billionaire playboy genius philanthropists.
Right?!
It's a shame we can't take a picture of you all dolled up.
Not without standing still for a few months, yeah. But I was thinking about that.
I picked up something else at another store downtown. Thought maybe it could help us with that.
Nancy Whitehead, I thought you and I might take up painting sometime.
WATERCOLOR
SHOP

Tony Stark moves from meeting to meeting, his body accumulating dozens of notes every second. He sighs. Stuff like this didn't happen before he knew Doreen. But then he smiles, because after all...stuff like this didn't happen before he knew Doreen.

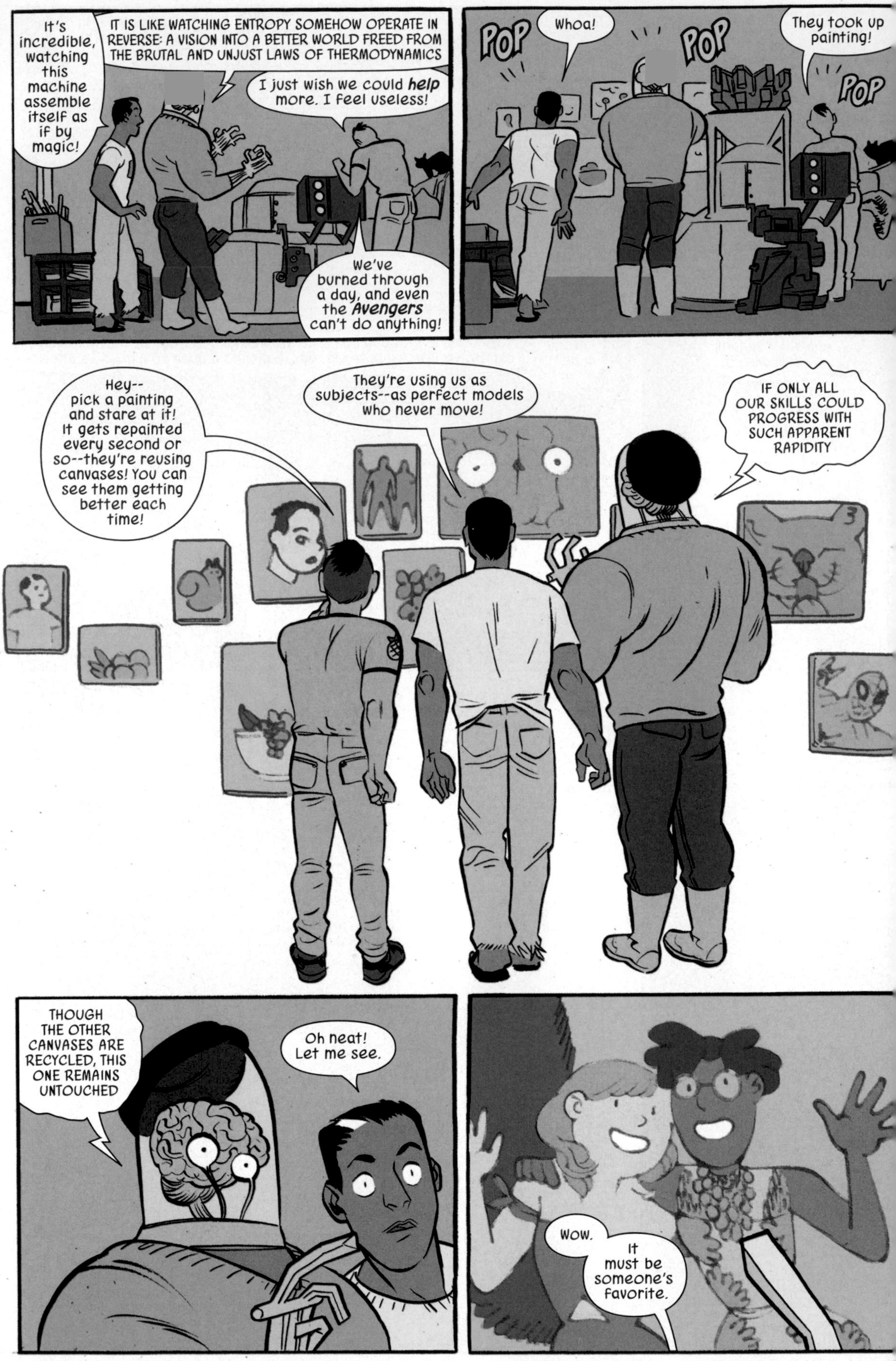

It's incredible, watching this machine assemble itself as if by magic!
IT IS LIKE WATCHING ENTROPY SOMEHOW OPERATE IN REVERSE: A VISION INTO A BETTER WORLD FREED FROM THE BRUTAL AND UNJUST LAWS OF THERMODYNAMICS
I just wish we could **help** more. I feel useless!
We've burned through a day, and even the *Avengers* can't do anything!
POP
Whoa!
POP
They took up painting!
POP
Hey-- pick a painting and stare at it! It gets repainted every second or so--they're reusing canvases! You can see them getting better each time!
They're using us as subjects--as perfect models who never move!
IF ONLY ALL OUR SKILLS COULD PROGRESS WITH SUCH APPARENT RAPIDITY
THOUGH THE OTHER CANVASES ARE RECYCLED, THIS ONE REMAINS UNTOUCHED
Oh neat! Let me see.
WOW.
It must be someone's favorite.

Brain Drain legitimately fantasizes about a world in which entropy operates in reverse. You could scramble an egg back into its shell! You could fire a leaf blower into your room and your clothes would fold themselves in the air and land back in the closet! *You could save so much time on household tasks.*

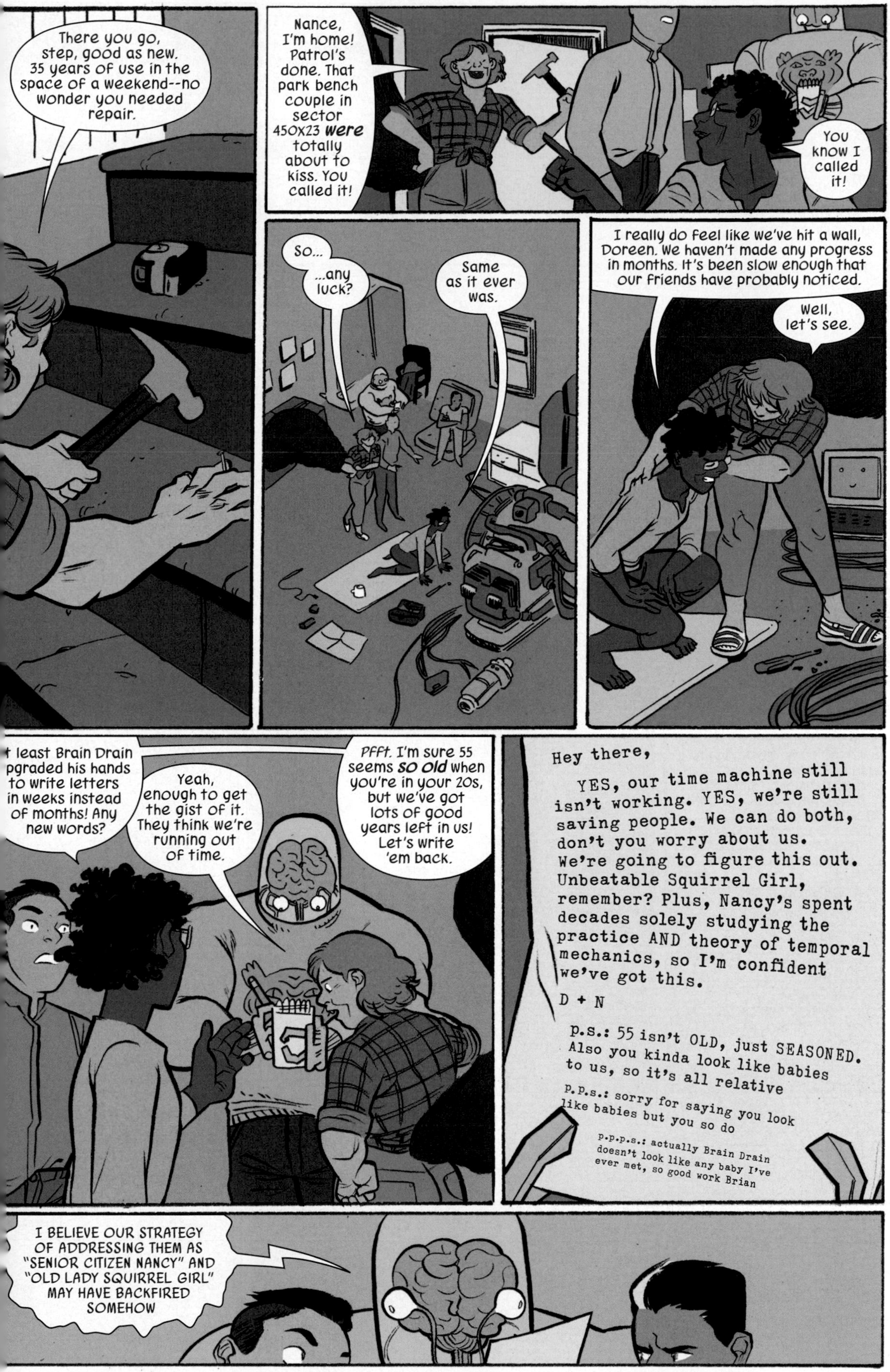
There you go, step, good as new. 35 years of use in the space of a weekend--no wonder you needed repair.
Nance, I'm home! Patrol's done. That park bench couple in sector 450X23 *were* totally about to kiss. You called it!
You know I called it!
So...
...any luck?
Same as it ever was.
I really do feel like we've hit a wall, Doreen. We haven't made any progress in months. It's been slow enough that our friends have probably noticed.
Well, let's see.
t least Brain Drain pgraded his hands to write letters in weeks instead of months! Any new words?
Yeah, enough to get the gist of it. They think we're running out of time.
Pfft. I'm sure 55 seems ***so old*** when you're in your 20s, but we've got lots of good years left in us! Let's write 'em back.
Hey there,
YES, our time machine still isn't working. YES, we're still saving people. We can do both, don't you worry about us. We're going to figure this out. Unbeatable Squirrel Girl, remember? Plus, Nancy's spent decades solely studying the practice AND theory of temporal mechanics, so I'm confident we've got this.
D + N
p.s.: 55 isn't OLD, just SEASONED. Also you kinda look like babies to us, so it's all relative
p.p.s.: sorry for saying you look like babies but you so do
p.p.p.s.: actually Brain Drain doesn't look like any baby I've ever met, so good work Brian
I BELIEVE OUR STRATEGY OF ADDRESSING THEM AS "SENIOR CITIZEN NANCY" AND "OLD LADY SQUIRREL GIRL" MAY HAVE BACKFIRED SOMEHOW

IN MY EXPERIENCE IT IS EXTREMELY HARD TO PREDICT WHAT THE ELDERLY ENJOY BEING ADDRESSED AS. GRANDMA BRAIN DRAIN HERSELF HAS PERSONALLY REJECTED "SENIOR CITIZEN," "CITIZEN SENIOR," "LONGEVITRON," AND EVEN "THE SILVER TSUNAMI"

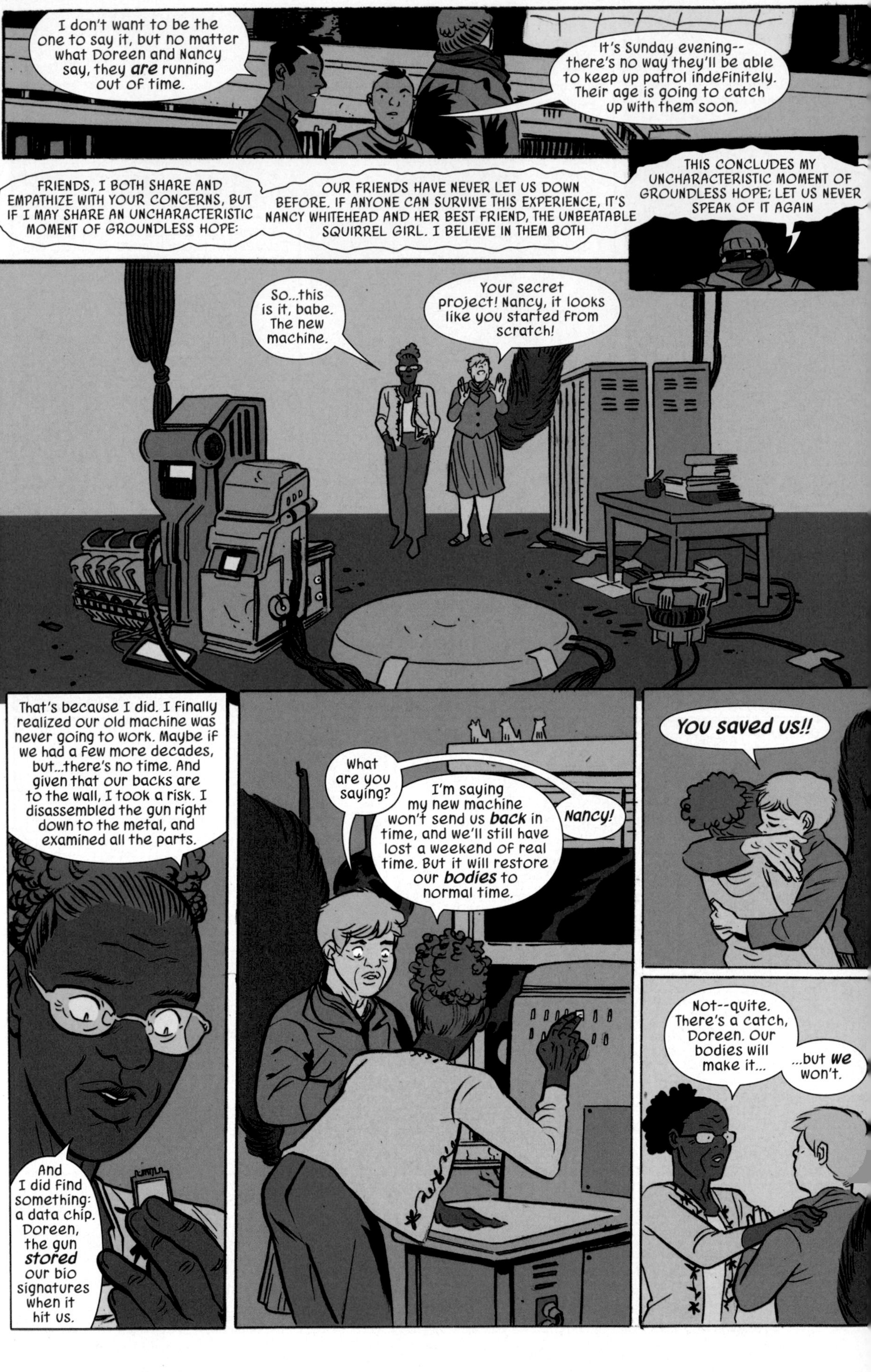
I don't want to be the one to say it, but no matter what Doreen and Nancy say, they *are* running out of time.
It's Sunday evening-- there's no way they'll be able to keep up patrol indefinitely. Their age is going to catch up with them soon.
FRIENDS, I BOTH SHARE AND EMPATHIZE WITH YOUR CONCERNS, BUT IF I MAY SHARE AN UNCHARACTERISTIC MOMENT OF GROUNDLESS HOPE:
OUR FRIENDS HAVE NEVER LET US DOWN BEFORE. IF ANYONE CAN SURVIVE THIS EXPERIENCE, IT'S NANCY WHITEHEAD AND HER BEST FRIEND, THE UNBEATABLE SQUIRREL GIRL. I BELIEVE IN THEM BOTH
THIS CONCLUDES MY UNCHARACTERISTIC MOMENT OF GROUNDLESS HOPE; LET US NEVER SPEAK OF IT AGAIN
So...this is it, babe. The new machine.
Your secret project! Nancy, it looks like you started from scratch!
That's because I did. I finally realized our old machine was never going to work. Maybe if we had a few more decades, but...there's no time. And given that our backs are to the wall, I took a risk. I disassembled the gun right down to the metal, and examined all the parts.
And I did find something: a data chip. Doreen, the gun *stored* our bio signatures when it hit us.
What are you saying?
Nancy!
I'm saying my new machine won't send us *back* in time, and we'll still have lost a weekend of real time. But it will restore our *bodies* to normal time.
You saved us!!
Not--quite. There's a catch, Doreen. Our bodies will make it...
...but *we* won't.

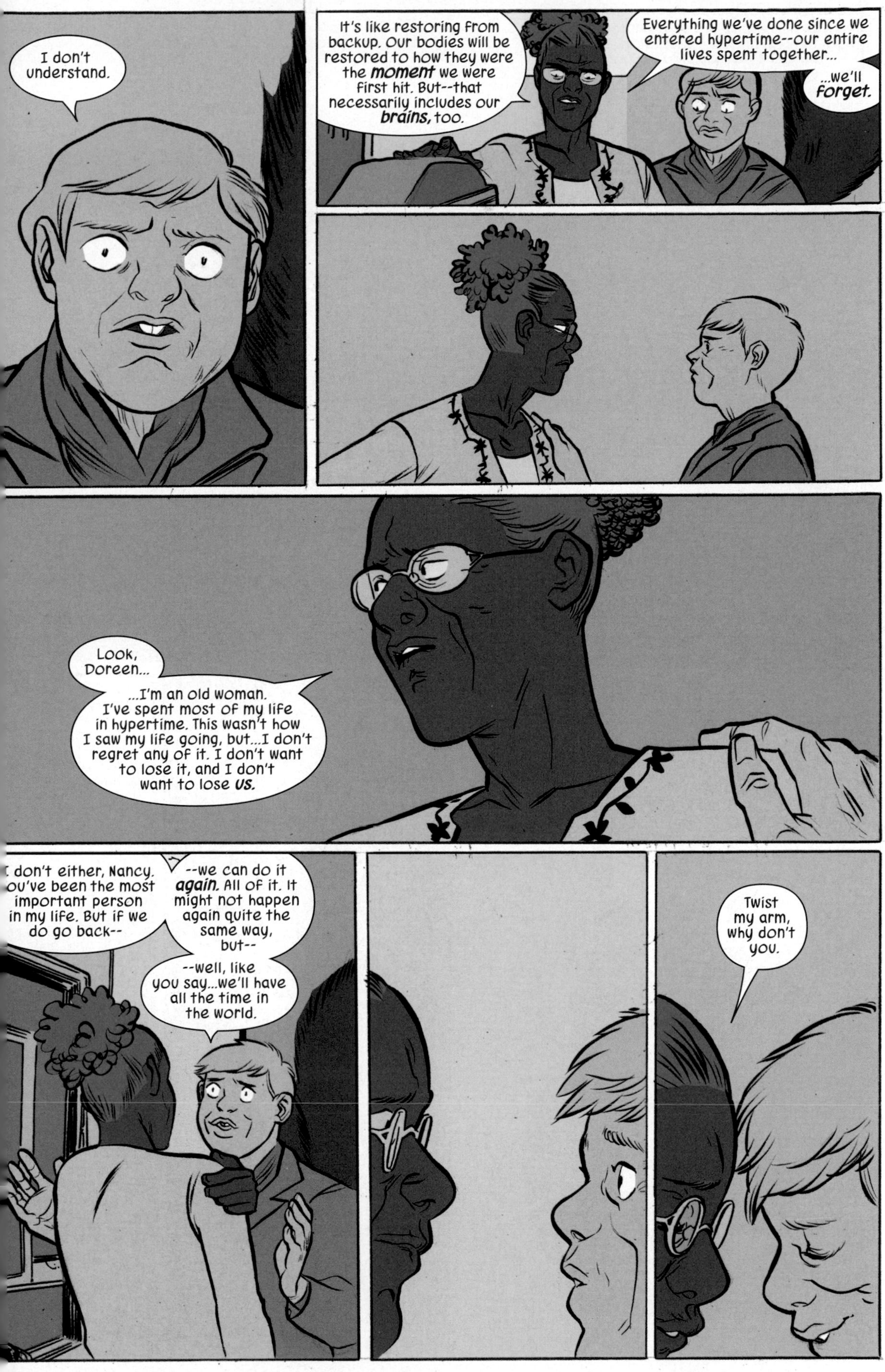
I don't understand.
It's like restoring from backup. Our bodies will be restored to how they were the *moment* we were first hit. But--that necessarily includes our *brains*, too.
Everything we've done since we entered hypertime--our entire lives spent together...
...we'll *forget.*
Look, Doreen...
...I'm an old woman. I've spent most of my life in hypertime. This wasn't how I saw my life going, but...I don't regret any of it. I don't want to lose it, and I don't want to lose *US.*
I don't either, Nancy. You've been the most important person in my life. But if we do go back--
--we can do it *again.* All of it. It might not happen again quite the same way, but--
--well, like you say...we'll have all the time in the world.
Twist my arm, why don't you.

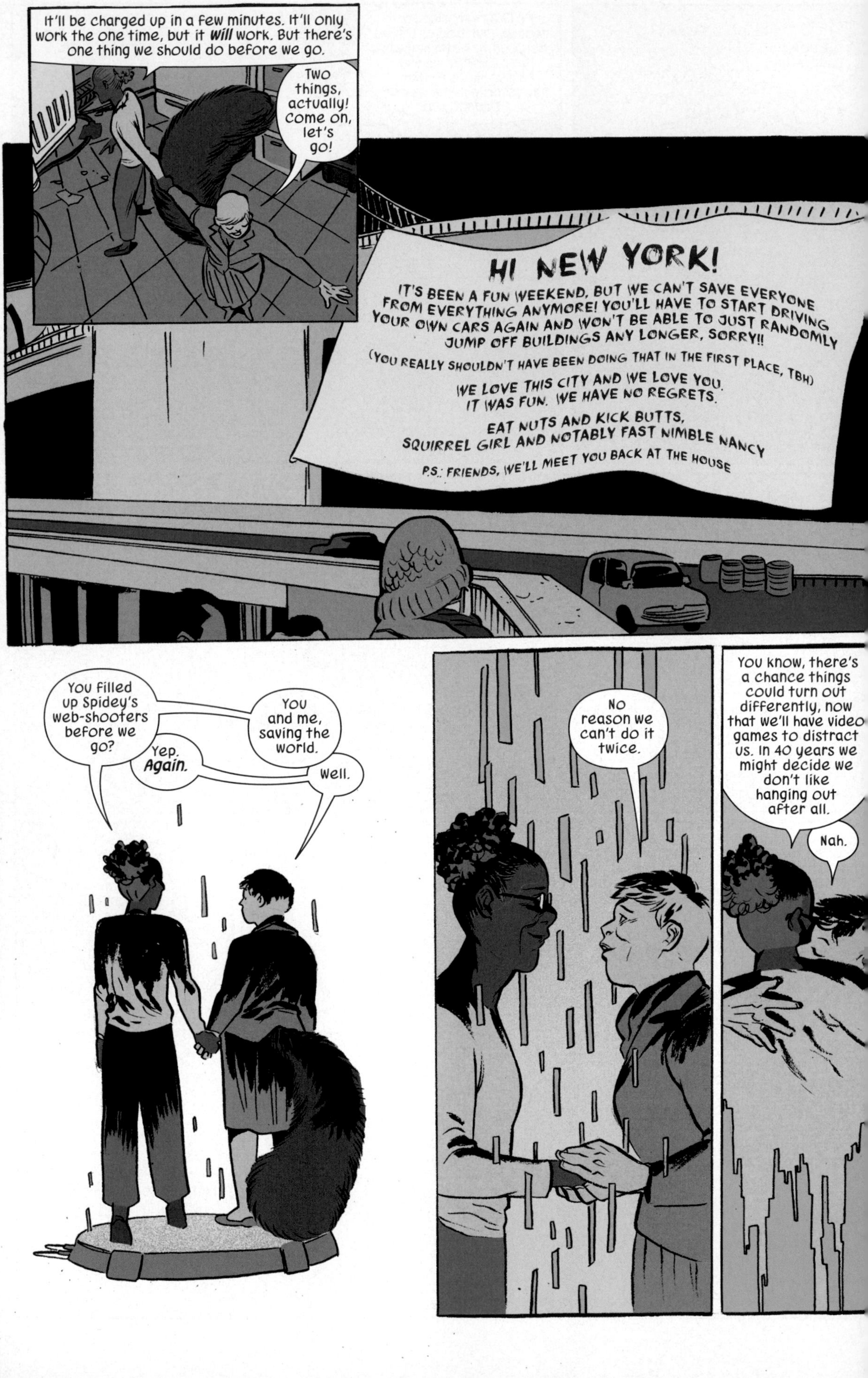
It'll be charged up in a few minutes. It'll only work the one time, but it *will* work. But there's one thing we should do before we go.
Two things, actually! Come on, let's go!
HI NEW YORK!
IT'S BEEN A FUN WEEKEND, BUT WE CAN'T SAVE EVERYONE FROM EVERYTHING ANYMORE! YOU'LL HAVE TO START DRIVING YOUR OWN CARS AGAIN AND WON'T BE ABLE TO JUST RANDOMLY JUMP OFF BUILDINGS ANY LONGER, SORRY!!
(YOU REALLY SHOULDN'T HAVE BEEN DOING THAT IN THE FIRST PLACE, TBH)
WE LOVE THIS CITY AND WE LOVE YOU.
IT WAS FUN. WE HAVE NO REGRETS.
EAT NUTS AND KICK BUTTS,
SQUIRREL GIRL AND NOTABLY FAST NIMBLE NANCY
P.S.: FRIENDS, WE'LL MEET YOU BACK AT THE HOUSE
You filled up Spidey's web-shooters before we go?
You and me, saving the world.
Yep. *Again.*
Well.
No reason we can't do it twice.
You know, there's a chance things could turn out differently, now that we'll have video games to distract us. In 40 years we might decide we don't like hanging out after all.
Nah.

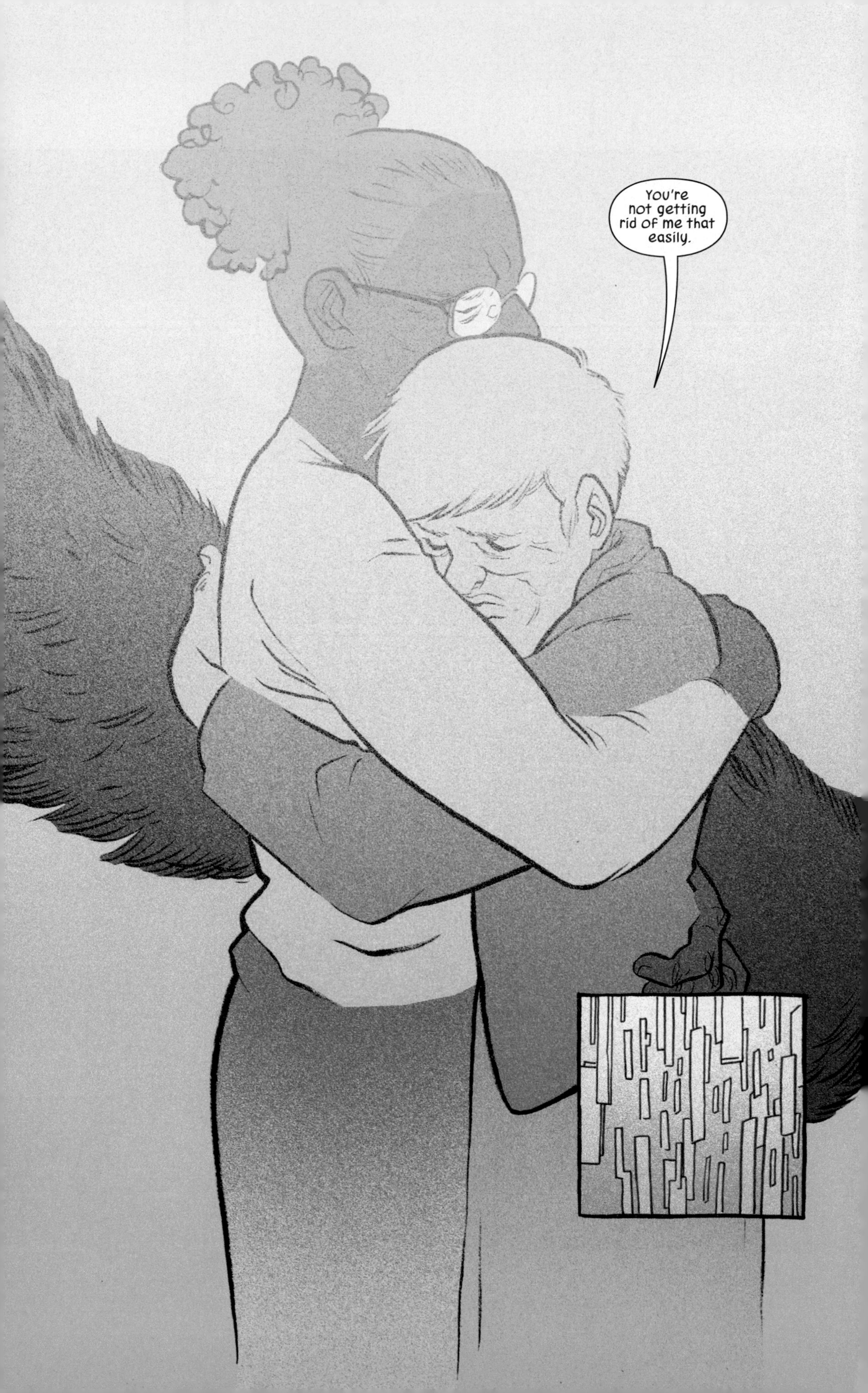
You're not getting rid of me that easily.

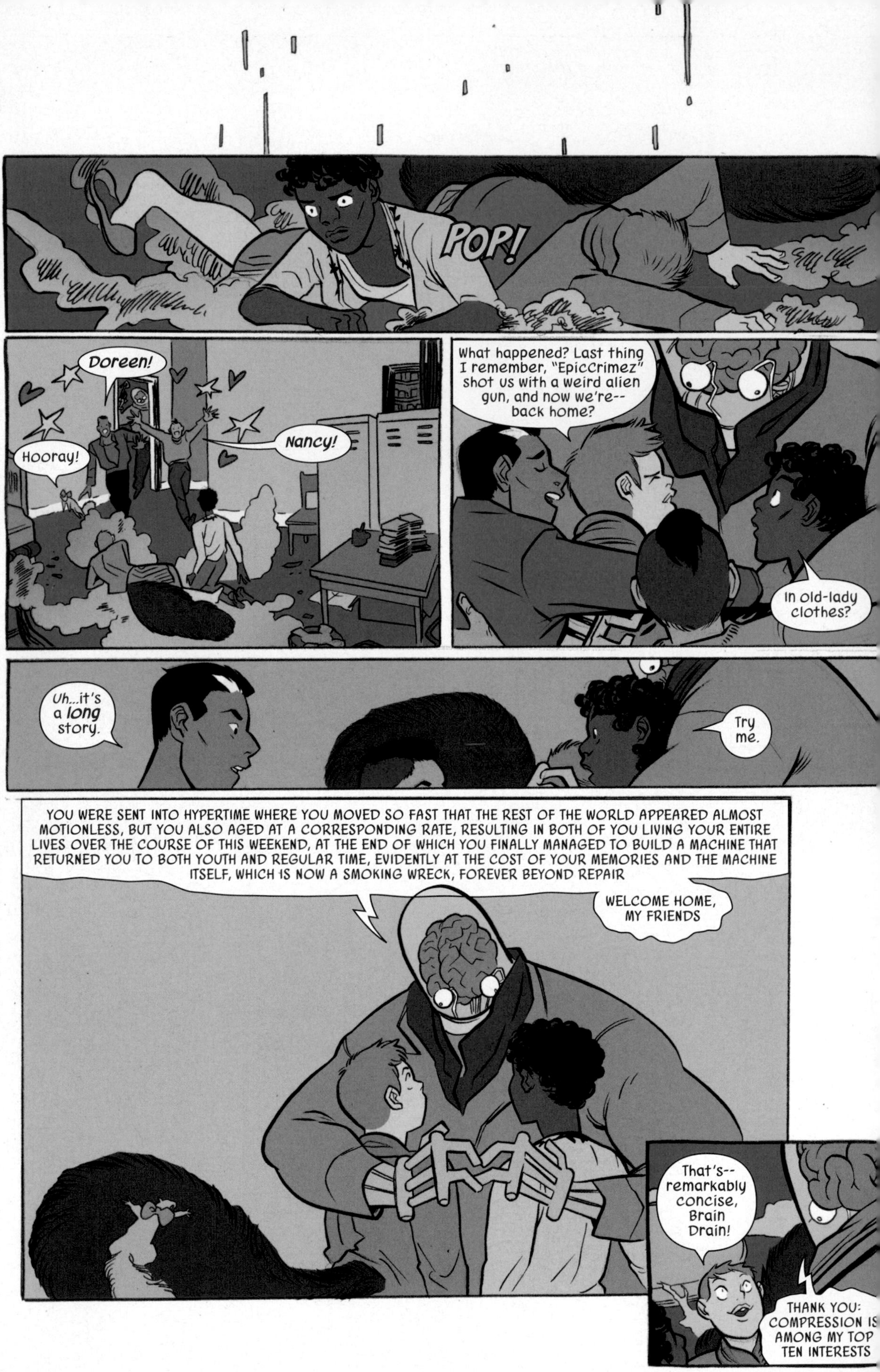
POP!
Doreen!
Hooray!
Nancy!
What happened? Last thing I remember, "EpicCrimez" shot us with a weird alien gun, and now we're-- back home?
In old-lady clothes?
Uh...it's a *long* story.
Try me.
YOU WERE SENT INTO HYPERTIME WHERE YOU MOVED SO FAST THAT THE REST OF THE WORLD APPEARED ALMOST MOTIONLESS, BUT YOU ALSO AGED AT A CORRESPONDING RATE, RESULTING IN BOTH OF YOU LIVING YOUR ENTIRE LIVES OVER THE COURSE OF THIS WEEKEND, AT THE END OF WHICH YOU FINALLY MANAGED TO BUILD A MACHINE THAT RETURNED YOU TO BOTH YOUTH AND REGULAR TIME, EVIDENTLY AT THE COST OF YOUR MEMORIES AND THE MACHINE ITSELF, WHICH IS NOW A SMOKING WRECK, FOREVER BEYOND REPAIR
WELCOME HOME, MY FRIENDS
That's-- remarkably concise, Brain Drain!
THANK YOU: COMPRESSION IS AMONG MY TOP TEN INTERESTS

OR SHOULD I SAY, "CMPRSN<=10th INTRST"

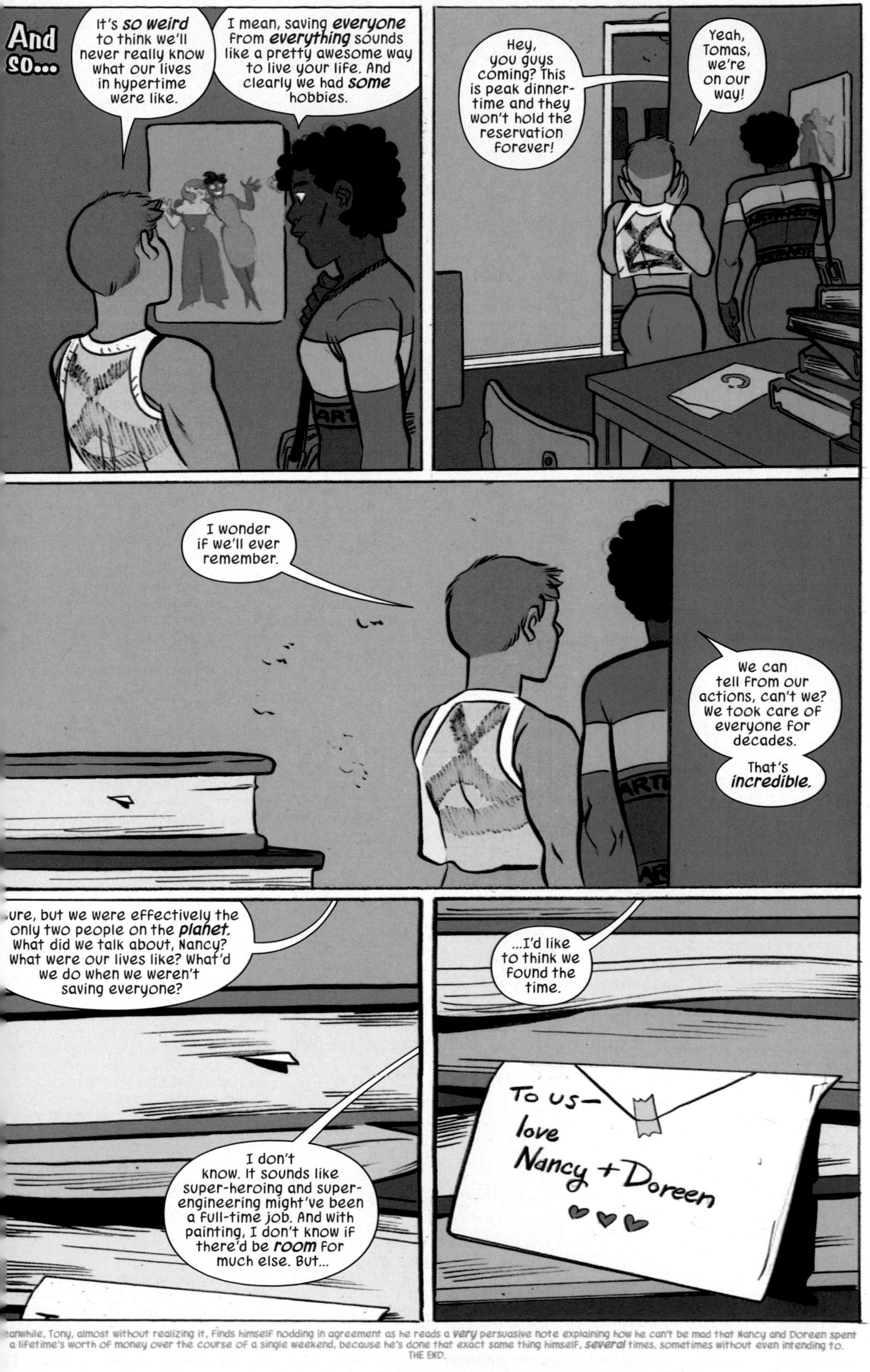
And so...
It's *so weird* to think we'll never really know what our lives in hypertime were like.
I mean, saving *everyone* from *everything* sounds like a pretty awesome way to live your life. And clearly we had *some* hobbies.
Hey, you guys coming? This is peak dinner-time and they won't hold the reservation forever!
Yeah, Tomas, we're on our way!
I wonder if we'll ever remember.
We can tell from our actions, can't we? We took care of everyone for decades.
That's *incredible.*
ure, but we were effectively the only two people on the *planet.* What did we talk about, Nancy? What were our lives like? What'd we do when we weren't saving everyone?
I don't know. It sounds like super-heroing and super-engineering might've been a full-time job. And with painting, I don't know if there'd be *room* for much else. But...
...I'd like to think we found the time.
To us— love Nancy + Doreen

eanwhile, Tony, almost without realizing it, finds himself nodding in agreement as he reads a *very* persuasive note explaining how he can't be mad that Nancy and Doreen spent a lifetime's worth of money over the course of a single weekend, because he's done that exact same thing himself, *several* times, sometimes without even intending to.

THE END.

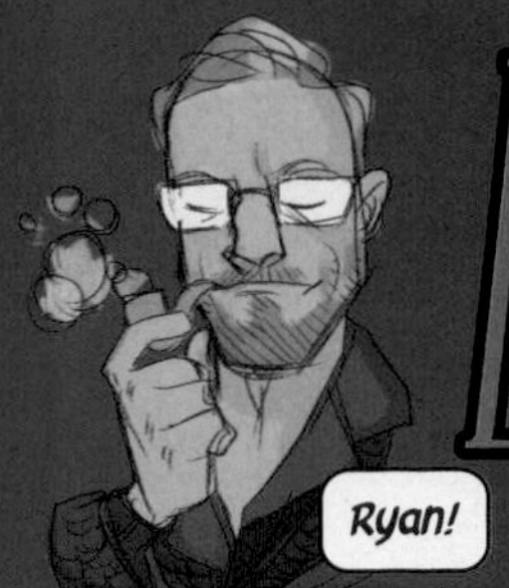
Ryan!

Letters From Nuts

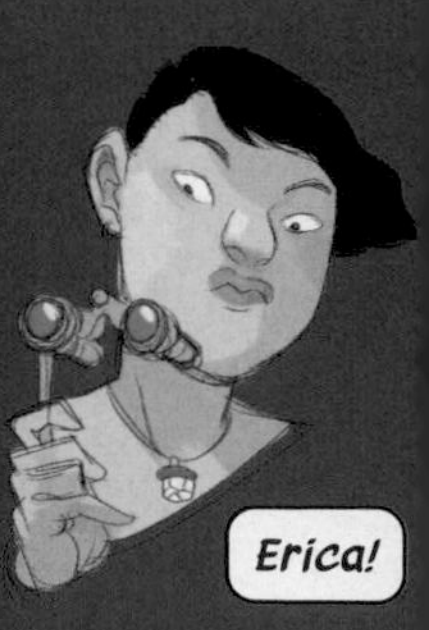
Erica!

Send letters to mheroes@marvel.com or 135 W 50th St, 7th Floor, New York, NY 10020 (Please mark "OKAY TO PRINT"

My six-year-old twin daughters have been wanting to send you photos of their Marvel Bishoujo Statues of Squirrel Girl for months. We recently moved, so time has been a bit tight with getting that accomplished.

After I told them that today was National Squirrel Appreciation Day, they insisted that we had to mail you the photograph now! Along with their little statues, they're also sporting their second batch of licensed Doreen shirts.

Also, I have one question. Any word on when they'll be releasing a Marvel Legends action figure of Squirrel Girl? We can't wait to each buy our own copies of them!

Darrick Patrick
Dayton, Ohio

P.S. Here is the photograph of Logann and Nola with their new Squirrel Girl swag.

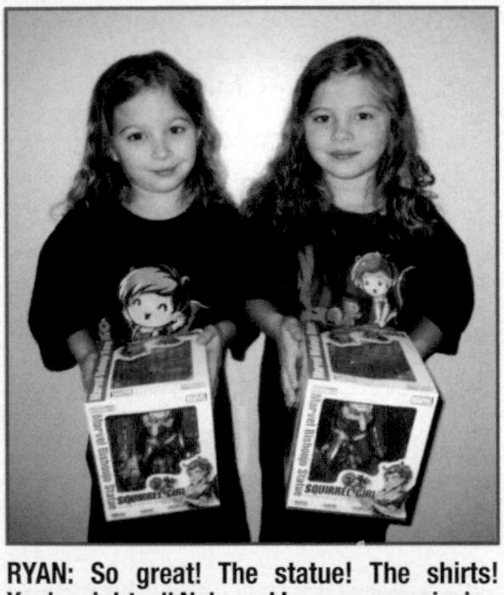
SQUIRREL GIRL
SQUIRREL GIRL

RYAN: So great! The statue! The shirts! You're right, all Nola and Logann are missing is the action figure, and I wish whoever was in charge of Turning Marvel Heroes Into Figures With At Least 14 Points Of Articulation would hurry up and make that happen! (Before I wrote comics I was big into action figures, so I have Opinions over how many points of articulation a figure should have for Maximum Battle/Empathy Action.)

ERICA: I love this! And--oh, wow. Two of everything! I'm jealous! My cousin and I kept track of our VHS tapes so we could trade our clamshell case Disney movies back and forth. I'm glad you guys are settled in enough to start taking photos and writing into comics letters pages.

Hi SQUIRREL GIRL crew,

I love your series! I look forward to each volume and love giving away copies of your comics to people whom I love. I was never really into comics and didn't understand the allure, but I decided just to try it out and see what happens. I always loved Batman; Iron Man and Spider-Man are also some of my top faves. But I heard about Squirrel Girl simply due to a meme my FB bestie Kayla posted and was instantly intrigued. I purchased Vol. 1 and a few pages in I was hooked! I very soon purchased Vol. 2 and just had to wait a few weeks for Vol. 3 at the time. I then sent a copy of Vol. 1 to my favorite feminist Facebook page as a thank you and also as a means to fortify her with extra misogynist-butt-kicking prowess! Well, she loved it and over a year later I still see her page posting lots of Squirrel Girl things!

I also dressed up as Squirrel Girl this last Halloween! This next Halloween I may just try to get a better jacket, so I may be Miss Green again!

THEORY TIME!

Mary--okay, there is something up with her, huh? Yeah, like, I predict she is gunna attain some sort of super-power due to her technological expertise, but she won't be fully good or bad! Right? She's pretty, I can see why Tomas likes her, but dude, Tomas needs to date Doreen! Please!

Thank you for creating such a great comic and a means both to escape and inspire, which is what the best art does. I'm a writer and working on my own fantasy novel series now about faeries with a focus on world religions and diversity. I hope that my work can have the same type of impact that yours does!

Eric

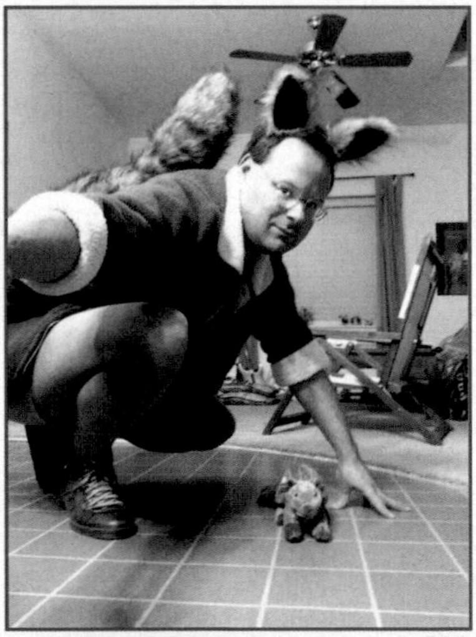

RYAN: All I can say about Mary is there's a bit more about her in THE VERY NEXT ISSUE OF THIS SERIES! I like her a lot, mainly because she reminds me of every engineer I've ever known: just a wee bit of mad scientist in the mix. And, also like all engineers I've also known, she wouldn't need a super-power to take ove[r] the world. Thank you for these super-kin[d] words, and your costume looks amazin[g]

ERICA: There's so much here so I'm jus[t] going to go down a list: 1. I love Mary and he[r] efficient '90s hacker-themed apartment. 2 I'm glad you like the book so much and ar[e] getting other people into it! 3. That costum[e] is great! 4. Good luck with your own work; [I] hope it makes the impact you're looking fo[r]

Hey Squirrel People,

You probably guessed this based on the fact tha[t] I'm writing you, but I love this comic! You migh[t] even say I'm...NUTS about it? (Sorry.) In m[y] personal opinion, it's the best comic Marvel i[s] currently publishing. (Admittedly, I've only rea[d] issues from seven-ish titles being publishe[d] right now, but still.) It's got great writing an[d] humor and awesomesauce art; it's pretty sel[f] contained, completely ignoring all the gian[t] crossovers other than mentioning them in th[e] delightful Twitter recaps (as someone wh[o] got into Marvel comics reading back issue[s] from the '70s and early '80s, when annu[al] company-wide crossovers weren't exactly [a] thing, this gives me life); it's not bogged dow[n] with lots of confusing repeatedly retconne[d] continuity; and it's got these complete[ly] random things like Negative Zone ice cream [o]r weird montages or nihilist robots with huma[n] brains or Canadian Avengers action figures [o]r dinosaur Ultron or Alfredo and Chef Bear oka[y] this is a huge run-on sentence I should sto[p] now. Basically, your comic is lighthearted an[d] awesome and weirdly educational and I lov[e] it. Also I think your version of Count Nefaria [is] the best and should be the 616 canon versio[n]. Literally the only reason I haven't got this thi[ng] on a pull list is that I'm not in one place yea[r] round because of college and breaks and stuf[f].

Also, I introduced the comic to my 8-year-o[ld] sister over winter break and she enjoys it a[s] well! I checked out the first volume from th[e] library, we read the first few issues togethe[r] and then she went and read the rest without m[e] when I was working and she was home sick. [If] you publish this letter I'll send some picture[s] she drew. Actually, I'll send them either way, it['s] just that I can't right now because they are [in] her room and I am in my dorm. I fail at bribin[g]. Aaaand this letter is kind of long an[d] meandering and you probably won['t] publish it, but if you did that would be coo[l]. Until Doreen calls Animal Control o[n] Tippy-Toe, Make Mine Marvel, I gues[s].

Éowy[n]

RYAN: Éowyn, you are now officially o[n] the hook to send us pictures! And than[k] you--the recaps are a lot of fun, and th[e] goal there was: Since every issue cou[ld] be someone's first, we wanted to make [it] so things would be understandable. B[ut]

ince every issue (except our [first] first ne) is also NOT someone's first, we wanted o make things a little more interesting han just reading a "here's what happened" age--great to hear we succeeded in hat! Chef Bear is my favorite and I'm ery happy he's living happily ever after.

RICA: Well, Alfredo is MY favorite because like learning about new types of fancy hickens. He's a Sumatra, by the way. hey're not new, just new to me. Sumatras re rare, and generally closer to wild fowl han domestic. They're kept more for show han food because they're gorgeous but also on't lay a lot of eggs and are very skinny. I'm oing to go off on a totally different tangent ecause I'm thinking about it right now. When had to draw Alfredo I was thinking about an rticle I read in high school, probably in the Aetro, about how Fifth Avenue types were eeping designer chickens and then getting id of them because chickens are actually eally filthy (poop and salmonella, kids). So Aelissa HAD to have a beautiful, impractical hicken, but also the fact that these birds are errible eats means that her ordering him to e killed was 100% about her being a jerk, ecause a $3 pack of thighs at the corner tore would be tastier than this prized bird.

'm sorry, I've forgotten the question.

o, I just wanted to first thank you for onsistently putting out freaking PHENOMENAL vork. I've loved SQUIRREL GIRL from day one, and 100% of that love comes from how easy it is to empathize with her and the way she handles everything. I'm an adult man, and I still have a LOT to learn about how to handle situations in pretty much every aspect of my life, which usually does NOT mean reading comics. I was reading the Mole Man arc though, and while I'm well past the fedora-wearing "m'lady"-ing phase of my life (thankfully) it really hit home to see precisely how that kind of treatment actually hurts people. I knew before reading that arc that how I used to behave was wrong, but much more as a statement of fact, like a line of code or something, another parameter to avoid. Seeing the way Doreen was affected by Mole Man's actions made the impact of that kind of behavior much easier for me to understand and empathize with. It's one thing to not be a creep because you understand that it IS the wrong thing, and another entirely to understand WHY it's the wrong thing. Beyond that, the arc with Doreen and Tomas' relationship (or lack thereof) also helped me cope a bit with a similar situation in my own life. Being reminded that if you really love someone, their happiness should be what matters to you, is outrageously helpful. It's not always easy to cope with those emotions, so being able to channel what was a very toxic feeling into a SIGNIFICANTLY more wholesome one made my pretty crappy (no offense to Ken!) day into a much, much better one. So thanks for all of the emotional support, laughter and unusually helpful life counseling. Keep up the good work!

Tyler

RYAN: Oh heck, we all have things we look back on where we thought, "This is definitely a cool and good thing to say and do," and then now we think, "Oh no, oh no, I was not cool or good at all." It feels bad but it's also a terrific metric that you're growing as a person, so I try to hold tight to that when I feel ridiculous remembering the stupid stuff I've done when I was much younger/ also one week ago. Also: The mental trick of deciding "I like someone so I want them to be happy even if that happiness doesn't involve me" is something we should all have in our repertoire, so props for pulling it off!

ERICA: I'm glad that story resonated with you. When we first started the book we had every intention of setting up Doreen and Tomas. But after a year and a half--which included the "Secret Wars" break that represented, I want to say, eight months of time in the Marvel U--it seemed ridiculous, but we still wanted to address this thread we had started. So the idea that just because you're the protagonist it doesn't mean you're going to get what you want and that other people are separate from you and have other valid feelings were things we wanted to put in there. Also, I'm not gonna lie: I'm sick of movies where the hero is into someone and then the movie does everything it can to convince you that the love interest's significant other is "less than" in some way so that the hero can have this person.

Hey everyone. The issue of SQUIRREL GIRL you're holding right now is my last for the foreseeable future. The lovely and talented DEREK CHARM is going to be drawing the next arc, which I'll be doing the covers for.

I'm so glad I got to spend the past three and a half years working on this book. It has changed my life, and that is not an exaggeration. I'm going to tell a story that not a lot of people know because, frankly, I don't discuss this much.

When Wil Moss first asked me if I wanted to draw SQUIRREL GIRL (and this was literally just A drawing of SG because he was still pitching the book to his bosses), I had ended a seven-year relationship about a month earlier but was still in the same apartment as my ex, and my father had just died maybe two weeks prior, AND I was low on cash because I wasn't taking a lot of work and was traveling back home constantly. I asked Wil if I could redesign her, he said sure, and then I drew about four pages of Squirrel Girl sketches for this mystery book. When I was in the middle of working on those first sketches, I met Dave, the man I'm soon going to marry. So I turn in the drawings, and two weeks later the comics news sites are talking about how Marvel has trademarked "Squirrel Girl"--my first clue! Two weeks after that, I get an e-mail from Ryan North introducing himself and saying the book is happening.

Since then, I've drawn 905 pages of Squirrel Girl (including covers). I've traveled across the country and to other countries meeting fans. I've won two Eisners. And most importantly, I've spent a portion of my life on a book that people tell me they share with their family and loved ones, that brightens their day, that makes them evaluate their lives, that reflects their lived experiences in ways they haven't seen elsewhere.

So yes, my life is completely different than it was before even the idea of working on SQUIRREL GIRL came into my consciousness. And it's so much better for it.

To Wil, thanks for taking a chance on a new artist.

To Ryan, it's been a pleasure working with you and becoming your friend.

To Rico, you bring color into the lives of everyone around you and...uh... thanks for rolling with the punches every time I was slow or late.

To the readers, thank you all for picking up the book and writing in every month. We couldn't have done it without your support.

-Erica

P.S. I feel a little like a ghost fading off into the sky whispering "my job here is done" because Ryan made me cry with the end of the SQUIRREL GIRL BEATS UP THE MARVEL UNIVERSE! graphic novel, but he just now told me that I made him cry with this issue so BOOM! We're even, baby!

Next Issue:

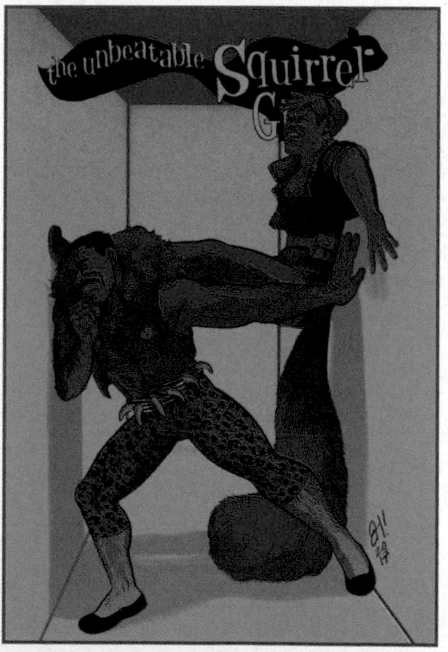
the unbeatable Squirrel

Ryan and artist Derek Charm kick off a new storyarc that will finally answer the question: If Kraven the Hunter is a bad guy, how come he's always, like, so nice and helpful? Plus: a "shocking" revelation!

Attention, Squirrel Scouts! Make sure to check out our production blog, **unbeatablesquirrelgirl.tumblr.com**, where we post behind-the-scenes stuff on how the book gets made, along with all sorts of cool things *you* make: fanart, cosplay, whatever!

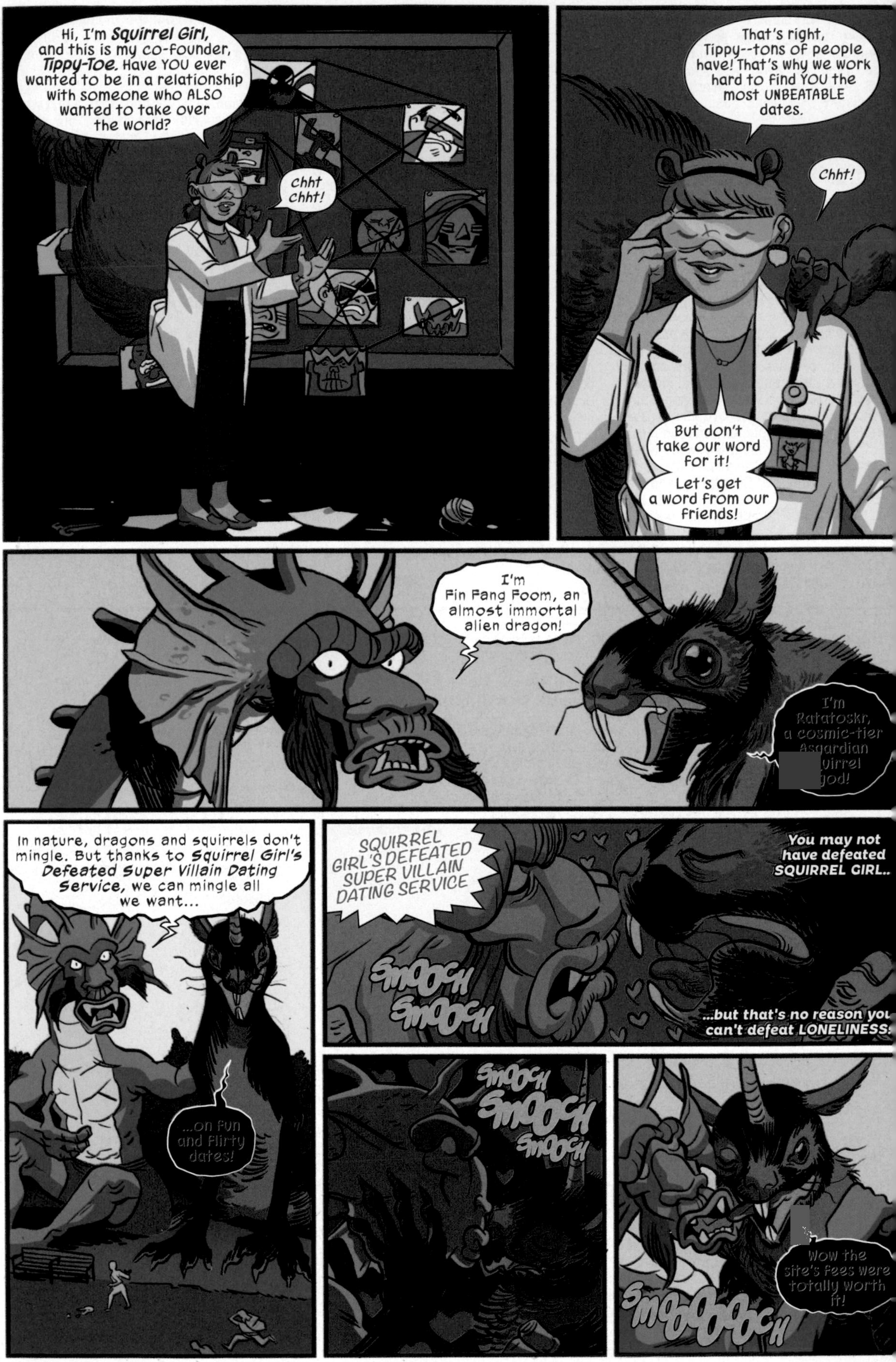
Hi, I'm Squirrel Girl, and this is my co-founder, Tippy-Toe. Have YOU ever wanted to be in a relationship with someone who ALSO wanted to take over the world?
Chht Chht!
That's right, Tippy--tons of people have! That's why we work hard to find YOU the most UNBEATABLE dates.
Chht!
But don't take our word for it!
Let's get a word from our friends!
I'm Fin Fang Foom, an almost immortal alien dragon!
I'm Ratatoskr, a cosmic-tier Asgardian
In nature, dragons and squirrels don't mingle. But thanks to Squirrel Girl's Defeated Super Villain Dating Service, we can mingle all we want...
...on fun and flirty dates!
SQUIRREL GIRL'S DEFEATED SUPER VILLAIN DATING SERVICE
You may not have defeated SQUIRREL GIRL..
SMOOCH SMOOCH
...but that's no reason you can't defeat LONELINESS.
SMOOCH SMOOCH SMOOCH
Wow the site's fees were totally worth it!
SMOOOOOOCH

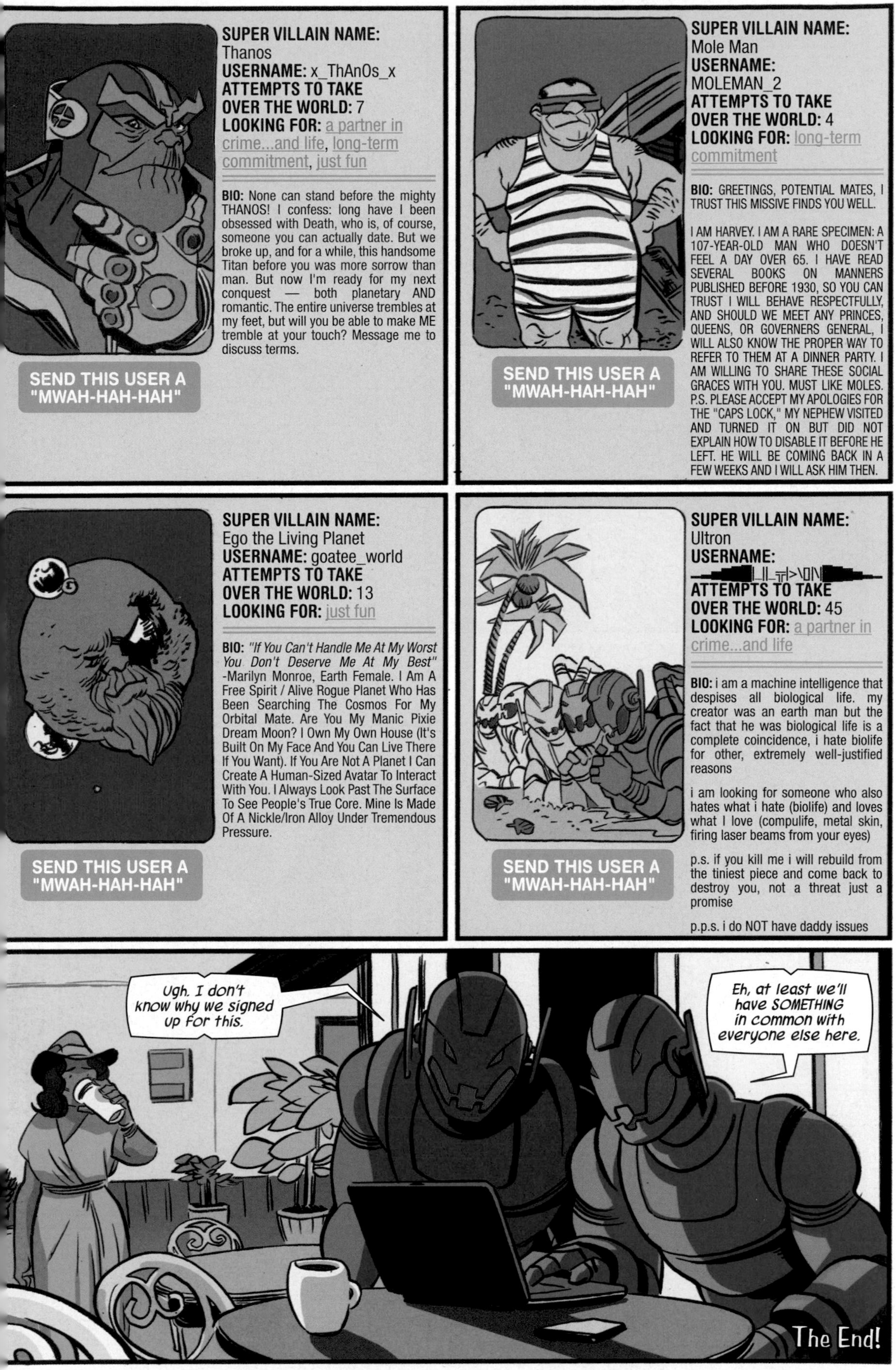
SUPER VILLAIN NAME: Thanos
USERNAME: x_ThAnOs_x
ATTEMPTS TO TAKE OVER THE WORLD: 7
LOOKING FOR: a partner in crime...and life, long-term commitment, just fun
BIO: None can stand before the mighty THANOS! I confess: long have I been obsessed with Death, who is, of course, someone you can actually date. But we broke up, and for a while, this handsome Titan before you was more sorrow than man. But now I'm ready for my next conquest — both planetary AND romantic. The entire universe trembles at my feet, but will you be able to make ME tremble at your touch? Message me to discuss terms.
SEND THIS USER A "MWAH-HAH-HAH"
SUPER VILLAIN NAME: Mole Man
USERNAME: MOLEMAN_2
ATTEMPTS TO TAKE OVER THE WORLD: 4
LOOKING FOR: long-term commitment
BIO: GREETINGS, POTENTIAL MATES, I TRUST THIS MISSIVE FINDS YOU WELL.
I AM HARVEY. I AM A RARE SPECIMEN: A 107-YEAR-OLD MAN WHO DOESN'T FEEL A DAY OVER 65. I HAVE READ SEVERAL BOOKS ON MANNERS PUBLISHED BEFORE 1930, SO YOU CAN TRUST I WILL BEHAVE RESPECTFULLY, AND SHOULD WE MEET ANY PRINCES, QUEENS, OR GOVERNERS GENERAL, I WILL ALSO KNOW THE PROPER WAY TO REFER TO THEM AT A DINNER PARTY. I AM WILLING TO SHARE THESE SOCIAL GRACES WITH YOU. MUST LIKE MOLES.
P.S. PLEASE ACCEPT MY APOLOGIES FOR THE "CAPS LOCK," MY NEPHEW VISITED AND TURNED IT ON BUT DID NOT EXPLAIN HOW TO DISABLE IT BEFORE HE LEFT. HE WILL BE COMING BACK IN A FEW WEEKS AND I WILL ASK HIM THEN.
SEND THIS USER A "MWAH-HAH-HAH"
SUPER VILLAIN NAME: Ego the Living Planet
USERNAME: goatee_world
ATTEMPTS TO TAKE OVER THE WORLD: 13
LOOKING FOR: just fun
BIO: "If You Can't Handle Me At My Worst You Don't Deserve Me At My Best" -Marilyn Monroe, Earth Female. I Am A Free Spirit / Alive Rogue Planet Who Has Been Searching The Cosmos For My Orbital Mate. Are You My Manic Pixie Dream Moon? I Own My Own House (It's Built On My Face And You Can Live There If You Want). If You Are Not A Planet I Can Create A Human-Sized Avatar To Interact With You. I Always Look Past The Surface To See People's True Core. Mine Is Made Of A Nickle/Iron Alloy Under Tremendous Pressure.
SEND THIS USER A "MWAH-HAH-HAH"
SUPER VILLAIN NAME: Ultron
USERNAME:
ATTEMPTS TO TAKE OVER THE WORLD: 45
LOOKING FOR: a partner in crime...and life
BIO: i am a machine intelligence that despises all biological life. my creator was an earth man but the fact that he was biological life is a complete coincidence, i hate biolife for other, extremely well-justified reasons
i am looking for someone who also hates what i hate (biolife) and loves what I love (compulife, metal skin, firing laser beams from your eyes)
p.s. if you kill me i will rebuild from the tiniest piece and come back to destroy you, not a threat just a promise
p.p.s. i do NOT have daddy issues
SEND THIS USER A "MWAH-HAH-HAH"
Ugh. I don't know why we signed up for this.
Eh, at least we'll have SOMETHING in common with everyone else here.
The End!

Writer: Ryan North Artist: Erica Henderson Letterer: VC's Clayton Cowles Editor: Heather Antos

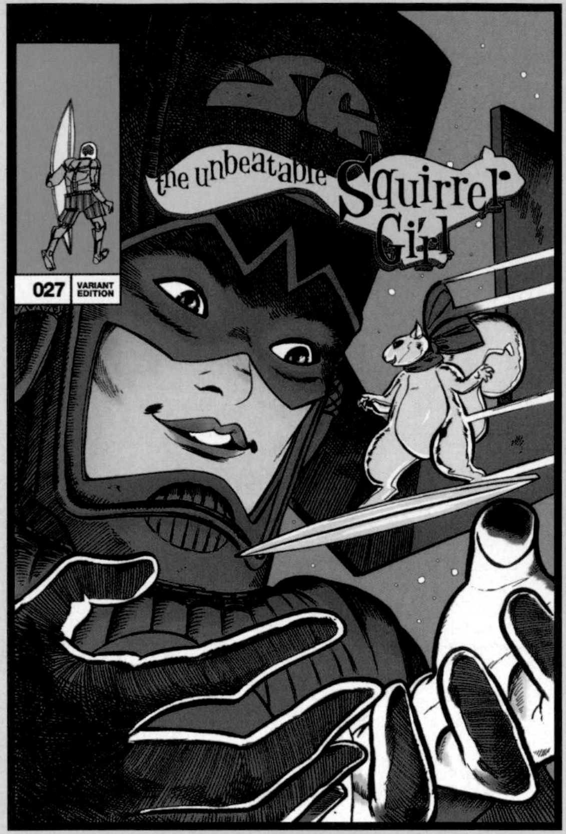
the unbeatable Squirrel Girl
027
VARIANT EDITION

#27 HOMAGE VARIANT
BY **VERONICA FISH**

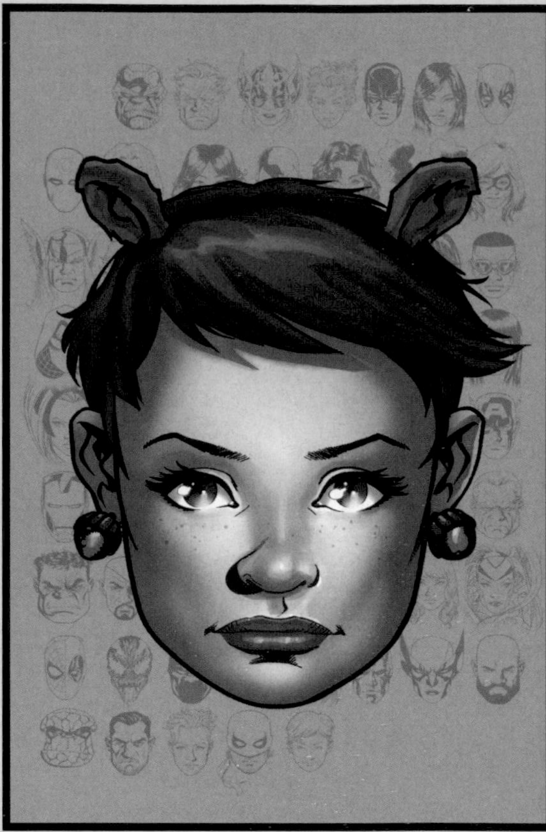

#27 LEGACY HEADSHOT VARIANT
BY **MIKE McKONE** & **ANDY TROY**

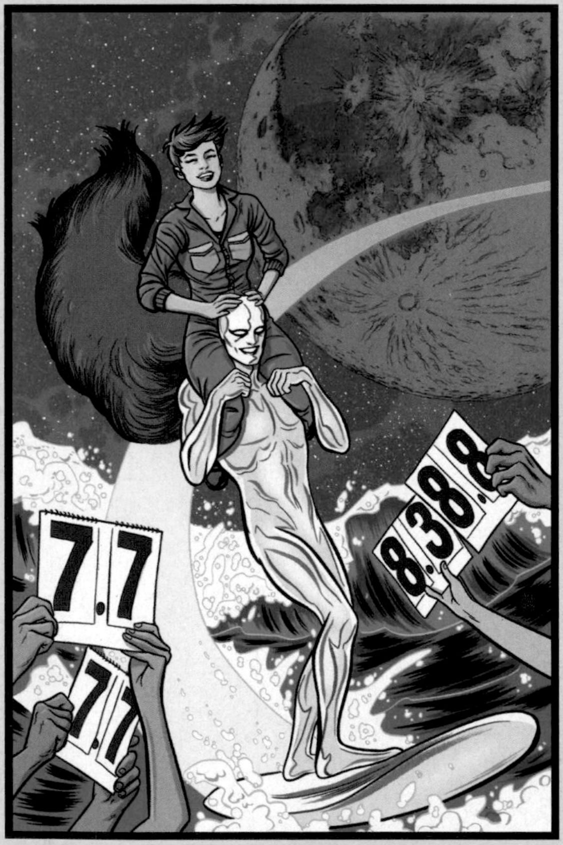
7.7
7.7
8.3
8.8

#27 VARIANT
BY **MICHAEL ALLRED** & **LAURA ALLRED**

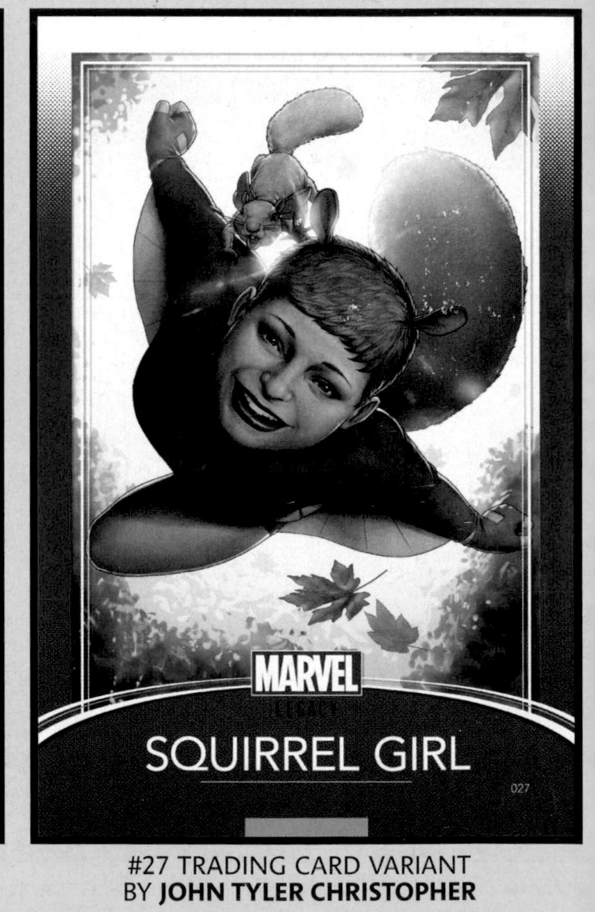
MARVEL
SQUIRREL GIRL
027

#27 TRADING CARD VARIANT
BY **JOHN TYLER CHRISTOPHER**